The Pioneer Woman

The Pioneer Woman

A Canadian Character Type

ELIZABETH THOMPSON

McGill-Queen's University Press
Montreal & Kingston • London • Buffalo

© McGill-Queen's University Press 1991
ISBN 0-7735-0832-5

Legal deposit second quarter 1991
Bibliothèque nationale du Québec

Printed in Canada on acid-free paper

This book has been published with the help of a grant
from the Social Science Federation of Canada, using
funds provided by the Social Sciences and Humanities
Research Council of Canada.

Canadian Cataloguing in Publication Data

Thompson, Elizabeth
    The pioneer woman
    Includes bibliographical references.
    ISBN 0-7735-0832-5
    1. Women pioneers in literature. 2. Canadian fiction
    (English) – 20th century – History and criticism.
    3. Canadian fiction – 19th century – History and
    criticism. I. Title.
    PS8103.P58T48 1991 C813'.509.352042 C90-090518-2
    PR9185.6.P58T48 1991

This book was set in Baskerville 10/12
by Caractéra inc., Quebec City.

To D.M.R. Bentley and K. Kingsmill.

Without their support, this book would not have been written.

Contents

The Pioneer Woman

Introduction

A female character type, one which is arguably unique to Canada, can be found in English-Canadian fiction from the time of the earliest Canadian creative writing, up to and including the present time. By virtue of her historical origins, this character type should be labelled the "pioneer woman," since her creation was, in fact, grounded in the actuality of the pioneer experience, and on details of the experience that were reconstructed and reinterpreted in fiction, often through a moralistic or idealistic filter. The pioneer woman has made the transition from being a "mythical concept,"[1] evident in the work of the pioneer writer Catharine Parr Trail, as in her *The Backwoods of Canada* (1836) and *The Canadian Settler's Guide* (1855), to being an accepted and essential aspect of female characterization in Canadian fiction. As Northrop Frye says in his Conclusion to the *Literary History of Canada:*

Literature is conscious mythology: as society develops, its mythical stories become structural principles of story-telling, its mythical concepts, sun-gods and the like, become habits of metaphorical thought. In a fully mature literary tradition, the writer enters into a structure of traditional stories and images.[2]

The longevity of the pioneer woman as character type in English-Canadian fiction and her recurrent use as a metaphor for Canadian femininity indicate that the character appeals to some common perception of a woman's role in Canadian society, and that the role for women proposed by the early emigrants was indeed an appropriate choice for the Canadian frontier, regardless of the location and nature of that frontier.

The direct antecedents of the pioneer as literary character were the real pioneers who settled in Upper Canada during the early nineteenth century and who created a new life and a new social mythology for themselves. Pioneering in Canada must have been a disorienting experience for the nineteenth-century female emigrants.[3] Far from home, separated from friends and family, such emigrants as Catharine Parr Traill, who documented her pioneer experiences in *The Backwoods of Canada* and *The Canadian Settler's Guide* (Traill's sister, Susanna Moodie, also a pioneer, described her life in Canada in *Roughing It in the Bush* [1852] and *Life in the Clearings* [1853]), faced daunting new tasks in a strange and occasionally dangerous environment. In order to cope with their situation, women were forced to learn new domestic skills and to redefine their feminine role within the family unit and within the society around them. In "The Intelligent Woman's Guide to Pioneering in Canada," Virginia Rouslin defines Canadian pioneer women as "heroines,"[4] drawing attention specifically to a small group of highly educated and articulate settlers – Susanna Moodie, Mary O'Brien, Catharine Traill, and Anna Jameson (Rouslin includes Jameson despite the fact that this particular woman was a pioneer traveller rather than a pioneer settler) – women who were able not only to cope with their new environment but also to provide suggestions for others. Drawing upon her academic background and upon her social training as an English gentlewoman, each woman outlines a new role for women, a role suited to "a new land which had not yet had the time to make social proscriptions as to who should do what."[5] The picture of the typical pioneer woman which emerges from these (and other)[6] pioneer writings is of a self-assured, confident woman, one who adapts cheerfully to adverse circumstances, one who is capable and active in an emergency, one who plays a vital role in pioneering. In short, in the course of their own pioneering endeavours, women such as Catharine Parr Traill and Susanna Moodie outlined a new feminine ideal – the Canadian pioneer woman. As Rouslin points out:

one sees that these women writers were fighting to establish a new tradition in non-fiction for female readers, both in Europe and in Canada. It involved reflecting, as best they could, the actual environment in which they lived, from the distinctly female point of view – something that was not covered in male versions, which often idealized pioneering. It was an attempt to translate and transmit what might well be termed a minority point of view, in terms of its publication ... Jameson (along with the other writers), recorded and gave to us a new role for the intelligent and well-educated woman. It was a celebration of another facet of women's lives – and not the dirge we might have believed was the only song written for our pioneer women.[7]

As has been noted, Catharine Traill was one of these articulate women who defined a pioneer woman's role on the Canadian frontier. Rouslin does not isolate Traill for special consideration, yet, because she published her conclusions in fiction such as *Canadian Crusoes* (1852) as well as non-fictional works such as *The Backwoods of Canada* and *The Canadian Settler's Guide*, Traill becomes the single most important contributor to the creation of this new, Canadian, concept of women in both an historical and a literary sense. Through an examination of Traill's work, it will be seen that Rouslin's analysis of the creation of the pioneer "heroine" in non-fiction applies equally well to fiction.[8]

In *The Backwoods of Canada* and *The Canadian Settler's Guide*, Traill was as accurate as possible in her depiction of a Canadian settler's life because she was attempting to help other emigrant women to master the difficulties encountered and develop the skills required in the course of the pioneering experience. Yet Traill offsets her basic pragmatism with a strong moral bias and an obvious tendency to colour real events with a cheerful idealism. She transposes the highly idealized figure of the Canadian pioneer woman which results from this combination of realism and idealism into her fiction and creates what is, in effect, a new fictional character type. When *Canadian Crusoes* is viewed against the background of *The Backwoods of Canada* and *The Canadian Settler's Guide*, it becomes clear that Traill's pioneer heroine, Catharine Maxwell, is a mixture of fact and fancy – an idealistic reinterpretation of real life on the frontier of nineteenth-century Upper Canada.

The continuity between Traill's characterization of women and the characterization of women in subsequent Canadian fiction cannot be denied or ignored. Various versions of the pioneer woman appear with great regularity in English-Canadian fiction throughout the hundred years following her development of the character type in the middle of the nineteenth century. By the end of the nineteenth century, frontier days in Canada, certainly in eastern Canada, were rapidly coming to an end, and the pioneer woman, as she had been identified by Traill, was becoming a figure from the past. Yet, the pioneer woman continued to appear in such English-Canadian fiction as, for example, Sara Jeannette Duncan's *The Imperialist* (1904) and Ralph Connor's *The Man from Glengarry* (1901) and *Glengarry School Days* (1902).

The pattern of settlement in Canada – a slow movement from the East to the West and the North – ensures that any date assigned as the ending period of a Canadian frontier must be an arbitrary one. It is certain, however, that, by the end of the nineteenth century, pioneer days in southern Ontario, and in eastern Canada generally, had ended, while the northern and western frontiers were still being settled well into the twentieth century. (Indeed, the Canadian North can, with some justification, be regarded as the last remaining frontier.) The turn of the century, then, constitutes a turning point of sorts in the settlement of English Canada, and, in their fiction, Duncan and Connor document this period of transition from frontier to civilization. Consequently, their novels echo back to the past in featuring pioneer women who cope on a real, physical frontier, and forward to the future in featuring pioneer women who cope with a new type of frontier environment, one grounded in social and personal concerns rather than in the physical landscape.

In *The Imperialist*, Duncan creates an heir to Traill's ideal pioneer woman in her characterization of Mrs Murchison. With the figure of Advena Murchison, however, Duncan creates a revitalized version of the pioneer woman as character type in fiction, one which is influenced by Duncan's awareness of contemporary social issues in Canada. Advena's frontier – her choice of a career as a teacher – is closely related to the social theories of Canadian feminists of the late nineteenth and early twentieth centuries. In his Glengarry books, Connor also utilizes the character of the pioneer woman as she had been defined by Traill. His Mrs Murray in such novels as *The Man from Glengarry* and *Glengarry School Days* is based on his knowledge of the lives of pioneer women in nineteenth-century Ontario, and his Mrs Mavor of *Black Rock* (1898) is based on his knowledge of pioneer life in the North-West. Like Duncan, Connor continues to develop and to expand the character type so that the pioneer woman can have relevance in a post-frontier society. Thus, while the historical origins of Connor's female pioneers are always apparent, his modification of the pioneer woman and the frontier that she inhabits ventures into the realm of religious metaphor. It will be argued in the following pages that these later appearances of the pioneer woman in fiction, for example Duncan's Advena Murchison and Connor's Mrs Murray, are derived from Traill's pioneer woman, or, when no such debt can be demonstrated, that all exhibit traits which link them to the original model.

In their use of the pioneer woman in fiction, Duncan and Connor tend to be representative of Canadian writers of the late nineteenth and early twentieth centuries. This indicates that by this point there was a widespread acceptance of the pioneer woman as a Canadian character type, as this type had been defined by Traill. Such writers as Marian Keith in *Duncan Polite* (1905), L.M. Montgomery in *Anne of Green Gables* (1908), Robert Stead in *The Homesteaders* (1916), and Nellie McClung in *Purple Springs* (1921) include versions of the pioneer woman in their fiction. The general acceptance of the character is indicated by the variety of settings used: Prince Edward Island in Montgomery's *Anne of Green Gables,* Ontario in Keith's *Duncan Polite,* Manitoba in McClung's *Purple Springs,* and Alberta in Stead's *The Homesteaders.*

The longevity of the pioneer woman as character type is further demonstrated in the twentieth-century fiction of Margaret Laurence. Hagar Sphipley of *The Stone Angel* (1964), Rachel Cameron of *A Jest of God* (1966), and Morag Gunn of *The Diviners* (1974) inhabit a frontier which would be unfamiliar territory to Traill, since, in Laurence's work, the frontier is an internal, personal one. Yet, each of Laurence's protagonists, like Duncan's Advena in *The Imperialist* and Connor's Mrs Murray in *The Man from Glengarry* and *Glengarry School Days,* is a later version of Traill's pioneer woman. The appearance of Traill in *The Diviners* effectively establishes a connection between Catharine Traill, the nineteenth-century backwoods pioneer, and Morag Gunn, the twentieth-century pioneer. While the differences between Catharine and Morag are immediately obvious to Morag, she learns, in the course of the narrative, to recognize and to appreciate their similarities. Morag admires Traill and seeks her counsel, only to discover that she knows what Traill has to say; furthermore, she realizes that she already acts correctly on her individual frontier. Traill's advice to pioneer women is a part of Morag's personal legacy; Morag is the descendant of pioneers and is a pioneer herself.

Nor is Laurence alone in her use of the pioneer woman in twentieth-century fiction. Works such as L.M. Montgomery's *The Blue Castle* (1926), Ethel Wilson's *Swamp Angel* (1954), Constance Beresford-Howe's *The Book of Eve* (1973), Joan Barfoot's *Abra* (1978), Aretha van Herk's *Judith* (1978), and Katherine Govier's *Between Men* (1987) include contemporary versions of the pioneer woman. Laurence, however, by virtue of several factors – for example, her literary prominence, her inclusion of Traill in *The Diviners,* and her evident awareness of an historical continuum – merits special attention.

The pioneer woman as character type changes and evolves in the century which separates Traill's work from Laurence's fiction. The frontier is redefined several times, and with the redefinition comes a corresponding change in the nature of the pioneering process (or in the pioneer woman's interaction with the frontier). To begin with, the term "pioneering process," used in connection with Traill's fiction, refers to the pioneer woman's interaction with a real, physical place. Then, in later fiction, such as that of Duncan and Connor, the pioneering process also becomes a metaphor for social and religious conflict. Finally, in the contemporary fiction of Laurence, the pioneering process is internalized, referring to a personal dilemma to be solved by the protagonist. Despite the shifting nature of the frontier territory, however, the pioneer woman as character type remains readily identifiable. Certain essential qualities are retained: the ability to act decisively and quickly in cases of emergency, and the strength to accept adverse circumstances on the frontier, combined with the courage to attempt an improvement of these frontier conditions. In Canadian fiction, then, "the gray little woman back home, standing over the coal stove"[9] is often a heroine. While Frederick Philip Grove may be correct when he says, "A pioneering world ... is a man's world," a world in which "woman is the slave" and is "relegated to the tasks of a helper,"[10] it becomes clear that many writers have approached the pioneering experiences of Canadian women with a much more positive attitude. Rouslin comments:

it seems fit to reconsider whom we should include in our list of past heroes *and* heroines who have gone before us into the wilderness, prepared the way for others to follow, and who have left us, as Frye believes, a "legacy of dignity and high courage."[11]

Chief among any list of Canadian heroines should be Catharine Parr Traill. Traill's model for the ideal Canadian pioneer "prepared the way for others to follow." Traill's "conscious mythology"[12] – her creation of the pioneer woman – left a "legacy of dignity and high courage"[13] which other women might emulate in their lives and which other writers might employ in their fiction. As Northrop Frye points out: "there does seem to be such a thing as an imaginative continuum, and ... writers are conditioned in their attitudes by their predecessors, whether there is a conscious influence or not."[14] A direct link can seldom be established between Traill and following writers; nor is the establishment of such a link necessary. The lack of "conscious influence" has not hindered the reproduction of the pioneer woman in fiction. And the appearance of the pioneer woman as heroine is part of a Canadian artistic continuity that stretches from Traill to Laurence and beyond.

CHAPTER ONE

The Fiction of Catharine Parr Traill

Catharine Parr Traill is probably best known for her two non-fictional accounts of pioneer life in Upper Canada – *The Backwoods of Canada* (1836) and *The Canadian Settler's Guide* (1855). In both of these works Traill wrote about her personal experiences in the Canadian backwoods, describing Canadian life for a primarily British reading public and offering useful advice to new and prospective Canadian emigrants. What is less commonly known, however, is that, in addition to *The Backwoods of Canada* and *The Canadian Settler's Guide*, Traill also produced a large quantity of fiction. Although Traill's best fiction, such as *Canadian Crusoes* (1852), was written in Canada, and hence probably reflects her Canadian experiences, her writing career did not begin here. Nor were her fictional topics restricted to the retelling of her Canadian adventures. *Pearls and Pebbles*, for example, published in 1895, contains a collection of stories which span Traill's long career as a writer, from "The Swiss Herdboy and his Alpine Mouse," written when Traill was fifteen years old, to "The First Death in the Clearing," a story based on Traill's own Canadian experiences that originally appeared as "The Bereavement" in the *Literary Garland* in 1866. Unfortunately, much of Traill's fiction seems dated and tedious today. This stems from Traill's apparent desire to instruct rather than to entertain her reader. Traill continually interrupts her narratives to clarify a point, to relate an anecdote that is somehow connected to the main narrative, to add details of natural history which are, at best, only tenuously relevant to the story, or to reiterate and to reinforce a moral issue. Consequently, Traill's fiction is, for the most part, incompatible with contemporary tastes, and has remained in relative obscurity.

Yet the obscurity into which Traill's fiction has fallen remains regrettable because, despite the unevenness of a narrative style that derives from the author's determination to instruct and to enlighten her reader, some aspects of her fiction were fresh and innovative at the time of writing. Even in her earliest works she was, on occasion, a breaker of new fictional ground, particularly in the realm of female characterization. Of central importance for the present discussion is the fact that a number of Traill's female protagonists – most notably the women in her Canadian books – differ markedly from standard depictions of women in popular mid-nineteenth-century British fiction. While she could recreate common type characters in her fiction (such as Emma in "The Primrose Girl" of 1823), Traill was able to go beyond the boundaries imposed by typecasting and to create some unique and truly memorable heroines (such as Downy in *Little Downy* of 1822). Moreover, in her Canadian books, Traill was somewhat of a pioneer in the writing of fiction that could with some justification be labelled "Canadian." She was one of the first writers to use a Canadian setting throughout a work of fiction and one of the first to feature a Canadian-born heroine in a novel – the Catharine Maxwell of *Canadian Crusoes*. Other writers, such as Traill's own sister, Susanna Moodie, who was also a Canadian emigrant, continued to produce fiction with a British setting and to employ female protagonists who represented the most commonly selected heroine of nineteenth-century British fiction – the English lady.[1] The two sisters responded very differently to Canada, in a literary sense at any rate. While Traill incorporated her new experiences into her fiction, Moodie continued resolutely to ignore Canada, and her *Mark Hurdlestone, The Gold Worshipper* (1853) and *Geoffrey Moncton: or, The Faithless Guardian* (1855), both written after her emigration to Canada, feature English gentlewomen in their native English setting.

A standard and relatively unchanging list of traits continued to define an English lady throughout the greater part of nineteenth-century British fiction, and a lady was always immediately recognizable as such by her appearance, her skills, her manners, and her way of life.[2] In brief, the lady belongs to the middle and upper classes of English society, and is accustomed to a life of leisure in which she can display her many decorative, drawing-room talents. (This is the character type which appears in the novels of Susanna Moodie.) Catharine Traill was no doubt aware of this particular tradition of female characterization in fiction. Indeed, Emma, the youthful protagonist of "The Primrose Girl," is a stereotypical example of a lady of the period: she is wealthy, pampered, and accustomed to an idle existence. Yet one of Traill's most important contributions to literature, specifically to Canadian literature, was to break with this tradition of female characterization and to begin the development of a character type which did not fit the rather rigid set of conditions and terms defining a lady. While the inclination to literary independence that would lead to the development of the pioneer heroine may have begun before Traill's emigration to Canada, it was quite likely aided by her exposure to a new way of life in the Canadian backwoods, where old standards governing the behaviour appropriate to a lady were no longer applicable.

One of Traill's earliest and most enjoyable children's books, *Little Downy; or, The History of a Field-Mouse* (1822), a work which sets a precedent for much of the later female character delineation in Traill's Canadian-based books, features the life and times of a female field-mouse. While this particular work has no connection with Canada, with Traill's subsequent emigration to Canada, or with her production of literature with Canadian settings, themes, and characters, it is an important beginning-point in a study of Traill's fiction from a feminine perspective. It substantiates the idea that Traill was capable of ignoring, or, rather, of rising above, the limitations imposed by a strict observance of convention. Despite her evident belief that moral instruction was an essential aspect of children's literature, Traill produced in *Little Downy* a work that was innovative and, more important, a heroine who is engaging and real – both as a mouse and as a female. For example, Downy's lapse into slothful enjoyment of the kitchen garden, after her previous experiences of constant hard work and danger, makes her one of the most delightfully fallible heroines of Traill's fiction. And this early refusal to be bound by convention in the development of a female character anticipates the characterization of women in Traill's Canadian books.

There are several factors which separate Downy from the general rank and file of ordinary heroines of English fiction and which anticipate Traill's creation of a new character type in her Canadian fiction. For example, although Downy could perhaps be termed "ladylike" in her habits and her appearance, she is not a "lady."[3] She is neat, but plain in appearance. She is neither beautiful nor delicate, and her daily existence in no way resembles the life of a lady.[4] Except for a brief hiatus in the kitchen garden when she lives in "idleness and luxury,"[5] Downy is hard-working. She builds her own house, finds her food, and supports her family, including her husband. Unlike Emma Selwhyn, the young lady of "The Primrose Girl," she must fend for herself. She is never sheltered or protected. Her survival depends on her consistently quick reactions in times of danger. This is a daily struggle which is far removed from the pampered life of the English lady. Of course, Downy is a mouse. Yet the fact remains that the character of Downy promotes a vastly different image of femininity than that projected by Emma Selwhyn.

The appearance of the worker as opposed to the lady as protagonist is relatively rare in English fiction of the early nineteenth century.[6] Independent, self-sufficient, working-class women were seldom the topic of fiction. When they appeared, they were often unimportant, peripheral figures, or they were rapidly promoted to a higher class.[7] By using a mouse as heroine Traill can begin to explore the possibilities of development and change in female characterization without challenging her readers' expectations or offending their sensibilites. Downy can thus be seen as a cautious experiment. On the one hand, Traill conforms to social and literary tradition by insisting that appropriate behaviour is defined by one's background and personal life. On the other hand, through Downy, Traill begins to redefine appropriate behaviour for female protagonists in fiction and to indicate that more than one female character type may be a suitable heroine.

During this same period of time (the early nineteenth century), before her own emigration to Canada, Traill's sister Susanna was publishing fiction as well; she wrote a number of children's books, the majority of which were indistinguishable from Traill's in plot, theme, and characterization. Traill, however, most importantly in *Little Downy,* demonstrated a greater interest in natural history – an interest which, incidentally, anticipated the work of Beatrix Potter later in the century, and which also anticipated Traill's eager curiosity about life in Canada.

The other female protagonists in Traill's pre-Canadian fiction, such as *The Young Emigrants* (1826), generally fail to live up to the promise indicated in the characterization of the field-mouse in *Little Downy.* By and large, the women in *The Young Emigrants,* Mrs Clarence, Ellen, and Agnes, resemble Emma Selwhyn of "The Primrose Girl" and are recreations of a model English lady of the nineteenth century. For the most part, the stories that feature these stereotypical female characters are moral tales. The result is that plot action revolves around the development of the moral purpose and characterization is flat as it is designed solely to illustrate and to augment the story's moral precepts.[8] In *The Young Emigrants,* for example, Traill employs standard character types and continues her practice of using fiction to instruct. But, to a certain extent, the novel deviates from the ordinary, and Ruth Marks in her Preface to *The Young Emigrants* notes that this particular story is an important, and, indeed, a pivotal one in the development of Traill's fiction:

In surveying Catharine Parr Traill's work it is apparent that the major factor in its development was her emigration to Canada. It released her from the strictures which made her early stories for little children immature in style, palely reflecting the qualities of warmth and grace, honesty and candor which she later revealed. *The Young Emigrants* anticipated the vigorous writer she was to become.[9]

While Marks may be overstating the case somewhat, *The Young Emigrants* does illustrate some of Traill's major concerns as a writer, as well as indicating the direction her later fiction was to take, In "Traill's Canadian Settlers," Clara Thomas makes the point that "both Catharine's attitude to life and her philosophy of emigration are already formed in *The Young Emigrants.*"[10] For present purposes, however, it is important to examine Traill's early development of a feminine ideal in an analysis which is related to Thomas's work, but which sets the stage for Traill's creation of a new character type in fiction.

In *The Young Emigrants* Traill follows the fortunes of a middle-class English family which is forced by decreased income to choose between, on the one hand, reduced circumstances and the inevitable fall in stocial status which would accompany poverty, and, on the other, the possibility of building a new life in Canada. As characters, the female members of the Clarence family are, like Emma Selwhyn of "The Primrose Girl," included in the narrative primarily to serve a purpose; they are distinct from Emma, however, in that the purpose is not limited to the illustration of a particular moral precept. Like the Selwhyns, the Clarence women belong to an affluent English middle class and have been accustomed to a life of ease and luxury. As a result, Ellen and Agnes Clarence are, at the outset of *The Young Emigrants,* essentially uninteresting representatives of the standard English lady. They possess the traits and qualities typical of their social rank, and are reproductions of the ideal pattern. Their story becomes interesting (and Ruth Marks's high praise of *The Young Emigrants* is somewhat justified) when Traill deals with the plight of this type of woman in Canadian frontier environment and analyses the changes in daily life which would necessarily accompany a move to the New World.

The Young Emigrants can be divided into three interconnected and overlapping sections: the life and habits of the Clarence women as middle-class English ladies; the preparations made for emigration by the Clarence family; and the experiences of these women as pioneers in Canada. The central dilemma of the book – the question of most concern to the young female emigrants, and also, one would assume, of greatest interest to a British middle-class reading public – is the issue of one's social status in Canada. Can a woman remain a lady in Canada, living as a Canadian pioneer, and performing what are essentially "unladylike" tasks? Each section of the story tackles this crucial issue.

The Clarence women are most definitely ladies. The social status of the Clarence family, and by extension the status of its female members, is established quite quickly in the first segment of *The Young Emigrants*. Because of the family's middle-class background, certain assumptions can be made about the daily life, the education, and the social habits and skills of its female members. The women, Ellen, Agnes, and Mrs Clarence, have been sheltered and protected; they have been accustomed to a life in which women are expected to be somewhat frail, decorative ornaments rather than robust, useful household workers. Consider the reactions of the women to the news of the declining family fortunes which will necessitate giving up the family estate and accepting a lower rank in society:

"Give up Roselands, papa!" exclaimed Ellen, bursting into tears. "Where shall we go if we leave this place, so dear to us all?" "Ah! dearest mamma, what will become of us all?" asked Agnes, in a tone of great distress.[11]

The men generally are made of sterner stuff than the women, however, and Mr Clarence proposes emigration. Richard, his son, supports the plan. As befits their frail, emotional, female nature, the women are less optimistic. Ellen says, "I am sure I never can bear to live in America" (5). Agnes is reduced to total silence: "Agnes did not speak but her tears flowed silently over the work she vainly attempted to continue" (5). The real concern to these women is the consequence to them of a fall in social standing. Since Ellen and Agnes define themselves as ladies, a loss of status would be tantamount to a loss of personal identity. Moreover, being pampered, they are physically untrained and mentally unprepared for the impending switch to a labouring-class existence in either North America or England. Ellen raises the most important issue confronting the prospective gentle-woman emigrant when she asks her brother:

In America, what will be the use of those accomplishments, that Agnes and I have spent so much time in attaining? Will not our skill in music, French, and drawing, be all thrown away, among the wild woods of Canada? (11)

Richard Clarence's response indicates Traill's own solution to the problem, and, incidentally, anticipates her backwoods books of advice to emigrant women. Richard feels that the girls will be able to reconcile the two apparently incompatible roles of refined lady and hard-working pioneer woman. He further states that the accomplishments known only to a lady will be certain to enrich her life as an emigrant, making her a better pioneer. He says to Ellen:

"My dear sister ... if you see things in their right light, you will perceive that your French will be useful to you in conversing with the Canadians, who speak that language. Music will cheer our evenings, after the toils of the day; and as to drawing, remember, Ellen, how many beautiful flowers Canada produces, which will form new and interesting studies for your pencil. You have hitherto made these accomplishments the sole employment of your life; but now a higher duty awaits you, and more active pursuits. Your more elegant attainments will still serve as a pleasing relaxation from graver studies, and more toilsome occupation; but they must no longer form the business of your life." (11–12)

Traill indicates here that a lady will always maintain her status as a lady, even on a wild Canadian frontier, and, moreover, she states her enduring belief that a lady's many decorative accomplishments will continue to enrich her life no matter what her circumstances.

The Clarence girls accept Richard's well-meant and extremely optimistic advice and, in the second segment of *The Young Emigrants,* Agnes begins to seek practical solutions to her dilemma, and to prepare for emigration. In the process, she starts to alter some of her normal patterns of behaviour. Agnes's first practical decision is to follow her brother's lead. She stays on an English farm for a short period of time in order to acquire the knowledge and skills she will need in the Canadian backwoods. In what is seen as kind condescension by the farmer and his wife, Agnes lives in the farmer's "humble home" (19) and learns the tasks of a farm woman. For example, she is taught "the management of cows and poultry" (19). This, of course, is not ordinarily part of the education of the English lady, and may be perceived as degrading, since, in the Clarence family's experience, menial tasks are more commonly performed by members of an inferior, labouring class. Yet, in this portion of *The Young Emigrants,* Traill endeavours to preserve the impression of the gentility of her characters. She insists that Agnes is no less a lady because she can make butter and cheese. Mrs Clarence is pleased with her daughter's pragmatism and defends her actions: "'Why,' said she, 'should these offices be unbecoming to a lady, merely because they are useful'" (20). With the expression of this point of view by Mrs Clarence, Traill has begun her crusade of insisting that the tasks performed by Canadian pioneer women are not incompatible with gentility, and are, in fact, appropriate duties for a lady on a frontier. In *The Young Emigrants*, Traill is developing her own theories about emigration and about a woman's role in a new environment. These theories are repeated at greater length in Traill's two backwoods memoirs, *The Backwoods of Canada* and *The Canadian Settler's Guide*, and are most fully utilized in fiction through the creation of Catharine Maxwell, the Canadian-born pioneer heroine of *Canadian Crusoes*.

The pivotal moral issue in the story of the young emigrants in the Clarence family, as well as the major determining factor in the girls' change of heart regarding emigration and the single most important ingredient in successful pioneering, is the belief that one must submit cheerfully to the will of God. Once the Clarence girls have faced the fact that their poverty and their emigration are the will of God, they become resigned to their fate. They decide to accept willingly the necessary changes which will accompany emigration. Traill notes with approbation that the Clarence women have found "mental strength enough to determine on doing their duty, in that state of life to which it had pleased God to call them" (19). The desirability of cheerful submission to providence is the central moral lesson in *The Young Emigrants*. This theme dominates the novel and reappears throughout the work written by Traill after her own emigration to Canada. In "Traill's Canadian Settlers," Clara Thomas notes that this belief in "a divinely ordained structure with every part appointed" (33) is part of Traill's "personal faith," and is, moreover, "the accepted ethos of British middle class society" (33). There is, generally speaking, a decline in moral emphasis in Traill's later works, with the exception of this single theme, which continues to dominate and to shape the fiction and the non-fiction. Traill's adaptation of British middle-class beliefs to suit Canadian conditions is nowhere more evident than in this one area. As Traill emphasizes in *The Young Emigrants:* "It is always wisest and best to submit, without murmuring, to those things which we have not the power to remedy" (28).

In the third segment of the *The Young Emigrants,* the Clarence ladies have relocated to Canada. They begin to perform new tasks, tasks which in England (or in English fiction) would be deemed inappropriate. Agnes's tasks include the management of the poultry. She also supervises and takes an active part in the baking, the preserving, and the sewing. In addition, she establishes a school and takes pride in her garden. This union of a working-class daily existence with gentility represents a notable departure in fiction; in her creation of pioneer lady, Traill has few, if any literary precedents. The optimistic tone and moral orientation of the narrative are carefully preserved in the final section of the *The Young Emigrants*, where the Clarence women jealously guard their illusions of gentility on the frontier, maintaining that, despite their new working habits, they are ladies. In fact, it is hinted that they may be even better persons as a result of emigration, since they have demonstrated a superior moral ability to bow obediently to the will of God in all things.

It should be noted that the inclusion of the description of typical Canadian pioneer activities in the final part of *The Young Emigrants* gives Traill the opportunity to instruct her readers in little-known facts about Canada. She was still a resident of England at the time of writing *The Young Emigrants*, and her knowledge had been collected from sources other than direct experience of Canadian life. Limited information does not hinder Traill, however; she loves to teach her reading public. It is also worth mentioning that Traill obviously has by this time developed some quite decided views on pioneers and pioneering, specifically with respect to the role of women ("ladies") on the frontier. The view that a lady could remain identifiable as a lady no matter where she might be and no matter what she might be doing, and the idea that one must always seek to obey the will of God willingly and cheerfully were apparently part of Traill's own efforts to adapt to her new country.

In the Canadian fiction, Traill's moralizing tends to become rather more muted and subtle. Following the lead of *The Young Emigrants*, she focuses in *Canadian Crusoes* only on the moral aspects of successful pioneering. Traill's natural inclination to instruct her readers, especially in natural science, is perhaps better suited to a Canadian background as well, since the details she is providing would, for the most part, be foreign to an English reading public. Although in Traill's later work there is a decline in moral instruction (which is in proportion to the increase in the number of Canadian anecdotes and the amount of natural history instruction), she continues to quote from the Bible to prove a point, and to interrupt her narratives to give moral advice and direction. But stories no longer hinge entirely on a moral issue as did, for example, "The Primrose Girl," and, in broad terms, the detached stance of the scientist and observer, first apparent in *Little Downy*, is used more extensively in Canadian works such as *Canadian Crusoes* (1852), *Lady Mary and her Nurse* (1856), and *Pearls and Pebbles* (1894). For Traill, the detached stance is perhaps a more natural, and therefore a more successful, approach to fiction than the sentimental, moralistic perspective adopted in earlier works. The descriptions of Canadian people, plants, and animals, and the Canadian anecdotes and asides based on facts and experiences, have a greater ring of truth than do the artificially contrived English tales.

On the negative side, however, it must be reiterated that Traill's fiction, even the middle and later work, is seldom entirely successful. Major narrative problems continue to mar her stories. The digressions which explain, describe, and elaborate a point are often the best part of such works as *Lady Mary and Her Nurse* and *Canadian Crusoes*, even as they interrupt and destroy the flow of a narrative. It is a paradox of Traill's writing that in these longer narratives. the digressions into natural history, the activities of the animal characters, and the "true" stories about Canadian settlers tend to be more vividly written than the main story and its characters. The interaction of Mary and her nurse, Mrs Frazer, for example, serves only as a frame upon which to hang various Canadian anecdotes.

While it continues to demonstrate Traill's narrative weaknesses and irregularities, *Lady Mary and Her Nurse* is a useful work to examine from the point of view of Traill's awareness of, and ability to reproduce, standard representations of fictional female characters as well as her ability to break away from the norm and to develop a new type of female character in her fiction. *Lady Mary* juxtaposes two vastly different character types: Lady Mary, a young English lady, and Mrs Frazer, a Canadian pioneer. Unfortunately, Mary and Mrs Frazer are interesting only as types. They merit critical attention in a study of female characterization, but they are never very engaging as people.

Mary, as a visitor to Canada, like Mrs Jameson in real life, is allowed to observe and to comment on the local scene. Her father has been appointed governor, and hence the family will, at some point, return to England with its social standing unharmed by the Canadian visit. During her stay in Canada, Mary remains an English lady, and follows such a character's habitual pursuits. She belongs to an upper-class, wealthy, leisured, social élite, and she maintains this status in Canada by virtue of her father's distinguished position in the government. Throughout *Lady Mary and Her Nurse*, Mary leads a relatively idle existence. In a typical day she rides in the sleigh with her parents, plays with her dolls, or takes care of her pet animals. In the midst of pioneer Canada, where the majority of little girls her age are performing important household tasks, Mary is being given drawing lessons by her governess. Her pastimes, neither useful nor essential for survival, are vastly different from the pastimes of another of Traill's young protagonists, Catharine Maxwell of *Canadian Crusoes*, a true Canadian with little, if any, leisure time, no servants, and a scanty education. Mary's life is related in only a peripheral way to the Canadian setting. Indeed, her principal contact with the country comes through her nurse, a Canadian woman who is instructing her in facts about Canada. This structure means that the book consists of a series of short anecdotes and descriptions of Canadian customs, and Canadian plant and animal life.

Although she does not engage the reader's interest and never becomes a fully rounded character, Mary serves a relatively important narrative function in *Lady Mary*. She is necessary to provide an audience for the nurse, a listener to Mrs Frazer's stories about Canada. The instruction of Mary becomes the narrative excuse for the book's digressions into natural history, plant life, animal life, Canadian Indians and their customs, northern lights, maple syrup, lost children, snakes, bears, and wolves. Since Mary is a model child – a lady in her actions as well as in her ancestry – she listens eagerly:

Many little girls, as young as the Governor's daughter, would have thought it dull to listen to what her nurse had to say about plants and trees; but Lady Mary would put aside her dolls and toys, to stand beside her to ask questions, and listen to her answers; the more she heard, the more she desired to hear, about these things.[12]

Mrs Frazer is of a vastly different social background and possesses different knowledge and skills from her charge. Her function is to pass on her unique knowledge to Mary, and to the reader as well. A Canadian pioneer woman who was born in a log cabin in the Canadian backwoods, Mary's nurse is accustomed to a life of hard work. She is a widow and has had to support her son by herself. In an English sense, she belongs to a lower, labouring class in which women (and men) must earn their living, a class in which women cannot lead a pampered and leisured existence. Traill modifies her description of Mrs Frazer somewhat by claiming that the woman has known better days:

she was a person of good education, who had seen and noticed as well as read a good deal. She had been a poor woman, but had once been a respectable farmer's wife, though her husband's death had reduced her to a state of servitude; and she had earned money enough while in the Governor's service to educate her son, and this was how she came to be Lady Mary's nurse. (203)

The implication here is that Mrs Frazer is somewhat of a "distressed gentlewoman." This concession to popular social and literary taste (the lady is a "better" woman, more worthy of inclusion as a protagonist in fiction, more likely to be educated, and to possess the various social graces) may perhaps have seemed necessary to Traill, for, in *Lady Mary*, the roles of the servant and the lady tend to be reversed. Mrs Frazer is given the superior role of instructor. She has useful information, something of value to give to her pupil. Lady Mary listens obediently and willingly to her nurse's stories.

This is quite different from the situation in "The Primrose Girl" where Emma Selwhyn, the young lady, is in a position to dispense charity to her poor old nurse, Susannah, and to the flower seller. In "The Primrose Girl," the lady has something of value to give to her social subordinates; they receive her charity with gratitude, whether the gift be money, food, or kind condescension. By contrast in *Lady Mary* the wealthy young lady is the recipient from her social subordinate of a gift of knowledge, knowledge which, in Traill's eyes at least, is not to be undervalued. Mrs Frazer is not an object of pity; she is, rather, a woman worthy of a great deal of respect. Capable of earning her own living, she possesses important information and is very ladylike but has none of the social background necessary to define herself as a lady equal in status to Lady Mary. At the conclusion of *Lady Mary*, the Governor gives Mrs Frazer a deed for land as a gift. The gift establishes the fact that Mrs Frazer, despite her low social status in an English frame of reference, is a woman to be respected. The gift of land ensures that she no longer has to work for a living. She has gained her independence. Yet, the gift also represents a return to the established English social order in which the wealthy, upper-class family can dispense charity while the poor, lower-class family must accept it. Mrs Frazer may in fact be financially independent, but she owes it to the charity of another person.

The most successfully realized female characters in *Lady Mary* are the squirrels, the protagonists of one of the book's digressions. As in *Little Downy*, the adventures of a rodent family dominate the tales, and the humans seem to have been added merely to narrate the story and to provide it with a frame. In the short story about Canadian squirrels, Traill proves once again that she is more at ease in the role of scientific observer of animal life than as analyst of human behaviour. The squirrels are accurately described as animals, and, like Downy, are engagingly human and fallible as well. As in *Little Downy*, the consequences of error or of poor judgment on the part of an animal are both swift and severe. Silver-nose is caught and tamed by Indians; Velvet-paw is crushed to death by a mill-wheel. Although these disasters could quite conceivably happen to a real squirrel, Traill makes them appear to be the result of "human" frailties in the animals. Velvet-paw meets her untimely demise, for example, because she has grown fat and lazy living in the mill and cannot escape the mill-wheel. The animal characters emerge as more believable, more fully realized, and, paradoxically, more human, than the human characters for precisely one reason: they are permitted to have flaws. Traill's animal characters (and, to a lesser extent, this includes Downy as well) are often used as moral examples in a negative rather than a positive sense: their errors stand as warnings to the human reader. This contrasts sharply with the human female protagonists, who remain static, unchanging representations of perfection throughout *Lady Mary*. Just as Mary is the perfect English lady, so Mrs Frazer is the ideal pioneer woman. Perhaps the underlying amorality of animal life and the natural world temporarily frees Traill from her efforts to depict in her fiction a moral, balanced, and Christian view. It seems a pity that Traill was unable to utilize her accurate scientist's eye more freely in her fiction, and that she limited her honest reporting to animal and plant life rather than expanding it to the creation of realistic and believable characters.

Although *Canadian Crusoes* (1852) was written before *Lady Mary and Her Nurse* (1856), it actually represents a further development in Traill's conception and use of a Canadian female character type in fiction. While Mrs Frazer can be seen as an adult version of the Catharine Maxwell of *Canadian Crusoes,* the latter character is more fully realized as a person, and more fully developed as the representative of the Canadian pioneer woman. Yet both characters were doubtless intended to be typical. They share a similar background, common experiences, and display the same skills and knowledge. In the later book, Mrs Frazer's own life and her personal experiences as a pioneer are seldom mentioned, except in a peripheral, allusive sense. In the earlier story, Catharine Maxwell's life and actions are essential to the narrative. As a result, Catharine Maxwell in *Canadian Crusoes* is ultimately the more important female protagonist of the two.

In many ways, Catharine Maxwell is the literary antithesis of Lady Mary and Emma Selwhyn. Certainly, her way of life is quite different from that of a young English lady. Catharine's family background, her education (or rather her lack of education), and her skills and daily habits are not at all similar to those of the English-born characters found in Traill's fiction. As a type, Catharine probably has more in common with Traill's animal characters than with her human ones. Moreover, the characterization of Catharine represents an important departure from standard depictions of women in English popular fiction. Catharine is not an English lady. Nor is she intended to embody and to demonstrate one particular moral virtue. She does become a model of perfection and is someone to be emulated, but for neither of the above reasons. She is, rather, a model pioneer, the ideal Canadian girl.

Catharine's uniqueness as a female protagonist is grounded in her social background – her ancestry. She is a Canadian-born girl with no pretensions to gentility. Her family is not connected to the British middle or upper classes. Before settling in Canada, her father was a British soldier; he was neither an officer nor a member of the gentry.

Maxwell met and married a French-Canadian girl while he was on duty in Canada. His daughter is, therefore, a native-born Canadian. Furthermore, with her French-English heritage, Catharine represents an ideal, almost allegorical, union of Canada's two founding cultures. (Unfortunately for her significance as a Canadian symbol of perfect union, Catharine has no Indian ancestry, but Traill later adds this motif when Catharine's brother marries the Indian girl adopted by the children during their residence in the bush; Catharine thus becomes the Indian girl's sister-in-law.) In any event, Catharine is a truly Canadian girl with no connection by birth or by marriage to the English gentility. Indeed, the Maxwell family could for all intents and purposes be members of a lower, labouring class. They have no servants to perform the menial household chores. Catharine can and does handle much of the responsibility of the home. She is first introduced to the reader as she stands working industriously at her spinning wheel:

Under the shade of the luxuriant hop-vines, that covered the rustic porch in front of the little dwelling, the light step of Catharine Maxwell might be heard mixed with the drowsy whirring of the big wheel, as she passed to and fro guiding the thread of yarn in its course.[13]

The background is set. The Maxwell family has no middle-class pretensions. They have little money, and they survive by working hard.

Nor are Catharine's personal traits those of an English lady. Not only does she possess none of the decorative skills of the typical English gentlewoman but she is poorly educated – in fact, virtually illiterate. Traill comments, "of book-learning she knew nothing beyond a little reading, and that but imperfectly, acquired from her father's teaching" (6). And at one point in her adventures in the bush, Catharine wonders if the hills she can see in the distance are the highlands of Scotland. A poor, ignorant girl growing up in the Ontario backwoods seems an unlikely heroine. Certainly, few of the nineteenth-century English readers of *Canadian Crusoes* would be able to sympathize with Catharine or to understand even remotely her origins and her way of life. Yet Traill defends both herself and her ignorant young heroine. When Catharine has mistaken the hills in the distance for the highlands of Scotland, Traill says:

Let not the youthful and more learned reader smile at the ignorance of the Canadian girl; she knew nothing of maps, and globes, and hemispheres, – her only book of study had been the Holy Scriptures, her only teacher a poor Highland soldier. (87)

By creating an illiterate and socially unskilled female protagonist, and by indicating at this and at several other points of *Canadian Crusoes* that she is to be viewed with sympathy, Traill reverses some common notions of the way of life and the habits of the ideal woman, the woman suitable for use as heroine in fiction. Traill takes her sympathetic stance one step further when she insists that, despite her lack of a "proper" education, Catharine Maxwell is not to be pitied. She is, rather, an example of a model child, worthy of respect and emulation. Catharine's performance of household chores is, according to Traill, a source of pride rather than a cause of shame. Traill points out that, although her heroine is uneducated and has none of the correct drawing-room accomplishments of a lady, she is, nevertheless, clever and skilled in other areas of expertise.

Perhaps a new interpretation of education and of "accomplishment" is being proposed by Traill in her spirited defence of Catharine Maxwell. Catharine has been educated in the ways of the bush rather than in the social or literary skills known to English ladies. She knows and understands her own world and her role in that world. She is able to perform her special duties well. In Canadian terms, she is a model woman. Despite her lack of social background and acquired accomplishments, she is someone to be admired and copied.

Catharine Maxwell demonstrates a further exploration by Traill in *Canadian Crusoes* of the possibilities inherent in developing a working-class pioneer heroine in fiction. Like Little Downy, Catharine is practical, capable, and hard-working; she is able to support herself and to take care of others. Downy's traits are linked to her unique experiences as a mouse, and are well suited to biological fact; Catharine's traits are the product of her pioneer background. The descriptions of her duties are historically accurate, and undoubtedly are based on Traill's own knowledge of pioneer life in Canada. In *Little Downy*, Downy is the strongest member of her family. She is able to build a home for herself and her growing family; she can find food for herself and her children. And it is Downy, not her husband Silket, who takes care of the children. Like Downy, Catharine Maxwell is a strong, practical, and intelligent member of her small family group. But Catharine is more fortunate than Downy, since her brother and cousin are both helpful and sensible. They shoulder much of the work when the children are lost in the bush. Nevertheless, Catharine plays the important role of the mother of the lost children. She becomes the emotional centre of her bush "family":

Ardently attached to each other, they seemed bound together by a yet more sacred tie of brotherhood. They were now all the world to one another, and no cloud of disunion came to mar their happiness. Hector's habitual gravity and caution were tempered by Louis's lively vivacity and ardour of temper, and they both loved Catharine, and strove to smoothe, as much as possible, the hard life to which she was exposed, by the most affectionate consideration for her comfort, and she in return endeavoured to repay them by cheerfully enduring all privations, and making light of all their trials, and taking a lively interest in all their plans and contrivances. (94)

Catharine is responsible for her fair share of the work required for survival. Yet she is, in a sense, stronger than the two boys; she is the moral centre of the family. As Clara Thomas comments in "Traill's Canadian Settlers," "If there is an edge between the male and female roles, it is in fact, Catharine's" (36). It is because of Catharine that the group of children is harmonious in spite of the apparently hopeless situation.

Both Little Downy and Catharine Maxwell owe a debt as characters to a Puritan work ethic, to an ideal of behaviour which stresses the value of hard work, rather than to the tradition in fiction which demands that the ideal woman be an idle, decorative member of a leisured class. By taking this point of view, Traill broke with a tradition of feminine characterization that endured in popular English fiction throughout the eighteenth and nineteenth centuries. Yet it is important to qualify this praise somewhat, and to point out that Traill neither denies nor ignores a tradition of femininity which emphasizes the benefits to be gained by membership in the English middle and upper classes. Her protagonists are not removed entirely from the traditional depictions of women in fiction. Catharine, like her predecessor Downy and her fellow pioneer Mrs Frazer, has enough of the qualities of a lady to make her an appropriate heroine in the eyes of an English reading public. Catharine is stripped of the non-essential, decorative skills that serve no practical purpose on a frontier, but she retains some of the essential traits of an English lady. Her appearance, her good manners, her gentle, loving nature, all mark her as someone who is naturally "ladylike." Near the beginning of *Canadian Crusoes*, Traill says:

With the gaiety and naïveté of the Frenchwoman, Catharine possessed, when occasion called it into action, a thoughtful and well-regulated mind, abilities which would well have repaid the care of mental cultivation. (6)

Thus, Catharine is not an entirely new and different character type, despite her foreign habitat and foreign customs. What Traill has done in essence is to rewrite and revise the definition of a feminine ideal so that it becomes compatible with a backwoods, Canadian setting.

Possibly the single most important feature of *Canadian Crusoes,* certainly the feature of the book which dramatically complements Traill's delineation of the pioneer heroine, is Traill's application of the Robinson Crusoe story in a Canadian context.[14] Although Traill's version of the story features three children who are lost in the Canadian bush rather than an English man who is a castaway on a tropical island, there are many parallels between Daniel Defoe's 1719 novel and Traill's *Canadian Crusoes.* Like Crusoe, the Maxwell children and their cousin Louis are, through misadventure, cut off from civilization and must rely on their own resources to survive. Again like Crusoe, they develop ingenious methods to aid their survival: they build a home; they learn to survive without help; they plant and harvest crops; they make clothing from animal skins; they "tame" and Christianize a native. At the end of both *Robinson Crusoe* and *Canadian Crusoes,* the lost characters are rescued.

The use of the Crusoe story permits Traill to embark on descriptions of the Canadian landscape, to describe Canadian plants and animals, and to study at length the daily life of the Canadian pioneer. While such digressions are by no means uncommon in Traill's fiction, the use of the Crusoe plot warrants, and may even demand, digressions which in other works appear to be the result of personal indulgence on the part of the author. In this type of story, Traill can be permitted her descririptions of the surroundings and the survival methods of her young Crusoes. The result is that *Canadian Crusoes* is a more cohesive story than many of Traill's works of fiction. More significantly, perhaps, the Crusoe motif complements Traill's development in fiction of a Canadian, working-class pioneer heroine. The Crusoe story, reworked in *Canadian Crusoes* with a Canadian setting and characters, promotes and justifies Traill's personal vision of Catharine Maxwell as the representative of a new feminine ideal. Only a pioneer girl, one who is accustomed to the rigours of Canadian life and who is already proficient in the performance of the duties of a pioneer household, could survive in this particular situation. Although Traill's presentation of Catharine as an ideal is related to a number of the themes, moral attitudes, and views on emigration which she has expressed elsewhere, the Crusoe story is an ideal way in which to introduce a particular type of character in fiction. Catharine Maxwell is a Canadian, feminine, and idealized version of Defoe's Robinson Crusoe.

Catharine, in her role as a female Crusoe, must work hard to survive. This is not a new attitude for Traill, but her the work ethic is linked to the Crusoe situation where a heroine who is willing to work hard is very much required. Furthermore, Traill indicates that English children, despite any commendable willingness to submit to their fate and despite any laudable efforts to learn new skills, would not survive alone in the Canadian bush. The Canadian pioneer children are superior in this situation:

Early accustomed to the hardships incidental to the lives of the settlers in the bush, these young people had learned to bear with patience and cheerfulness privations that would have crushed the spirits of children more delicately nurtured ... Now it was that they learned to value in its fullest extent this useful and practical knowledge, which enabled them to face with fortitude the privations of a life so precarious as that to which they were now exposed. (28)

The pioneer is, therefore, established as a type of ideal character in this particular situation, in spite of his or her lack of education, gentility, or wealth. It is very important for an understanding of Traill's creation of a new type of female protagonist that there be a recognition of the fact that the pioneer girl must be perceived as an ideal, at least in her native backwoods setting. Traill takes great pains to foster this attitude in her readers.

It should be noted in conclusion that several themes, interests, and preoccupations reappear frequently throughout Traill's fiction. An important theme is the way in which a woman relates herself to the world around her. Each of Traill's female characters, from Little Emma of "The Primrose Girl" to Catharine Maxwell of *Canadian Crusoes,* is defined by her environment, and defines herself in relation to that environment. Chief among Traill's personal interests, as becomes evident in *The Young Emigrants, Lady Mary and Her Nurse,* and *Canadian Crusoes,* is her love of new, or little-known, facts and anecdotes. Very evidently, her fascination for the New World, its social customs, and its natural history influenced her writing, even before her departure for Canada. Traill also loves to display her erudition to her readers, often interrupting a narrative to instruct or to offer bits of advice, as in *Lady Mary and Her Nurse* and *Canadian Crusoes.* Her calm assumption that her readers will find her experiences and her information fascinating is a constant motivating factor in her writing. Traill brings an inquiring mind to her fiction, whether she is explaining obscure points of natural history or of pioneer life in Canada. She approaches all new situations as problems to be confronted and solved. She has a strong moral bias which colours and influences all her fiction. Finally, she attempts to understand, to analyse, and to explicate what she sees around her. This last point is most evident in her use of Canada in her fiction from *The Young Emigrants* to *Canadian Crusoes.* Traill not only describes the Canadian backwoods, but also develops a female character type who will suit that particular setting and set of circumstances. While Traill had experimented with the characterization of women as early as *Little Downy*, one of her major accomplishements in the writing of fiction is her creation in *Canadian Crusoes* of a backwoods heroine, a uniquely Canadian character type.

I have argued that Traill was unique among her contemporaries for her inclusion of the New World, and of the New World woman, in her fiction. Indeed, a comparison of Traill's fiction with some other Canadian fiction of the nineteenth century serves to point up Traill's literary isolation.

Traill's sister, Susanna Moodie, has already been mentioned. Like Traill, Moodie was a capable pioneer woman. In spite of frequent appeals to reader sympathy, Moodie's two accounts of pioneering, *Roughing It in the Bush* (1852) and *Life in the Clearings* (1853), have a strong self-congratulatory tone. Moodie has succeeded in the bush, and is proud of the fact. Unlike Traill, however, Moodie continued to produce in fiction a steady stream of English gentlewomen: for example, Margaretta Moncton of *Geoffrey Moncton: or, the Faithless Guardian*, and Juliet Whitmore of *Mark Hurdlestone*. Margaretta Moncton is a beautiful, frail, rich, pampered, middle-class English lady who excels at many of the pastimes recommended for ladies: she is a "fine pianist,"[15] an "excellent equestrian" (231), and she demonstrates "an exquisite taste" (232) when she paints "groups of flowers from nature" (232). Margaretta is affectingly frail, a "poor, fading, white rose" (354). None of these traits was at all relevant to Canadian pioneer life as it was being experienced by Moodie herself during the time she was writing about the delicate Margaretta and her adventures. If faced with the emergencies of Canadian pioneer life, Margaretta Moncton would surely expire. Indeed, she does not survive her pampered existence as an English lady; she dies in her husband's arms at the end of *Geoffrey Moncton*.

The topic of Canada arises periodically in Moodie's fiction, as in "Waiting for Dead Men's Shoes" in *Matrimonial Speculations* (1854), and *Flora Lyndsay* (1854), but the reality of backwoods life is, for the most part, not confronted directly. Like the Clarence family of Traill's *The Young Emigrants*, the Harford family of "Waiting for Dead Men's Shoes" considers itself to be impoverished; consequently, several family members emigrate to Canada in order to escape embarrassment. Moodie does not follow their exploits, choosing rather to focus on the romantic adventures of Rosamond, the sister who remains in England: "My present purpose is to stay at home, and see what befel Rosamond, and how her old uncle left his property."[16] *Flora Lyndsay* is ostensibly a novel about emigration. Yet Moodie follows the fortunes of the Lyndsay family only as far as their arrival in Canada; she leaves them on board ship, and summarizes their pioneering experiences as briefly as possible:

The Lyndsay's [sic] settled upon wild land, and suffered, for some years, great hardships in the backwoods. Ultimately, Mr. Lyndsay obtained an official appointment which enabled him to remove his wife and family to one of the fast-rising and flourishing towns of the Upper Providence [sic], where they have since resided in great happiness and comfort, and no longer regret their voyage to Canada, but bless the kind Providence that led them hither.[17]

Given the fact that her non-fiction, set as it is in Canada, has had a much greater impact than her fiction, it seems a pity that Moodie chose in *Flora Lyndsay* to ignore once again her knowledge of Canadian life.[18]

In the orientation towards the Old World that is demonstrated in her fiction, Moodie is more representative of her era than is Traill. Most of the fictional prose published in the *Literary Garland,* for example, echoes Moodie's preoccupation with sentimental English fiction.[19] Even a writer like John Richardson, who used a Canadian setting in his *Wacousta or the Prophecy* (1832) and *The Canadian Brothers; or, The Prophecy Fulfilled: A Tale of the Late American War* (1840), reverts to standard English characterizations of women despite the fact that an English lady (for instance, Clara De Haldimar of *Wacousta*) is clearly an incongruous figure in the midst of bloody Indian wars. Richardson was aware, evidently, that a Canadian "type" existed, a type which differed from the English lady as commonly perceived: witness his description in *The Canadian Brothers* of the intrepid Canadian women who risk life and limb in crossing a dangerous ice-filled river merely to attend a dance. Lieutenant Villiers comments to his brother officers that the women sit calmly in their sleighs,

as quietly and as unconcernedly, wrapped in their furs, as if they were merely taking their customary drive on terra firma ... nay, I am persuaded that if they ever entertain an anxiety on those occasions, it is either least the absence of one of those formidable masses should compel them to abandon an enterprize, the bare idea of entering upon which would give an European woman an attack of nerves or that the delayed aid should be a means of depriving them of one half minute of their anticipated pleasure.[20]

Richardson's female protagonists in *Wacousta,* the De Haldimar cousins, Madeline and Clara, tend to ignore the possibilities inherent in the model of the courageous Canadian women described in the above passage. Clara is beautiful and frail; she faints at every danger – real and imagined. Appropriately, she does not survive; the stresses of Canadian life prove to be too much for her. Madeline is more hardy; she can rouse herself to action in some cases, but, by and large, she falls short of the ideal of the capable and active pioneer woman. While Richardson chose to write about Canadian events and to use Canadian characters, he failed to exploit the dramatic potential inherent in the type of woman who would risk death to attend a dance. The Indian woman, Oucanasta of *Wacousta,* is the closest approximation to the active Canadian pioneer woman in Richardson's work; she twice saves Madeline De Haldimar from death because of her ability to act correctly in times of emergency. More generally, however, Richardson prefers to exploit the sentimental rather than to develop the possibilities of real pioneer life.

Set against a background of these and other writers,[21] Traill's efforts to Canadianize her fiction appear both innovative and courageous. As has been noted before, Traill's Canadian pioneer heroine, Catharine Maxwell, is far removed from the standard sentimental view of the English lady of the nineteenth century, reflecting, rather, the life of the pioneer women of that particular period in Canada. The importance of this literary legacy should not be ignored in any consideration of versions of the pioneer woman who appear in Canadian fiction up to and during the present time, and who are still perceived as the representatives of a particular type of ideal.

CHAPTER TWO

The Non-Fiction of Catharine Parr Traill

Catharine Parr Traill's emigration to Canada coincides with a major shift in the focus and the subjects of her writing. After her settlement in Upper Canada in the 1830s, she began, as has already been seen, to use Canada in her writing and to incorporate her collection of facts and anecdotes about pioneering into both her fiction and her non-fiction. As has also been seen, her literary interest in Canada had, in fact, been indicated earlier, specifically in her short novel, *The Young Emigrants or Pictures of Canada* (1826), which deals with the emigration to Canada of a middle-class English family. The focus in this particular story remains fixed on the English characters, however, while the later fiction, as for example, *Canadian Crusoes* (1852), utilizes Canadian characters. The later work's greater appeal, particularly to Canadian readers, is related to the author's first-hand knowledge of Canada. A further shift in the focus of Traill's writing is evident in her general movement away from the writing of fiction to the production of non-fiction. This shift probably reflects the fact that non-fiction could more directly reproduce Traill's own experiences as a pioneer, and provided a better forum for the expression of her views on pioneering. In any event, Traill's two most important and accomplished works, *The Backwoods of Canada* (1836) and *The Canadian Settler's Guide* (1855), are non-fiction, and both are based on the author's life as a pioneer in the Ontario backwoods. It is in these two works that she develops most fully her definition of the ideal pioneer woman, a definition which she transferred into her fiction.

It is unfortunate that relatively few first-hand accounts, particularly accounts written from a woman's perspective, of pioneering in nineteenth-century Ontario are available.[1] The diaries and letters of a small number of female pioneers have been published, notably

Susanna Moodie's *Roughing It in the Bush* (1852) and *Life in the Clearings* (1853), Frances Stewart's *Our Forest Home* (1889), Anne Langton's *A Gentlewoman in Upper Canada, The Journals of Anne Langton* (1950), and Mary Gapper O'Brien's *The Journals of Mary O'Brien, 1828–1838* (1968). Anna Jameson's *Winter Studies and Summer Rambles in Canada* (1838) should also be mentioned here. Although Jameson was not a pioneer, she travelled extensively throughout Upper Canada, and in *Winter Studies and Summer Rambles* she commented on the Canadian society she had seen. Taken together, these works give a fairly comprehensive view of a woman's life in pioneer Canada – more specifically, in pioneer Upper Canada. It has been noted that in her article "The Intelligent Woman's Guide to Pioneering in Canada," Virginia Rouslin has described the formulation by these women of a new female role, one which suited frontier life. In all major areas, these women were in agreement, and Traill's conclusions can be reinforced by reference to the work of any of the others. Yet, Traill emerges as a central figure in this group of pioneers, partly because she defined most clearly and succinctly the role of the pioneer woman, and partly because her work was published during the pioneer period; she intended to reach out and to influence other emigrants and prospective emigrants. Thus, in any discussion of the origins of the pioneer woman as both historical figure and literary type, Traill's work merits special attention.

Like Traill, Jameson and Moodie oriented their writing for immediate publication. Other women related their experiences either for their own benefit or for the purpose of maintaining contact with a small intimate circle of friends and family in Britain. Publication of their writing came long after the time of actual pioneering. Thus, they had little or no impact on women of their own generation. Traill, Moodie, and Jameson, however, described a particular place and time as accurately as possible for the benefit of a curious, intelligent, and more general reading public. While the larger focus in their work results, to some extent, in a more general, less intimate tone, a personal quality is maintained because each writer interprets what she sees.

Traill, for example, adds her opinions and comments to her lists of facts and to her narration of anecdotes. In the process of explicating Canada for her readers, she thus applies her own system of values to the world about her. Her background, her personality, and her values all influence her observations and help to change her non-fiction from simple factual reports to highly creative interpretations of pioneer life. The result of all this is that in her non-fiction Traill displays both her talent as a creative writer and her ability to observe and to report on the world about her with a great deal of accuracy. In other words, she applies her ideals to the reality of Canada, creating a diverse, multifaceted, and entertaining glimpse of nineteenth-century Ontario. In her description of the life of a female pioneer in Upper Canada, Traill colours factual reporting with an idealistic and interpretive bias.

Like Traill, Moodie and Jameson coloured factual reporting with their biases as English gentlewomen. Many of their conclusions are similar to those made by Traill. Yet in the development of the pioneer woman as an ideal of Canadian femininity, Traill remains the central figure in this small group. On the one hand, despite her clear and accurate observations, Jameson was merely an observer of pioneer life rather than a participant. On the other hand, Moodie (unlike Langton, O'Brien, Stewart, and Traill) apparently never relinquished her belief that true gentility was incompatible with backwoods life. Whether this was Moodie's own personal belief or merely a writer's stance (used to heighten the dramatic effect of her various trials and tribulations as a pioneer) is difficult to determine. At any rate, Moodie did not idealize pioneer life. Nor was she able to synthesize pioneer life with gentility.

Traill and Moodie had intimate knowledge of the many differences between the life of an English gentlewoman and that of a Canadian pioneer, and both writers use this knowledge to shape their writing. Moodie's inability in her non-fiction to resolve the two ways of life may, in fact, be the more accurate rendering of a gentlewoman's plight when faced with the exigencies of the Canadian frontier; Traill's attempts in both her non-fiction and her fiction to fuse the two divergent ways of life may be too idealistic for practical application. Yet, while Moodie makes evident and heightens the problems faced by the emigrant, Traill begins to formulate the solutions to the problems. Moodie laments her loss of status; Traill cheerfully works on the formulation of a new status.

It could even be said that the greatest strength of *The Backwoods of Canada* and *The Canadian Settler's Guide* is derived from Traill's ability to make observations from two distinctly different perspectives – to juxtapose the real with the ideal. Accurate reporting is varied with creative, fanciful, idealistic, and philosophical asides. These asides provide a marked contrast to the relation of cold facts; moreover, they strengthen and broaden the literary and historical value of the works in question. A dual mode of perception at once scientific and poetic permeates all of Traill's non-fiction. For example, she observes Canadian plant life with the scientific detachment of a botanist. But, at the same time, she is strangely excited by the plants which are foreign to her, and takes great pleasure in naming them. It is also notable that in her major botanical work, *Canadian Wild Flowers* (1868), there is a juxtaposition of poetry with the scientific descriptions of the various native plants. On the one hand, Traill records geographic and topographic details with the eager curiosity of an explorer; on the other hand, she occasionally becomes lost in a Romantic and abstract contemplation of Nature. She lists facts and provides survival instructions for new emigrants, but she also retains a sense of overall perspective, and attempts to instil in her readers an appreciation of the beauty and the future promise of her adopted country. When discussing pioneer facts she does not try to disguise her opinion that her duties seem endless, but, in a manner consistent with her social perspective, she also begins to develop an attitude or an ideal that other women can adopt. She proposes that there is something intrinsically valuable in pioneer life, and she creates a model of an ideal pioneer woman, a model which combines the real physical necessities of life on a frontier both with her own personal system of values and with her continued perception of herself as an English lady. Thus, the pioneer woman, as she is envisioned by Traill, creatively synthesizes practicality with sensibility, and the central consciousness (or, the preconceptions and the biases) of the English gentlewoman is the medium through which the reality of pioneer life is filtered to produce Traill's Canadian pioneer woman.

Throughout her writing there is no indication that Traill is aware either of a possible discrepancy in her views or of a split in her focus as she describes Canada. Yet it is notable that the various diverse modes of perception which are so obvious in the two longer works, *The Backwoods of Canada* and *The Canadian Settler's Guide*, achieve a more harmonious union in a later, shorter, prose passage, "The Bereavement," first published in the *Literary Garland* in 1866, and revised and republished in *Pearls and Pebbles* (1894) as "The First Death in the Clearing." Moreover, in the depiction of the pioneer narrator, there is little evidence of a split focus. As will be seen in due course, this particular sample of Traill's writing contains a shorter, sharper focus that often leads directly into a larger view and/ or into contemplative thought. This is to anticipate a later stage of the discussion, however, and for the present, the argument will turn to *The Backwoods of Canada*.

The Backwoods of Canada is Traill's first major work to confront directly and honestly the reality of life in pioneer Canada. As has been seen, *The Young Emigrants*, written before Traill's emigration, demonstrates the author's early interest in Canada, but must have been based on second-hand knowledge. In contrast *The Backwoods of*

Canada is derived from Traill's own experiences during the early years of her residence in Upper Canada. The book consists of a series of letters, ostensibly written to family and friends in Britain. The letters are set in a roughly chronological sequence and cover the first few years of the Traills' settlement in Ontario – that is, from 1832 to 1835. Traill's purpose in publishing such a work was evidently to explicate Canada and Canadian society for the benefit primarily of British and uninformed readers.

Whether addressing a private audience (the recipients of the original letters) or a later, larger audience (the readers of the published work), Traill seems to have assumed that she has attracted a certain type of readership – a readership made up of people from her own social background: education, reasonably affluent members of the middle class. The apparent assumption of a relatively uninformed but highly literate and intelligent audience probably heightened and encouraged Traill's propensity to approach her writing from the two separate points of reference – the scientific and the artistic – already described. Certainly, in *The Backwoods of Canada* she describes places, events, objects, and characters in minute detail so that her readers will see nineteenth-century Canada as it really is, and interprets these descriptions, adding comments which employ the terms and perspective of an English lady, a woman of refined and informed sensibilities, so that her readers will see and comprehend Canada from another less tangilble, but more familiar, point of view.

From the tone of the letters in *The Backwoods of Canada*, it would appear that Catharine Traill approached Canada with the eager curiosity of an explorer. While still on board ship, she studies maps so that she can better undestand her new country. As the ship makes its way up the St Lawrence River she constantly wants to know the names of the Quebec villages on either side. She is dismayed when she cannot disembark with the men at the Isle of Bic, but is placated to some extent when her husband brings her a bouquet of flowers from the island. Traill derives pleasure from identifying and naming the flora, and her curiosity is piqued when she discovers several strange new plants: "Besides these were several small white and yellow flowers, with which I was totally unacquainted."[2] This desire to know and to understand, to define, and to list all aspects of Canada's terrain is an important component of Traill's ability to enjoy her new surroundings. She trains the observant eye of the amateur scientist[3] on the scene about her:

It is fortunate for me that my love of natural history enables me to draw amusement from objects that are deemed by many unworthy of attention.

To me they present an inexhaustible fund of interest. The simplest weed that grows in my path, or the fly that flutters about me, are subjects for reflection, admiration, and delight. (17)

Yet Traill's interest in nature can also be that of a landscape artist rather than that of a botanist. Before her husband returns from the Isle of Bic, she solaces herself by looking at the scenery and enjoying her distant perspective of the island. She writes that she allays her resentment at her confinement by "feasting my eyes on the rich masses of foliage" (16). This skipping back and forth between the careful scrutiny of minute details and the long-range observation of picturesque nature is one of Traill's personal quirks as a writer – a quirk which she continues to display at regular intervals throughout the remainder of the narrative in *The Backwoods of Canada*. This particular passage provides early evidence of the bifocal vision that later enables Traill to list and describe the many tasks performed by the Canadian pioneer woman as well as to place these tasks within a larger perspective.

After the arrival of the ship in Canada, Traill is doomed to further disappointments at both Gros Isle and Quebec City. Because of a cholera epidemic, she cannot disembark and explore. But, as she has already observed, she is quite capable of amusing herself in most situations. At Gros Isle she is sent a basket of strawberries, raspberries, and flowers which she examines and enjoys. In a demonstration of her artistic sensibilities, Traill comments on the colourful and picturesque quality of the scene on the island, as, from her distant perspective, she watches the emigrants move about Gros Isle. She further amuses herself "with making little sketches of the fort and the surrounding scenery" (21). The gentlewoman's appreciation of the beauty of nature is offset partially by the practical pioneer's interest in the minute particulars of the vegetation indigenous to her new country, and is dampened slightly by the information that" "'tis distance lends enchantment to the view" (21) of the island. A friendly officer tells her that closer examination will reveal the underlying grotesque qualities:

disease, vice, poverty, filth, and famine – human misery in its most disgusting and saddening form. Such pictures as Hogarth's pencil only could have pourtrayed or Crabbe's pen described. (22)

The last sentence in this passage, with its references to the William Hogarth of such works as *A Rake's Progress* (1735) and *Marriage à la Mode* (1745) and the George Crabbe of such works as *The Village*

(1783) and *The Parish Register* (1807), demonstrates that, although Traill has been enlightened as to the true state of affairs on the island, and has been given the ugly, close-range details, she continues to be able to step back and to take a long-range perspective – to see the reality in terms of art. The nature-painting is undercut by a reference to Hogarthian or Crabbean realism; the images are still pictorial, however, and the long-range perspective balances the closer scrutiny. So, too, Traill's interpretation of a pioneer woman's life creatively combines reality with the artistic sensibility and perspective of an English gentlewoman.

In *A Gentlewoman in Upper Canada,* Anne Langton demonstrates a similar ability to step back from the practical, mundane reality of pioneer life in order to get a different view:

The morning was devoted to clearing out the cellars ... in the afternoon I took a solitary walk to the wood, and skirted it for some time, in search of a point from which the house might look well in a sketch.[1]

Langton returns to a close scrutiny of the unpleasant realities of pioneer life by commenting on the long tear in her skirt, made during her pursuit of a picturesque perspective.

Traill's ability to remark on the overall picture and also to itemize the parts that make up that picture from a much closer perspective indicates the wide scope of her literary imagination. She is interested in truth and accuracy, and writes so that her readers will see Canada as it really is. But she also appeals to the sensibilities of her audience. Specifically, the application of the principles of the picturesque and the sublime to a Canadian landscape seems designed to appeal to the understanding and the sympathies of her educated, middle-class readers. Much of what Traill describes would be strange or amusing to an English reader. But an appeal to the artistic awareness of this reader is calculated to awaken a sympathetic interest in Canada. Her reader will "see" Canada; ideally, he or she will "like" Canada.

An extremely important passage in Traill's interpretation of Canadian nature is found later in *The Backwoods of Canada* when she and her husband are lost at night in the bush. Shortly after their arrival in Canada, while the Traills are travelling to the home of Catharine Traill's brother, they lose their way. This particular episode is a central example of Traill's dual approach to the natural world: her practical account is juxtaposed with her appeal to the Romantic sensibilities of her readers. At a time when many women might well succumb to hysterics, Traill forgets her fear and doubt in a meditative, Romantic contemplation of nature:

A holy and tranquil peace came down upon me, soothing and softening my spirits into a calmness that seemed as unruffled as was the bosom of the water that lay stretched out before my feet. (118)

The implication that one can sense the existence of the deity through an appreciation of nature is found elsewhere in Traill's writing. In Peterborough, for example, she notes that she has felt close to God in the primitive backwoods church: "Never did our beautiful Liturgy seem so touching and impressive as it did that day, – offered up in our lowly, log-built church in the wilderness" (92). Later in the narrative, in her description of being lost, Traill juxtaposes sublime nature with the more prosaic aspects of the situation. Traill's episodic writing style, her ability to leap from one topic to another with almost alarming rapidity, prevents too frequent rhapsodizing on the glories of Nature. In this case, she balances occasional Romantic indulgence and factual reporting, with no apparent sense of incongruity. The story ends when she cheerfully settles in at her brother's home.

The necessary coexistence of utility and beauty is a recurring topic of discussion in *The Backwoods of Canada*, and is related to Traill's dual approach to nature. She comments on the great natural beauty of Peterborough, and notes, with approbation, the growing industry in this small town. But while she perceives the advantages inherent in the development of industry, she is apprehensive about the potential loss of the scenic beauty of Peterborough:

The plains are sold off in park lots, and some pretty little dwellings are being built, but I much fear the natural beauties of this lovely spot will be soon spoiled. (89)

Traill faces a similar problem when she and her husband begin clearing the trees from their land. She understands the necessity for chopping down the trees but would like to leave a few about her home to add beauty to the setting. This proves to be impossible: the older trees are not strong enough to exist without support, the saplings she asks her husband to spare are scorched in a fire, and she admits disappointment in her failure.

More commonly Traill is pragmatic and sensible, even when that pragmatism dictates the acceptance of a loss of beauty. Take, for example, the English lady's dilemma when she faces, for the first time, the reality of the backwoods log cabin: small, cramped, ugly, a far cry from any middle-class English woman's previous experience. When Traill's sister, Susanna Moodie, saw her own cabin, she was overwhelmed, and sat down to cry in helpless despair.[5] Fortunately, as she demonstrated in *The Backwoods of Canada,* Traill adopted a far different approach:

As I felt a great curiosity to see the interior of a log-house, I entered the open door-way of the tavern, as the people termed it, under the pretext of buying a draught of milk. (72)

She then notes the flaws and deficiencies of this structure with detached, scientific interest:

Besides the various emigrants, men, women, and children, that lodged within the walls, the log-house had tenants of another description. A fine calf occupied a pen in a corner; some pigs roamed grunting about in company with some half-dozen fowls. The most attractive objects were three snow-white pigeons, that were meekly picking up crumbs, and looking as if they were too pure and innocent to be inhabitants of such a place. (73)

From such a dubious beginning, Traill moves to an explanation of the advantages and the practical usefulness of these Canadian dwellings. She explains that all bush settlers, regardless of rank, must live in such cabins until they have the time and the money to build something better.

Anne Langton is generally optimistic in her view of Canada. Her early dislike of the ugliness of the Canadian log cabin is very quickly mitigated. In *A Gentlewoman in Upper Canada* she writes:

What most strikes me is a greater degree of roughness in the farming, buildings, gardens, fences, and especially roads, than I had expected. But when one looks at the wild woods around, and thinks that from such a wilderness the present state of things has been brought out by a few hands, and how much there is for those few hands to be constantly doing, one's surprise vanishes, and one rather wonders that so much has been done, than that so much remains to be done. (31)

In *The Backwoods of Canada,* Traill counsels a mental acceptance of such houses, through an understanding of their function, and demonstrates her own ability to do so:

for all its roughness, I love Canada, and am as happy in my humble log-house as if it were courtly hall or bower; habit reconciles us to many things that at first were distasteful. It has ever been my way to extract the sweet rather than the bitter in the cup of life, and surely it is best and wisest so to do. (310)

A determined optimism and an ability to bow to the inevitable are trademark qualities of Traill – mental qualities which ideally suited her role as a Canadian pioneer. As she says, "Nothing argues a greater degree of good sense and good feeling than a cheerful conformity to circumstances, adverse though they be compared with a former lot" (182).

Again, Anne Langton's opinions closely resembled Traill's. Like Traill, she was a cheerful pragmatist; in *A Gentlewoman in Upper Canada* she writes:

When I mention any of these primitive ways of doing things it is with the desire of making you more exactly conceive the precise style of civilization to which we have attained, not at all in the spirit of a grumbler, indeed it would be absurd to make grievances of such things; and after fastening your window with a string round a nail, or shading it with a boat flag for a month, you are very apt to forget that there is any other sort of hasp or blind. (35)

Traill's love of beauty cannot be ignored, however, for time and again she insists that a vital function of women in the backwoods is to ensure that grace and beauty exist in even the rudest dwellings. Her first view of Canadian log homes, seen from the distant perspective of the river, disappoints her, but she argues that it is not the dwellings themselves that are unacceptable:

It was not the rudeness of the material so much as the barn-like form of the buildings of this kind, and the little attention that was paid to the picturesque, that displeased me. (29)

In this case, Traill sets an example for her neighbours and, by extension, to future readers seeking instances of the correct conduct for a pioneer woman. She and her husband make a number of improvements to their log house. As soon as possible, she plants a garden. She grows vegetables to feed her family, and also transplants wild flowers, native plants, and shrubs. She has her garden enclosed with a "wattled fence" (309), which, she notes with approval, "forms a much more picturesque fence than those usually put up of split timber" (309). Finally, the Traills add a stoop, or verandah, to their log house. In Mrs Traill's opinion, a verandah greatly enhances the beauty of any log building. To add a final touch to the scene, she plants hops and grapes at the base of the verandah pillars.

The Langton family had similar views on beauty, and in *A Gentlewoman in Upper Canada,* Anne Langton says:

I look with pleasure and admiration at our verandah when I take my morning walk in it. The vines are up to the ceiling, and one of the rose-trees (a wild one) is nearly as high, and is quite a picture, so covered with flowers, and giving a sweet perfume, the want of which I have felt in the flowers in general here. When I think of what we were four years ago, our progress about the premises is wonderful, and repays us for all our care and painstaking. (167)

The tensions between the picturesque and the mundane, between the beautiful and the practical, between a long-range perspective and a closer scrutiny, and between the ideal world and the real world, dominate all aspects of Traill's backwoods writing, and are also evident in *The Backwoods of Canada* in her depiction of her own life as a pioneer. Traill describes the tasks and the way of life of a pioneer woman; she lists the many unpleasant duties which would be perceived as menial and degrading by an English gentlewoman, but she continually returns to her theme of practical necessity. Most important, she clings to her belief that she is a lady, and that she will always remain a lady, no matter what circumstances might dictate. Nevertheless, Traill confronts the reality of the life of a backwoodswoman with direct, unflinching honesty:

The female of the middling or better class, in her turn, pines for the society of the circle of friends she has quitted, probably for ever. She sighs for those little domestic comforts, that display of the refinements and elegancies of life, that she had been accustomed to see around her. She has little time now for those pursuits that were even her business as well as amusement. The accomplishments she has now to acquire are of a different order: she must become skilled in the arts of sugar-boiling, candle and soap-making, the making and baking of huge loaves, cooked in the bake-kettle, unless she be the fortunate mistress of a stone or clay oven. She must know how to manufacture *hop-rising* or *salt-rising* for leavening her bread; salting meat and fish, knitting stockings and mittens and comforters, spinning yarn in the big wheel (the French Canadian spinning-wheel), and dyeing the yarn when spun to have manufactured into cloth and coloured flannels, to clothe her husband and children, making clothes for herself, her husband and children; – for there are no tailors nor mantua-makers in the bush.

The management of poultry and the dairy must not be omitted. (183–84)

In this passage and others like it, Traill notes the lack of domestic comforts, the loneliness of the pioneer, and lists the new and arduous tasks which the migrant woman will confront.

It is interesting to see the subtle ways in which Traill seeks to impress upon her readers that, while the life of a pioneer woman may be difficult, it is not degrading. Although she sets two female roles in opposition in the passage just quoted – the cultivated lady with a great deal of time to develop leisured pursuits and accomplishments is juxtaposed to the eternally busy Canadian pioneer woman – Traill continues to assume that the pioneer woman will be able to define herself as a lady, even in the backwoods. Note, for example, the softening of the details of pioneer life by the use of "accomplishment," a word previously connected to such decorative pursuits as music or painting, but now used to signify tasks of a "different order." In this way, household chores such as baking bread and making soap and candles are equated with (and shown to be superior to) the decorative, idle skills of an English lady. The pioneer woman should be "skilled in the arts" of the backwoods housewife; she must become a manufacturer of various items, and a manager in several domestic departments. Traill's perspective presents a novel interpretation of the pioneer woman's role: the refined gentlewoman merely switches her area of expertise, losing none of her gentility in the process.

Anna Jameson agreed with Traill. She too felt that Old- and New-World accomplishments were compatible. In *Winter Studies and Summer Rambles* she comments:

I have observed that really accomplished women, accustomed to what is called the best society, have more resources here, and manage better, than some women who have no pretensions of any kind, and whose claims to social distinction could not have been great any where, but whom I found lamenting over themselves as if they had been so many exiled princesses.[6]

Jameson goes on to describe the life of one such "accomplished" woman in the backwoods, a woman who has faced difficulties with "a cheerful spirit" (II, 135). This woman's daughter, although lacking in the decorative, drawing-room accomplishments known to her mother, is nevertheless perceived by Jameson as a model child:

Her eldest daughter meantime, a fair and elegant girl, was acquiring, at the age of fifteen, qualities and habits which might well make amends for the possessing of mere accomplisments. She acted as a manager-in-chief, and glided about in her household avocations with a serene and quiet grace which was quite charming. (II, 135)

The mother, a gentlewoman, has adapted cheerfully to pioneer life; the daughter, reminiscent of the Catharine Maxwell of Traill's *Canadian Crusoes,* is clearly an ideal young woman in a world where "accomplishments" have necessarily been replaced by "household avocations."

In *The Backwoods of Canada,* Traill is honest in her descriptions of pioneer life. She outlines the reality of her situation. But (like Jameson in the previous example) she uses a British frame of reference so that her audience will understand and accept the customs of Canadian pioneer life. Despite her honesty in admitting the hardships, the loneliness, and the despair faced by herself and by other pioneer women, Traill continues to insist that she is a lady. In one breath, she reiterates her view that all emigrant women must, because of frontier conditions, face unpleasant tasks. In the next, she claims that Canadian society can be very pleasant and congenial. She says, for example:

Our society is mostly military or naval; so that we meet on equal grounds, and are, of course, well acquainted with the rules of good breeding and polite life; too much so to allow any deviation from those laws that good taste, good sense, and good feeling have established among persons of our class.

Yet here it is considered by no means derogatory to the wife of an officer or gentleman to assist in the work of the house, or to perform its entire duties, if occasion requires it; to understand the mystery of soap, candle, and sugar-making; to make bread, butter, and cheese, or even to milk her own cows; to knit and spin, and prepare the wool for the loom. In these matters we bush-ladies have a wholesome disregard of what Mr. or Mrs. So-and-so thinks or says. We pride ourselves on conforming to circumstances; and as a British officer must needs be a gentleman and his wife a lady, perhaps we repose quietly on that incontestable proof of our gentility, and can afford to be useful without injuring it. (270–1)

This is a central, essential statement of the position taken by Traill with respect to her role in Canada. It combines and contrasts her pragmatic acceptance of adverse circumstances with her idealism. In essence Traill at once admits that all bush settlers, regardless of their rank and previous experience, must work hard, and claims that this change in daily habits does not endanger one's social standing.

The Gapper family clung to its middle-class gentility as well. In spite of (perhaps in defiance of) long, difficult days, the family members passed their evening hours in much the same fashion as they had in Britain: they read aloud, played musical instruments and sang, and discussed politics, literature, and philosophy. It was in such a manner that Mary Gapper became acquainted with her future husband, Edward O'Brien (a gentleman). In *The Journals of Mary O'Brien*, she describes a typical evening:

Mary and I talk [*sic*] and read over some of her poetry. Whilst she was at work, I read to her some of the "Fall of Nineveh". After tea we read the "Book of the Church" till Richard returned ... Then Bill accompanied Mary with his fiddle till half past nine, when we had prayers and then talked till bedtime. (20)

Mary even tried to integrate her former life as somewhat of a "bluestocking" into her daily routine:

I also stirred a bowl of cream into butter, in which I succeeded much to my heart's content, sitting under the verandah and reading Milton all the time. Only I found to my sorrow when my work was finished that I had ground off one of my nails (118)

The image of backwoods gentility is greatly enhanced by this picture of Mary O'Brien churning butter, reading Milton, and destroying her fingernails in the process.

Anne Langton laments the lack of servants in Canada. Yet, she, like Traill, advocates the willing participation of the emigrant gentlewoman in any and all work. In *A Gentlewoman in Upper Canada* she says:

This, I suppose, is one of the troubles of the backwoods; there is so much expense and loss of time in hunting for a servant here that it is doubly annoying. However, it is not such a calamity to be left without as it would be at home ... How strangely one's ideas accommodate themselves to the ways and necessities of the country one is in! This summer, when our bustling household made a little help from the ladies often necessary, I used to be amused at myself going so composedly about my duties at the cooking stove. (63)

Langton's amusement at her new role does not disguise the fact that she has joined wholeheartedly in the pioneering process. Mary O'Brien, in *The Journals of Mary O'Brien*, talks about the shift between lady and pioneer as well: "I had just finished the first stage of my cooking and was about to shift my character from cook to gentlewoman" (141). O'Brien, Langton, and Traill noted the differences between lady and pioneer, but they had little difficulty in accepting and reconciling the two roles.

In spite of her claims that she herself retains her status as a lady, Traill notes a general levelling of social rank in Canada. Her reactions to social change are thus somewhat ambivalent, for while she asserts that she is a lady, and therefore superior to many of her fellow emigrants, she also appears to enjoy a great deal of the personal independence that has resulted from the social freedom of Canadian pioneer life, noting with approval the absence of certain rules of etiquette and behaviour which characterize the rigid class structure of British society, and confessing that she found life in Britain somewhat constricting:

I was too much inclined to spurn with impatience the fetters that etiquette and fashion are wont to impose on society, till they rob its followers of all freedom and independence of will. (269)

And Traill admits that she has found greater freedom in Canada: "I must freely confess to you that I do prize and enjoy my present liberty in this country exceedingly" (269). A positive result, then, of the backwoods emphasis on practicality is a greater freedom from social restraint:

Now, we *bush-settlers* are more independent: we do what we like; we dress as we find most suitable, and most convenient; we are totally without the fear of any Mr. or Mrs. Grundy; and having shaken off the trammels of Grundyism, we laugh at the absurdity of those who voluntarily forge afresh and hug their chains. (270)

Anne Langton, in *A Gentlewoman in Upper Canada*, reports a sense of unease when several ladies move into their neighbourhood:

At all these arrivals of ladies I do not think I rejoice, as it would seem natural to do. I shall have to pay morning visits, etc., and I suppose I am growing savage, *alias* selfish, and unaccustomed to make sacrifice to society. (107)

While she revels in her personal freedom, Traill finds other aspects of the levelling of social rank distinctly unappealing. She continues to stand on her dignity as a lady, and would like to ensure the retention of the willing servility of a lower, labouring class. The arrogance and affectation of servants in Canada apparently causes Traill, like

Susanna Moodie, some feelings of uneasiness. Unlike the upper classes, the lower classes should not shake off their chains, and laugh at
Grundyism. Traill quite openly disapproves of what she considers an
inappropriate assumption of equality by the lower classes in Canada.
She complains to her reader:

You would be surprised to see how soon the new comers fall into this dis-
agreable manner and affectation of equality, especially the inferior class of
Irish and Scotch; the English less so. (83)

Traill does not seem to feel any sense of incongruity in her opinions
on New-World freedom.

In certain circumstances in *The Backwoods of Canada* Traill actually
defends the levelling of class structure in Canada. For example, when
she compliments Peterborough on its "genteel society" (81), she notes
that this society is composed of officers and their families and pro-
fessional men, as well as storekeepers (and here one is reminded of
the Murchisons of Sara Jeannette Duncan's *The Imperialist* [1904]),
and that many of the Canadian merchants are "persons of respectable family and good education" (81), thus warranting their inclusion
in the list. Traill tells her readers that the social standing of a store-
keeper in Upper Canada is superior to that of a shopkeeper in an
English village, chiefly because, in Canada, all men and women,
regardless of rank, must take part in the active physical labour of
pioneer settlement. This is the one great leveller of rank in Canadian
society. Yet Traill refuses to discard all of her preconceived ideas of
rank and privilege:

After all, it is education and manners that must distinguish the gentleman
in this country, seeing that the labouring man, if he is diligent and indus-
trious, may soon become his equal in point of wordly possessions. (81)

While Traill acknowledges the inevitability of social levelling in Canada, she seems to anticipate the formation of a new aristocracy – in
effect, a meritocracy based on education and manners, an upper-
class segment of society which is composed of the well educated, not
necessarily of the well born or the wealthy. To an extent, then, Traill
guards the intangible proofs of her own gentility and despairs of the
social presumptions of her neighbours; but she also takes an active
and eager part in the pioneering process, enjoys her freedom from
social constriction, and hopes that the final, positive result of the
social levelling apparent in a frontier society will be the creation of
an ideal aristocracy based on qualities of the mind.

In *The Backwoods of Canada* Traill has, in effect, produced a spirited defence of Canada and of her life as a pioneer woman. She has faced the difficulties of pioneering and has admitted that her role forces her to cope with situations far different from any of her previous experience. The mingling of honesty with idealism leads Traill to conclude: "I find, by impartial survey of my present life, that I am to the full as happy, if not really happier, than I was in the old country" (268). Contrast Traill's rational statement with Susanna Moodie's passionate outburst when she leaves the bush for Belleville:

Many painful and conflicting emotions agitated my mind, but found no utterance in words, as we entered the forest path, and I looked my last upon that humble home consecrated by the memory of a thousand sorrows. Every object had become endeared to me during my long exile from civilized life. I loved the lonely lake, with its magnificent belt of dark pines sighing in the breeze; the cedar swamp, the summer home of my dark Indian friends; my own dear little garden, with its rugged snake-fence which I had helped Jenny to place with my own hands, and which I had assisted the faithful woman in cultivating for the last three years, where I had so often braved the tormenting mosquitoes, black flies, and intense heat, to provide vegetables for the use of the family. Even the cows, that had given a breakfast for the last time to my children, were now regarded with mournful affection.[7]

Although Moodie was evidently proud of her successes as a pioneer (the pride creeps in, almost unnoticed), she treats her experiences in the Canadian bush as a never-ending series of trials and tribulations; even her home is "consecrated" only "by the memory of a thousand sorrows."

A sense of determined optimism is a trait of Traill's pioneer writing, presenting a stark contrast to Moodie's complaining tone. It is evident in her first pioneer narrative, and continues to be a dominant force throughout the rest of her writing career. It influences the way in which she perceives herself and her surroundings. It is the guiding principle in her development of a plan for successful emigration and in her creation of a model pioneer woman for other emigrant women to emulate.

Like *The Backwoods of Canada*, *The Canadian Settler's Guide* confronts the reality of pioneer life in the backwoods. The later work is, however, more immediately practical in its orientation than its predecessor, and is intended to serve as "a useful guide"[8] to Canada, to be "a Manual of Canadian housewifery" (xviii) for female emigrants. In *The Canadian Settler's Guide*, Traill attempts to help British female emigrants to cope with the stresses and the "emergencies of their new mode of life" (xvii) in the Canadian backwoods. She knows from personal experience that a book of basic instructions would be a welcome addition to any pioneer home:

Having myself suffered from the disadvantage of acquiring all my knowledge of Canadian housekeeping by personal experience, and having heard other females similarly situated lament the want of some simple useful book to give them an insight into the customs and occupations incidental to a Canadian settler's life, I have taken upon me to endeavor to supply this want, and have with much labour collected such useful matter as I thought best calculated to afford the instruction required. (xvii)

Many emigrant women clearly needed Traill's advice and guidance. As Anna Jameson had noted in *Winter Studies and Summer Rambles,*

I have not often in my life met with contented and cheerful-minded women, but I never met with so many repining and discontented women as in Canada. I never met with *one* woman recently settled here, who considered herself happy in her new home and country: I *heard* of one, and doubtless there are others, but they are exceptions to the general rule. (ii, 133)

Traill, as if heeding Jameson's complaint, sets out to rectify the situation.

The Canadian Settler's Guide was, like *The Backwoods of Canada,* intended for publication. But while Traill's first major work of non-fiction was written for a wealthy, middle-class audience, her second assumes a more general readership and is written to help all Canadian emigrants rather than to enlighten and entertain a sophisticated social group. Consequently, the style of writing differs in the second book. In her Preface, Traill writes:

As this little work has been written for all classes, and more particularly for the wives and daughters of the small farmers, and part of it is also addressed to the wives of the labourer[s] and mechanics, I aimed at no beauty of style. It was not written with the intention of amusing, but simply of instructing and advising. (xviii)

Very evidently Traill wishes to create a practical, useful guide; she hopes primarily to instruct rather than to entertain. As a result, her book covers a wide variety of topics, and presents a large number of facts about pioneering. Her writing style tends to reflect her apparent intention to focus on use and practicality rather than on beauty. There are fewer rambling excursions into philosophic thought, fewer asides, and fewer anecdotes. Traill covers her topics as thoroughly as possible and as concisely as possible. Nevertheless she cannot avoid entirely her propensity to moralize, speculate, or entertain, and her work continues to mirror a tension between pragmatism and sensibility. Despite what seem to have been her intentions, Traill offers in *The Canadian Settler's Guide* both practical advice and moral or philosophic musings to the readers.

Moreover, while Traill defends the propriety of concentrating on what is useful and practical in a pioneer setting, she cannot eliminate the importance of beauty in her world view. Consequently, she insists that beauty and grace should be included in pioneer life as well. In her section on gardening in *The Canadian Settler's Guide* she tells her readers when and how to plant the various essential fruits and vegetables. A garden is a necessary addition to every pioneer home, and Traill not only describes the uses of each plant but also provides instructions for planting and harvesting the crops. Nevertheless, Traill veers from merely pragmatic towards aesthetic concerns when she urges her readers to pay attention to the potential beauty of the backwoods garden. She quotes from the *Old Countryman* when she writes, "give a thought and an eye occasionally to the beautiful" (53). She advocates, for example, the removal of the surface stones around the garden for both practical and aesthetic reasons:

These surface stones may be made very serviceable in filling up the lower part of the fence, or, piled in large heaps, be rendered ornamental by giving them the effect of rockwork. (55)

In this instance, Traill gives her settlers the option of employing the garden stones in either a useful or an ornamental way, of being either – or both – practical and artistic.

It is appropriate that Traill concludes her section on gardens with an excursion into her personal theories on nature and the natural world. Whereas she began by giving practical advice, even though she modifies her practicality with her theories on garden beautification, she concludes by noting that, through an appreciation of beauty, specifically an appreciation of the beauty of nature, one can sense the presence of God:

There are very few persons totally insensible to the enjoyment of the beautiful, either in nature or art, and still fewer who are insensible to the approbation of their fellow men; this feeling is no doubt implanted in them by the Great Creator, to encourage them in the pursuit of purer, more intellectual pleasures than belong to their grosser natures. As men cultivate the mind they rise in the scale of creation, and become more capable of adoring the

Almighty through the works of his hands. – I think there can be no doubt but that whatever elevates the higher faculties of the soul, brings man a step nearer to his Maker. (55–6)

In spite of her primary emphasis on practical advice in *The Canadian Settler's Guide,* Traill thus demonstrates a Romantic belief in the immanence of God in nature, as, of course, she had done in *The Backwoods of Canada* when she described the experience of being lost in the bush.

Traill advises the female reader of *The Canadian Settler's Guide* to spend some time beautifying her home. She insists on the importance of "comfort and convenience before show and finery" (13), and manages to make each beautification project a practical necessity. After stating that a verandah is a sensible addition to a backwoods cabin, she notes that it adds beauty to the building, and, in a further return to practical advice, that it serves as a useful extra room during the summer months. Traill further recommends that settlers plant vines at the base of the verandah pillars. The hop plant provides a "graceful drapery of leaves and flowers" (15) which adds a touch of beauty and refinement to the home. The hop plant is also a common source for the yeast used in the baking of bread, and Traill provides instructions in her book for making bread with home-grown yeast. In this way, Traill justifies her beautification projects with a practical dimension, and, by extension, indicates the way in which the ideal pioneer woman can honour the needs of both practicality and sensibility.

Traill's eclectic mingling of the mundane and the ideal dominates all of her attempts at useful instruction, and is exemplified in another section of *The Canadian Settler's Guide,* this time in a passage on Indian corn. The section is a typical one in its demonstration of Traill's multifaceted or bifocal approach to her subject as well as her redefinition of a woman's role to suit new world conditions. She begins by instructing her readers, first in the identification and function of Indian corn, then in the explanation of the proper planting and harvesting procedures for this North American crop. The practical, detailed instructions follow closely Traill's mandate to teach emigrant women the basic skills required by frontier living. This section is followed by an anecdote about one woman's experiences with Indian corn, and Traill then moves into a discussion of woman and her role in Canada, beginning with a warning to her readers that a woman's role on the frontier is quite different from anything an emigrant woman has experienced before:

I have been particular in describing, as minutely as I could, all these things relating to the cultivation of this crop, so universally grown in Canada; for though it is not often left to the management of females, yet such things have sometimes occurred through sickness or accident befalling the head of the family, that the work or the direction of it, has fallen upon the wives and daughters of the farmer.

I have known women in Canada, who have not only planted and hoed the corn, but have also harvested it. (113–14)

This is a frank acknowledgment that life is difficult on the Canadian frontier: any woman can be called upon to do not only her own housework but also the field-work which is more commonly the domain of her husband.

At this point in *The Canadian Settler's Guide* Traill moves into her anecdote about a particular woman's experience in the backwoods. She uses the story to alter her focus as a writer, and she begins to proselytize. The main elements of the anecdote can be easily summarized. A pioneer woman with a sick husband is forced by necessity to take charge of the harvesting of their corn crop. Although she is unused to field labour, and unsuited physically to do men's work, she finds the strength to complete the harvesting, to nurse her husband, and to amuse her baby:

At first she was inclined to fret, and give up in despair, but when she looked upon her sick husband and her helpless babe, she remembered that duty required better things from her than to lie down and weep, and lament: she knew that other women had their trials, and she braced up her mind to do what was before her, praying to God to give her strength to do her duty, and she went on cheerfully and with a brave spirit. (114)

A cheerful conformity to adverse circumstances, and a willing acceptance of necessity – these are the basic requirements of a pioneer woman, and Traill is merely repeating her earlier arguments from *The Backwoods of Canada.*

In *The Canadian Settler's Guide* Traill insists that, aside from the chance to display one's moral fortitude, pioneer chores offer certain rewards to women who bravely accept their new lot in life. In *The Backwoods of Canada,* Traill, as has been seen, comments on her sense of greater personal freedom from constricting social rules. In the story about Indian corn, in *The Canadian Settler's Guide,* Traill claims that the heroine of her story is not ashamed of her field-work. She proposes that the performance of menial tasks is not a degradation in Canada, but is, rather, a source for pride:

In after years she has often with honest pride related to her children, how she gathered in the first Indian corn crop that was raised on their bush farm.

Possibly this very circumstance gave a tone of energy and manly independence of spirit to her children, which will mark them in their progress in
after life. (115)

Thus, there is a lasting reward for this woman's cheerful response to
adverse circumstances. Traill claims in *The Canadian Settler's Guide*
that she has received similar benefits from her residence in Canada:

At first I could hardly understand why it happened that I never felt the
same sensation of fear in Canada as I had done in England. My mind seemed
lightened of a heavy burden; and I, who had been so timid, grew brave and
fearless amid the gloomy forests of Canada. (46)

Pride, self-confidence, independence – these are the rewards for the
courageous pioneer woman.

The combination of "cheerfulness of mind and activity of body"
(1), as outlined in the Preface of *The Canadian Settler's Guide,* is the
main ingredient in Traill's ideal pioneer woman, a figure in whom
pragmatism must coexist with inner spiritual beauty. The pioneer
woman must be physically capable as well as mentally prepared to
meet all exigencies with immediate activity: "In cases of emergency,
it is folly to fold one's hands and sit down to bewail in abject terror:
it is better to be up and doing" (204). While all of this activity must
have seemed quite foreign and very bewildering to some English
emigrant women, Traill reiterates her firm belief that, despite her
changed circumstances, a woman's self-definition can remain intact
on the frontier: "One thing is certain, that a lady will be a lady, even
in the plainest dress; a vulgar minded woman will never be a lady,
in the most costly garments" (10). Traill forges ahead, confidently
and serenely. Secure in the knowledge that she herself is a lady and
will always remain a lady, she advocates some quite radical changes
in a woman's role. The pioneer woman must revise her focus, accept
adversity with a brave and confident spirit, perform new and arduous
tasks in the kitchen and in the fields. Her rewards for cheerful service
are intangible but the implication is that, if she can perform her tasks
in the right spirit, she can define herself as a heroine, that she will
feel a lasting sense of pride in accomplishment and a new sense of
self-confidence, that she will undoubtedly be rewarded in the after-
life.

The differences between *The Backwoods of Canada* and *The Canadian
Settler's Guide* are marginal, yet, for present purposes, these differences merit attention. In the later book Traill continues to employ
various disparate points of view, and to vacillate between her accurate
portrayal of the real world of the Canadian backwoods and her ide-

alized interpretation of pioneering. *The Canadian Settler's Guide* is oriented towards a wider reading public, however, and is intended to be a practical guide to emigration. It develops more fully many of Traill's theories about pioneering in Canada, specifically her view of the female pioneer and her role in Canadian life. Moreover, Traill's ideas may be better integrated in *The Canadian Settler's Guide*, for here she tends to point out the ideal aspects of every situation, and a certain balance is achieved. There is, for example, the story of the pioneer woman who harvests the corn. Traill comments that incidents such as this one are common in pioneer life. Women, called upon to perform work which is generally not within their sphere of duty, discover that they can carry out their unpleasant tasks, and that, surprisingly enough, they enjoy certain aspects of their work. As in *The Backwoods of Canada*, Traill insists on the propriety of conforming to necessity. But she insists equally that virtue is always rewarded, that there are intangible benefits which result from dutiful obedience. The woman who harvests the corn is merely bowing to the inevitable, and the reward she reaps is intangible as well as tangible. Traill is continually on the defensive in both books. She is aware that her readers may find her stories about Canada strange and even repulsive. She attempts to soften her tough stance by adopting a moral attitude which gives the reassurance that a cheerful acceptance of unpleasant tasks is both necessary and virtuous. According to Traill, virtue is often rewarded in Canada by a sense of pride in accomplishment and by a feeling of freedom from social restriction.

The defensive tone is missing from Traill's shorter non-fiction. In fact, Traill's best, most cohesive writing is found in her later collections of short stories, *Pearls and Pebbles* (1894) and *Cot and Cradle Stories* (1895), and in the anecdotes which are included as digressions within longer narratives. Because the majority of these shorter narratives and digressions are derived from Traill's personal experiences in the backwoods, they can be included in a discussion of her non-fiction. Many, including "The First Death in the Clearing" and "Something Gathers Up the Fragments" in *Pearls and Pebbles,* achieve what Clara Thomas has termed "a vignette perfection."[9] In the shorter works Traill is less concerned with developing her theories about pioneering and with justifying her ideas to her readers. Her points have been established: now she is employing her theories without fear of contradiction. Furthermore, the concentration on a single thought or incident means that the works are better unified. Otherwise, the themes and motifs of the longer non-fiction – particularly with respect to the ideal of the pioneer woman – seem to be essentially unchanged as they appear in the short stories.

Traill's short prose passage "The Bereavement," first published in the *Literary Garland* in 1866 and later rewritten and republished in *Pearls and Pebbles* in 1894 as "The First Death in the Clearing,"[10] is more personal in tone than the longer narratives where, more generally, she speaks with some detachment. In "The Bereavement," Traill continues to play a series of dual roles: she is a participant and an observer; she is the chief character in the drama and the narrator; she is an artist and a scientist; she is an English lady and a Canadian pioneer. Yet "The Bereavement" is unified and cohesive, largely because Traill, as unique person and also as character type, is at the centre of the work.

Traill pays close attention (as always) to small details. No object escapes her notice. In this story, unlike the more cumbersome longer works, however, this careful attention to detail is evident in her prose style. "The Bereavement" is carefully crafted as Traill reconstructs a scene or an incident as accurately as possible, assembling her details so that she can create a larger picture. In addition, she interprets what she sees; a small point, or a scene, or an incident, will act as a springboard for her movement into philosophic thought and speculation. Traill reassembles and rearranges the minute details of her landscape on a larger canvas so that she may narrate a story that has a moral purpose at its heart. In effect, the moral perspective of the author unites the various disparate points of view. That "The Bereavement" is based on the relation of one incident only, the death of a child, means that Traill has less opportunity to depart from her topic in order to impart useful or moral bits of wisdom. While Traill has not designed "The Bereavement" as a treatise on pioneering, she repeats many of the themes developed in earlier non-fiction, most notably her creation of an ideal Canadian pioneer woman.

In her initial evocation of a specific time and place in "The Bereavement," Traill produces minute details, things which would be noted only by the careful observer – the person who is interested in all parts which make up a composite whole. The episode begins on a spring morning:

The air was filled with insects which had either revived from their winter torpor or been prematurely awakened to the enjoyment of a bright but brief existence. A few sleepy, dusty looking flies had crept from their hiding places about the window – while some attenuated shadowy spider made vain attempts at commencing a web to entangle them.[11]

No object is seemingly too small or unimportant to escape enumeration by the scientist. But it takes the imaginative eye of an artist to portray these humble insects with sympathy, to grant them a "bright," albeit "brief" life. As she stands in her doorway, Traill, the scientist, observes the natural world outside her cabin. It is typical of Traill that she provides the proper latinate names for the plants and animals of the Canadian backwoods. She comments on "the neat snow-bird *(fringilla nivalis)*" (69). The effect of this display of erudition, unnecessary to the narrative, is rather odd. Nevertheless, it is part of Traill's general attempt to define and to classify the environment of the pioneer woman in her non-fiction.

Despite her scientific inclination and despite her propensity to list and to catalogue her surroundings, Traill is, as has been seen, almost always capable of observing the natural world with an artist's appreciation for colour and perspective. In all her descriptions of Canadian scenery Traill is as appreciative of the whole picture as she is of the picture's component parts; indeed, it could be said that the dual perspective is here again the epistemological counterpart of the ideal of the pioneer heroine, a figure who must be oriented towards both the useful and the beautiful. The writer who in "The Bereavement" comments on the flies in her window, and who can give the snow-bird its proper name, also reveals an awareness of the Romantic and picturesque value of nature:

I ... looked forth upon the face of Nature – and a lovely sight it was! The frosty earth was gemmed with countless diamonds – the mimic picture of those bright orbs above, which were still gleaming down from the clear blue sky; the saffron tint of early dawn was streaking the East. A light curling mist was gathering on the face of the rapid river, which lay before my eyes in all the majesty of its white crested waves, darkly shaded by the then unbroken line of forest on the opposite bank. (70–1)

An artistic awareness of the patterns of light and dark, of colour, and of foreground and background perspective, permeates this particular passage. Here, as in her account of being lost in the bush in *The Backwoods of Canada*, Traill demonstrates her belief in a God immanent in a nature that is comfortingly humanized: she looks upon "the face of Nature," and "the face of the rapid river." She loses herself in a Romantic contemplation of the beauty of nature; a contemplative side of her personality appears and balances the earlier glimpse of a practical orientation. Traill has once again demonstrated an ability to juxtapose, or perhaps to combine, several seemingly disparate ways of viewing the natural world. Yet, as already suggested, in "The Bereavement," the distinctions between the scientist and the artist tend to be less clearly marked and less important. There is more of an artistic balance between the two areas, less of a possible confusion in priorities.

The use of a single incident as the basis for "The Bereavement" allows the development of a more complex series of images in this story than in Traill's longer, rambling narratives, or in the shorter sketches based on the description of a single plant or animal. The longer narratives tend to be choppy and uneven. The shorter sketches – for example, the flower sketches published in the *Literary Garland*[12] or the descriptions of plants in *Canadian Wild Flowers* (1868) – while they display Traill's eclectic ability to perceive and portray a natural object in several ways, lack the greater artistic development of "The Bereavement." Furthermore, "The Bereavement" contains a series of consistent and well-developed patterns of imagery that augment and shape the narrative. One such pattern of imagery juxtaposes the interiors of various buildings with the exterior natural world. In this story, buildings are associated with imprisonment and death while nature is associated with springtime and new life. Yet, in both settings, Traill can sense the existence of the deity, and a consistent moral point of view unites the imagery. The narrator's desire to escape from the confinement of her cabin into the freedom of the spring sunshine is established in the initial scene:

Bright and blue as was the sky above, warm and genial as was the air around, and inviting as were the sounds of nature abroad, I yet found myself obliged to be an unwilling prisoner. (69)

The three senses of sight, touch, and sound unite in extending an invitation to this pioneer woman.

Traill states here and elsewhere (in both *The Backwoods of Canada* and *The Canadian Settler's Guide*) that she has noticed a feeling of personal freedom and independence in the backwoods. In "The Bereavement," the narrator's freedom would stem from her inclusion in the world outdoors:

How I envied the more fortunate flocks of wild geese and ducks that were revelling in the azure pools, that lay so invitingly open to them, on the ice-bound lake in front of our log house. Sorely tempted as I was by the bright sunshine, and all spring's pleasant harmonies, to go forth into the newly uncovered fields – yet I dared not risk wetting my feet, having but recently recovered from a severe fit of illness. (69)

Prevented by mundane human problems from going out into the spring sunshine, the narrator gazes longingly from behind her prison bars into a bright and vitally alive nature. In her earlier defences of Canada and of all things Canadian, Traill would have insisted on practical necessity; she would have noted that it is infinitely more sensible to remain indoors for a good reason. One ought to be pragmatic and practical. Certainly, she would not have referred to her cabin as a prison. Here in "The Bereavement" she seems no longer to be developing theories, with the result that she can relax and can use effective imagery, regardless of the impression she may be giving her readers concerning the interior of a log cabin.

In a further metaphoric use of building interiors, the narrator of "The Bereavement" describes the log cabin where a child has died. The narrator has been called from her own home to assist another woman with her sick baby, and, after the death of the child, the narrator returns to comfort the mother. The dim interior of the house and the child's death are juxtaposed with the "sunny brightness" (71) and the vitality of the spring day, on which Traill takes time to comment before she enters. Inside, however, the light dims, and as the narrator confronts sickness, grief, and death, her mood suffers a radical change: "A solemn feeling came over me, as I stepped across the threshold" (71).

Traill's religious convictions permeate and unite "The Bereavement." Religious metaphors and motifs, biblical allusions and parallels are used frequently in the narrative. Even the potentially threatening interior of a house where a child has died holds no fears for the narrator. The cabin, while it contains death, is, paradoxically, the centre of religious conviction as well, and becomes a holy place. The narrator has watched over the child throughout the night before its death; the third day after the death is a Sunday, and on this particular morning, the narrator returns to the cabin in order to assist the mourning parents. As she arrives she notes, "The door of the dwelling stood open, and I entered unbidden" (71). These parallels with the crucifixion and the resurrection of Christ – parallels which, of course, blur the distinctions between fiction and non-fiction – are augmented by the descriptions of the grief-stricken parents. The mother sits in the pose of a Madonna, "her face bowed over the pale shrouded form of the idol of her heart" (72), and mourns her loss with "the holy weeping of maternal love" (72). The father, a priestlike figure, is reading his Bible when Traill enters the cabin/tomb:

As I entered, he raised his head, and bowed with an air of deep reverence, but spoke no word, and I passed on, unwilling to intrude upon his wholesome meditation. (72)

Through the grief of its inhabitants, the log cabin becomes a church. With an allusion to Milton's "Il Penseroso," Traill observes the "dim religious light of the darkened room. In the centre was a table, decently covered with a snow white damask cloth."[13] That there is even a communion table of sorts in the centre of the room covered with a "snow white ... cloth" indicates that the death of the child becomes a commemoration of the death and resurrection of Christ.

The allusions and parallels to the Easter story are strengthened by the use of the springtime season, by Traill's firm belief in the renewal of all life, and by the departure of the dead child from its temporal home in the cabin into the spring sunshine for burial in the colonial cemetery. This movement, from a cabin to the outside world, typifies, for Traill, a movement into a freer, happier world. It denotes a movement from death into life, and it signifies a time of rejoicing rather than of mourning. The child's soul is in heaven. Its body, buried in the quiet Canadian cemetery, is surrounded by the beauty of nature and by nature's constant reminder of the existence of God:

the pines sigh above them a solemn requiem, the wild birds of the forest sing their lullaby, and the pure white lily of the woods and the blue violet, grow as freely on their green mossy graves, as though they slept within the holy shadow of the sanctuary. (72)

Despite the wealth of religious imagery surrounding the description of the interior of the log cabin, it is evident that Traill derives greater comfort from a contemplation of the outside world. Beauty is always a source of emotional strength and reassurance for Traill.

One of the most interesting aspects of "The Bereavement" is Traill's portrayal of herself, the pioneer woman, as narrator and as participant. She first describes herself as a woman torn between the desire to go outside on a beautiful day and the knowledge that there is a good, practical reason for staying inside. As elsewhere in her writing, she is clearly motivated by the pioneer heroine's devotion to both beauty and practical necessity, and clearly in possession of the ability to describe the natural world from both a scientific and a scenic perspective. A new note, however, is added in "The Bereavement" in the form of her role as healer. She has been called to assist with a sick child, and, later, she presides over the death of that child. The parents seem to perceive her as an almost holy figure: the father bows to her with reverence; she comforts the grieving mother. Traill has watched simultaneously a child dying and a spring day dawning. In both events, she can see the hand of God. Despite being given a somewhat mystical frame of reference, the narrator remains – like all Traill's pioneer heroines – an intensely practical woman. After her night-long vigil, she must leave the sick child and the sorrowing parents, and attend to the daily needs of her own family. And the young mother, sanctified into a Madonna figure by her sorrow, must, like Traill, turn her attention to the real and immediate demands of everyday life. When her child dies, she must continue to cook meals for several mill hands. There is a very real world around these women, a world that demands their active participation. In the spirit of the ideal pioneer, the two women obediently comply with the pressing needs of life and survival in the bush. As Traill has commented in *The Canadian Settler's Guide:*

The greatest heroine in life is she who knowing her duty, resolves not only to do it, but to do it to the best of her abilities, with heart and mind bent upon the work. (4)

"The Bereavement" dramatically illustrates Traill's definition of the true heroine.

Thus, throughout her non-fiction, Traill's dual focus, her ability to observe small details and her ability to rearrange these details within a larger framework, assists her in the development of an important theme – the pioneer heroine whose role, way of life, personal skills and knowledge, attitudes, and opinions constitute the most lasting feature of Traill's writing. Traill begins, in *The Backwoods of Canada*, with a typical emigrant – herself, the English lady – and sets her in the Ontario backwoods of the early nineteenth century. Starting with a familiar figure and pose, she shows how the English lady – a figure common in the fiction and the non-fiction of the nineteenth century[14] – is circumscribed by social class, by social history, by the demands of precedent and propriety. Once this lady, the well-educated and cultivated gentlewoman that was either Traill herself or a semi-fictionalized portrait of Traill, arrives in the backwoods, a process of redefinition begins. In effect, Traill uses her own experiences to bring about a redefinition of the role of women to suit the exigencies, realities, and demands of backwoods society. Traill describes Canada and Canadian life as accurately as possible. She has a clear perception of what a woman's role is like on the backwoods frontier of the early nineteenth century in Ontario. She agrees with Anne Langton, who, in *A Gentlewoman in Upper Canada,* says that "woman is a bit of a slave in this country" (95). But Traill justifies this new life; she defends the Canadian women who perform the menial work which is more commonly done by a lower, labouring class in Britain. She adds an interpretive analysis of pioneer life so that pioneer gentlewomen, despite their performance of unsuitable household chores, become idealized figures and even "heroines." By the time that Traill writes "The Bereavement," her narrator-heroine displays the various talents of a practical, active, capable pioneer, a mystical healer, and a lover of Romantic, humanized, and immanent Nature. She combines capability and activity of body with cheerful mental acceptance of her lot in life. In her non-fiction, then, Catharine Traill has defined an ideal pioneer for the benefit of her fellow Canadians and for the enlightenment of her British readers. Traill's ability as a writer to focus on minute details and the practical aspects of pioneering as well as on a long-range perspective and the ideal aspects of pioneering – specifically those aspects which relate to a woman's role on the frontier – has facilitated her creation of an idealized portrait of a multifaceted and talented pioneer woman.

While it cannot be denied that other pioneer writers articulated similar definitions and that Traill was not unique in her creation of a new feminine ideal, Traill merits special attention. Her works are not letters and diaries; rather, her writing is intended for publication and is directed towards a large reading public. Unfortunately, Traill's direct influence on her contemporaries and on following writers can never be assessed with any degree of accuracy. It cannot be assumed, for example, that such writers as Sara Jeannette Duncan, Ralph Connor, and Margaret Laurence were familiar with Traill's model pioneer when they began to use the pioneer woman as a character type in their fiction. It seems, rather, that these and other writers instinctively recreated in their work a model of Canadian femininity which is strikingly similar to that proposed by Traill. As will be demonstrated, although no direct causal link can be established between various generations of Canadian writers, the pioneer woman not only survives as a literary character type but also evolves to suit the changing social and literary climate. Traill is the first in a series of writers, a pioneer in her use of this Canadian character type.

The Pioneer Woman as Character Type in Sara Jeannette Duncan's "The Imperialist"

By the end of the nineteenth century, pioneer days had ended in Ontario, and the Canadian frontier had moved into the North and the West. In the West, as earlier in the East, pioneer women were required to perform superhuman feats of endurance, courage, and household skill as they faced the difficulties inherent in the settling of an often hostile physical environment.[1] While western women were taking an active part in the process of pioneering, eastern women were leaving pioneer days behind. But though in Ontario the role of the pioneer woman, as this role had been described by Catharine Parr Traill in *The Backwoods of Canada* (1836) and *The Canadian Settler's Guide* (1855), had ended and despite the social changes which were an inevitable result of increasing wealth and urbanization, the concept of the pioneer woman as a feminine ideal continued to flourish. While the ideal of the pioneer woman remained intact, however, the frontier which she inhabited no longer existed in a physical sense, and had to be redefined and relocated.

The recurrence of this character in Canadian literature indicates that the myth of the pioneer woman, as that myth had been articulated by Traill and others, continued to be applicable in an evolving social environment. Even where no connection can be established between Traill and following writers, it is clear that the pioneer woman who appears in the work of such nineteenth-century writers as Sara Jeannette Duncan is a direct literary descendant of Traill's. Moreover, while Traill may have been unique among her contemporaries in her use of the pioneer woman as a character in fiction, by the end of the nineteenth century this figure had begun to appear with great regularity in the work of many writers. Thus, by the turn of the century, the pioneer woman had become an archetype of the

Canadian consciousness and also a recognizable Canadian literary character type.

Social change was a direct and unavoidable result of the ending of pioneer society in Ontario, and Sara Jeannette Duncan's *The Imperialist* (1904) illustrates some of the major issues and dilemmas that were confronted by Ontario women at the turn of the century. To cite one example, in *The Imperialist,* Duncan defends the new career options which were becoming increasingly available for women in a post-frontier society. Her protagonist, Advena Murchison, has a university education and supports herself by working outside the home. Yet Duncan is also a traditionalist in her portrayal of female characters in *The Imperialist.* Advena's mother resembles the ideal pioneer woman as this woman was described by Catharine Parr Traill in *The Backwoods of Canada* and *The Canadian Settler's Guide.* But Advena and her mother are surprisingly similar, despite their vastly different career choices. Advena is, in fact, a new version of the pioneer woman, a pioneer woman on a new frontier. Through her characterization of Advena Murchison, Duncan redefines the frontier and the frontier woman to suit a new set of social circumstances. Thus, while Advena Murchison is undoubtedly a new, independent woman, she can still be defined as a pioneer: a feminine ideal, like her mother before her, Advena faces and seeks to change a frontier landscape.[2]

As has been noted, Duncan is representative rather than unique in her use of a redefined, more modern pioneer woman. Nellie McClung's *Purple Springs* (1921) and *Painted Fires* (1925), L.M. Montgomery's *Anne of Green Gables* (1908) and *Emily of New Moon* (1923), and Robert Stead's *The Homesteaders* (1916), to name only a few, also owe a debt to Traill's pioneer woman. Duncan's writing, however, is less sentimental and, arguably, less idealistic than that of a majority of Canadian writers at the turn of the century; certainly in her delineation of female characters in fiction she is both less sentimental and less idealistic than McClung, Montgomery, and Stead. As a result, her work tends to be more acceptable to a twentieth-century reader. Thus, while it is representative of its era, Duncan's *The Imperialist* is clearly a pivotal work and merits a close critical scrutiny: through its realism, it points the way towards later reincarnations of the pioneer woman.

Advena's frontier in *The Imperialist* is one which is composed of social attitudes and issues, a frontier which she could have chosen to avoid, as do her peers, Abby Murchison Johnson and Dora Milburn. Abby and Dora choose to emulate the circumscribed, outmoded roles of the women of their mothers' generation while Advena moves confidently into a new frontier region. At a time when few women worked for a living, and fewer still had acquired a university education, Advena has done both, making her something of a pioneer feminist. The perception of the development of women's rights as a pioneering process and the portrayal of feminists as pioneers are, in fact, common in Canadian social history.[3] The portrayal of feminists as pioneers was, moreover, a logical step in the evolution of the perception of the pioneer woman as a feminine ideal. When the physical frontiers had been conquered, Canadian women were obliged to look elsewhere for proof of their competence or, as the case may be, their superiority. As a result, the definition of a woman's proper role changed somewhat. The major emphasis was shifted from her contribution towards changing a hostile physical frontier to her participation in the process of improving an unfriendly or even injust social ore. Feminist crusaders in Canada were optimistic about their efforts and perceived themselves as powerful agents for positive social change. Theirs was a global point of view in many cases,[4] and they anticipated the advent of the millennium.[5] Evidently the definition of the frontier had expanded far beyond small backwoods farms to include humanity in general. It is important to note, however, that none of this process of the expansion of woman's proper sphere of activity involved a rejection of what were then seen as traditional feminine values in Canada.[6] The precedent of a capable, active pioneer woman who could overcome any obstacles in her path had been established by women such as Traill. Many of the qualities possessed by the original pioneers – for instance, activity in the face of an emergency,[7] a cheerful acceptance of adverse circumstances,[8] the courage and pragmatism necessary to begin to effect positive change on the frontier[9] – were seen as useful tools on the new social frontier, and a relatively easy transition was made from a physical landscape to a social arena.

Mrs Murchison conforms in virtually every aspect to Traill's definition of the woman who is suited to life on a frontier. When she is introduced in *The Imperialist*, Mrs Murchison is working in her kitchen, surrounded by her children. The kitchen, the centre of domestic activity, is an ideal backdrop for her, and, with gentle humour, Duncan uses this introductory setting and activity to establish certain essential aspects of her personality. More specifically, the setting is ideally suited to a demonstration of the sterling traits of the pioneer housekeeper. These traits, as they are demonstrated by Mrs Murchison, include the active participation in all aspects of domestic duties, a cheerful disposition, a pragmatic approach to adversity, and an appreciation of grace and beauty.[10]

The use of the house to define the character of the chief female inhabitant is an important part of the introductory scene and is a technique which is used throughout *The Imperialist* to describe Mrs Murchison. Mrs Murchison's struggles as a pioneer during the transition of Elgin from its rough frontier beginnings to its later prosperity are not described in any great detail. Rather, the changes made in the Murchison home throughout a period of several years are used to parallel the gradual shift in emphasis from a concentration on what is strictly necessary (the major focus of the pioneer struggle to survive) to an appreciation of comfort and luxury (the reward for success on the frontier) which denotes financial success.[11] In effect, Mrs Murchison's personal battle with her house becomes a metaphor for her pioneering years.[12] The metamorphosis of the house – the process of material improvement which results from a successful pioneering venture[13] – follows the transition of Elgin from frontier to establishment, the growth of the Murchison family from youth to maturity, and the fortunes of the Murchison family from poverty to material wealth:

They had grown up sturdily, emerging into sobriety and decorum by much the same degrees as the old house, under John Murchison's improving fortunes, grew cared for and presentable. The new roof went on, slate replacing shingles, the year Abby put her hair up; the bathroom was contemporary with Oliver's leaving school; the electric light was actually turned on for the first time in honour of Lorne's return from Toronto, a barrister and solicitor; several rooms had been done up for Abby's wedding.[14]

While the Murchison house is ultimately a showplace, in its initial state it was, for Mrs Murchison, "the bane of her existence" (28). At first the house required "far more looking after than the Murchisons could afford to give it" (28). The initial state of the Murchison family fortunes required Mrs Murchison's application of the various pioneer virtues and skills listed by Traill. In short, Mrs Murchison's early management of her home has demonstrated her capability, her adaptability, and her pragmatism. Mrs Murchison is among the last of the original pioneers in Elgin.[15] When she set up housekeeping, the town was rapidly changing from a small frontier town to a larger, more prosperous urban centre:

Elgin had begun as the centre of "trading" for the farmers of Fox County ... Main Street ... was now the chief artery of a thriving manufacturing town, with a collegiate institute, eleven churches, two newspapers, and an asylum for the deaf and dumb, to say nothing of a fire department unsurpassed for organization and achievement in the Province of Ontario. (25)

The initial scene introduces Mrs Murchison in a situation which demands her immediate, active, and capable participation in a domestic crisis. The servant has left without notice, and without having completed her work. Like a true pioneer, Mrs Murchison is equal to the occasion. She calls upon her children for assistance, and faces the calamity with poise and equanimity. She is obviously quite at home in the kitchen; the servant has been a luxury rather than a necessity. It also becomes apparent in this opening episode that Mrs Murchison retains many of the practical skills possessed by the frontier woman. For example, the servant has left her job because she objects to the home-made carpet in her room. Mrs Murchison takes offence at this because she made the rag carpet herself, and it is still a source of pride for her: "'Dear me!' she went on with a smile that lightened the whole situation, 'how proud I was of that performance! She didn't tell *me* she objected to rag carpet'" (16). Several pioneer traits are demonstrated in the making of this rag carpet. While the primary motivation was obviously practical and pragmatic (reshaping rags to make a useful household object), Mrs Murchison has also perceived it as a beautiful and decorative object, and the necessity to combine use and beauty in any situation is a central issue in Traill's philosophy of successful pioneering.[16] Finally, the making of the carpet has obviously given Mrs Murchison a great sense of accomplishment. She remembers, "sixty balls there were in it, and every one I sewed with my own fingers" (16).

Like the changing appearance of the Murchison home, the fortunes of the rag carpet follow the changes that take place within the Murchison family. Made during a pioneer era, at a time when economy was essential, and once the ornament of the spare room, it has since been relegated to a servant's bedroom. Furthermore, the rag carpet is no longer considered to be aesthetically pleasing. It is strictly functional, if it is necessary at all. The rag carpet is, in fact, a symbol of a past way of life, and of an outdated mode of perception. Yet, despite her present material prosperity, Mrs Murchison cannot forget her pioneer skills and economies. She continues to live as though pioneer days may return at any minute.

The soft soap that she uses in her kitchen is further evidence of Mrs Murchison's mastery of difficult pioneer tasks, as well as evidence of her later reluctance to abandon her pioneer economies:

The soft soap – Mrs Murchison had a barrelful boiled every spring in the back yard, an old colonial economy she hated to resign – made a fascinating brown lather with iridescent bubbles. (16)

Mrs Murchison's insistence on maintaining an outdated form of economy is emblematic of her difficulty in adapting to a modern, affluent, way of life. Moreover, in this particular scene, Duncan points out a basic contrast in point of view between Mrs Murchison and her daughter Advena. Both like the soft soap, but Mrs Murchison likes the economy while Advena likes the bubbles. The contrast which is established here becomes more pronounced as Advena proves to be almost totally lacking in the domestic skills which are the pride of her mother's existence.

In spite of her retention of various out-of-date pioneer practices, Mrs Murchison is neither an inadequate nor an unimportant figure in *The Imperialist*. She dominates the initial scene during the family crisis, surrounded by her children, and in control of the activity around her:

Mrs Murchison remains the central figure, nevertheless, with her family radiating from her, gathered to help or to hinder in one of those domestic crises which arose when the Murchisons were temporarily deprived of a "girl." (15)

Mrs Murchison is evidently the centre of her own small universe, like the centre of a wheel; the other family members revolve around her, seeming to derive much of their strength from her.

A similar tableau is arranged later in the narrative when the Murchisons entertain Dr Drummond and Mr and Mrs Williams. Once again Mrs Murchison's family is grouped around her, responding to her instructions. The movement in the characterization of Mrs Murchison from the kitchen to the dining-room follows the movement of the Murchison family from poverty to prosperity; the action shifts from a strictly functional room to a more formal one with a primarily social orientation, and from a family domestic crisis Duncan moves to a scene of entertainment.

But, while the different backgrounds for Mrs Murchison follow the changing family fortunes, both locations allow Mrs Murchison to dominate the action, and both permit her to demonstrate the many excellent domestic skills she has developed. Her capable management ensures that the meal served to her guests is a good one, eagerly anticipated and greatly enjoyed by her guests and her family alike. She controls the action by assigning various tasks to her children throughout the meal:

Lorne had charge of the cold tongue and Advena was entrusted with the pickled pears. The rest of the family were expected to think about the tea biscuits and the cake. (38)

Earlier in the narrative, Mrs Murchison has understood her children's disappointment at having no money to spend on Victoria Day (Mr Murchison has refused to give them any), and she secretly gives them twenty cents to buy ice cream. In this later chapter, Mrs Murchison's strongly protective maternal instincts prompt her to guess Lorne's news about a court case before he tells the family: "'Lorne, you've got it!' divined his mother instantly" (41). Practical housewifery skills and maternal domination are typical traits of Mrs Murchison, regardless of her surroundings in *The Imperialist*.

Throughout the dinner party Mrs Murchison demonstrates other excellent qualities which would have been recognized by Catharine Parr Traill as those belonging to a capable woman. For example, personal charm is clearly one of Mrs Murchison's traits, and the arrangement of her dinner table reveals her appreciation of beauty and elegance:

It was a table to do anybody credit, with its glossy damask and the old-fashioned silver and best china that Mrs Murchison had brought as a bride to her housekeeping – for, thank goodness, her mother had known what was what in such matters – a generous attractive table that you took some satisfaction in looking at. Mrs Murchison came of a family of noted housekeepers; where she got her charm I don't know. (38)

At Mrs Murchison's table, elegance and competence are displayed simultaneously. It will be recalled that in her analysis of backwoods life, Catharine Traill had insisted that beauty and practicality must, ideally, coexist. Duncan uses a similar approach in *The Imperialist* as one basis for her characterization of Mrs Murchison, using the woman's home as evidence of her personality.

True to the spirit of the pioneer woman, Mrs Murchison accepts her lot in life, if not always cheerfully (she often resents the amount of work involved in the upkeep of a large house), then at least with resignation. She has developed the skills necessary to succeed in a frontier environment. While she may not have chosen to be a pioneer, she evidently has decided to be good at her work. If there is a fault in Mrs Murchison, it is her inability to accept prosperity and to change with the times. When she has more money, more material possessions, and more leisure time, she continues to keep her old ways and habits. Duncan has attempted to create a realistic character, and as such Mrs Murchison is less than perfect;[17] but despite her faults she is also meant as a feminine ideal. At any rate, she has been a role model for her daughters Advena and Abby. To some extent, both follow in her footsteps.

The younger generation of women, as represented in *The Imperialist* by Advena, Abby, and Dora, has been influenced only indirectly by pioneer life in Ontario. These girls are at least one generation removed from the active process of pioneering; their actions are not dictated by the needs of survival. They have had access to a good education, and they enjoy the advantages of a more than adequate number of material goods and possessions. More important, they are self-determining in ways foreign to the women of their mothers' generation. This second generation of Canadians is at liberty to redefine itself (if it wishes to do so) by seeking new areas of interest, new types of employment.[18] The demands imposed by a physical frontier on its inhabitants no longer form the basis for the development of the ideal woman. This one factor is responsible, to a large extent, for the ambivalence in Duncan's characterization of Mrs Murchison, who is, perhaps, an ideal figure from an earlier time, but whose admirable qualities are not always relevant in a modern era. Certain of her traits stand the test of time; others do not.

Abby Murchison Johnson has chosen to emulate her mother, to extend the tradition of the active, capable woman who controls a domestic sphere with admirable efficiency. She marries early, and chooses her partner wisely; her husband is a doctor who is popular in Elgin. Abby begins almost immediately to start her own family, and she is well versed in the domestic skills that elude her less practical sister, Advena. Mrs Murchison is proud of Abby and boasts of her daughter's abilities as a housewife. Although Abby remains a relatively undeveloped character in *The Imperialist,* it seems clear from what is known of her that she and her household mirror her mother and her mother's home. When Abby needs baby clothes, she turns to her mother for help and advice, and borrows her mother's knitting patterns. In a burst of pride, thinly disguised as modesty, Mrs Murchison says:

Now that Abby's family is coming about her I seem to have my hands as full of children's clothes as ever I had. Abby seems to think there's nothing like my old patterns; I'm sure I'm sick of the sight of them! (101)

Mrs Murchison is, of course, satisfied with her daughter's choices because they reinforce her own system of values.

The characterization of Mrs Murchison in *The Imperialist* is, as has been shown, connected to her home. The rooms which she uses most frequently help to define her as a character. Unlike her mother, Abby is never seen in her own home; she is one of the few female characters not shown at work or entertaining guests in her drawing-room. Yet she is said to be a good homemaker and a social success. While Duncan does not describe Abby in any great detail, she notes that Abby does all the correct things: "she had taken no time at all to establish herself ... she was doing very well" (45). Abby is popular with her peers, and is visited often by her family: "Abby's housekeeping made an interest and Abby's baby a point of pilgrimage" (32). In spite of these hints concerning Abby and her habits, she remains an essentially flat character, important only for her acceptance of her mother's interests and way of life.

Abby may imitate her mother but she is not as admirable. While she possesses the practical skills of a pioneer woman, she has no major problems to solve, and, therefore, there is no evidence in her character of the mental and emotional strength of the pioneer woman who faces adversity with cheerful fortitude. Quite simply, Abby is a woman without a frontier, a housewife who has inherited some basic household skills from her mother.

Like Abby Murchison, Dora Milburn emulates her mother and accepts her mother's ideas about a woman's role. But Mrs Milburn and Dora project a far different image of femininity from that embodied in Mrs Murchison and Abby – an image that has very little in common with the tradition of an active, capable pioneer woman. The role adopted by the Milburn women is that of the English gentlewoman. The Milburns wish to emphasize the decorative helplessness of a more passive feminine way of life, and, at the same time, to impress others with the Milburn social superiority. These particular values are often at odds with the bustling, active Canadian town of Elgin, a town which is only one step removed from frontier conditions. The Milburn vision of ideal femininity is one which was discarded by pioneers like Catharine Parr Traill as they learned to set aside merely decorative pursuits and to take pride in their acquisition of new domestic accomplishments.

The Milburns are introduced to the reader as they sit, posed and poised, in their drawing-room. Duncan's choice of the drawing-room as a suitable frame of reference for the family group is significant. It is a room without a useful function in the daily life of the typical Canadian family of the period. Mrs Murchison also has a drawing-room, but is more often found in her kitchen, or, when she entertains, in her dining-room.[19] Once again the situation and the activity in which the female characters are first discovered help to define their personalities. Mrs Milburn, Miss Filkin, and Dora Milburn seem to have had nothing to do with the work of the party they are giving, and their lives seem to be spent in idle, decorative pursuits. Yet the irony of the situation is that this inactivity is merely an illusion:

No one would have supposed, from the way in which the family disposed itself in the drawing-room, that Miss Filkin had only just finished making the claret cup, or that Dora had been cutting sandwiches till the last minute, or that Mrs Milburn had been obliged to have a distinct understanding with the maid – Mrs Milburns' servants were all "maids," even the charwoman, who had buried three husbands – on the subject of wearing a cap when she answered the door. Mrs Milburn sat on a chair she had worked herself, occupied with something in the new stich; Dora performed lightly at the piano; Miss Filkin dipped into *Selections from the Poets of the Century,* placed as remotely as possible from the others; Mr Milburn, with his legs crossed, turned and folded a Toronto evening paper ... when Mr Lorne Murchison arrived ... they looked almost surprised to see him. (52–3).

The Milburn family probably works as hard as any family in Elgin, and Dora may be able to tackle any household chore, but this aspect of their lives is carefully disguised. The drawing-room plays an important part in the life of this particular family. Not without significance, it is the room where Dora entertains Lorne Murchison: when the Milburns pose themselves in the drawing-room, they create the illusion of leisure and ignore the reality of hard work; similarly, Dora's relationship with Lorne is based on illusion.

The Milburns' pose is clearly an artificial one, and clashes with the direct honesty and the pride in accomplishment common to many of the other characters in *The Imperialist.* The bustling activity of Mrs Murchison contrasts with Mrs Milburn's affectation of leisure. A sample of Mrs Murchison's handiwork is her practical rag carpet; Mrs Milburn sits on a sample of her embroidery and fancy-work in her drawing room. Two vastly different women have developed quite different skills to suit their personal views of a woman's role. Mrs Milburn, her sister, and her daughter attempt to retain the attitudes, the appearance, and the skills of the English gentlewoman, the woman who could come to grief on the frontier.[20]

The Milburns have ignored the social levelling which is a common characteristic of the New World:

Almost alone among those who had slipped into wider and more promiscuous circles with the widening of the stream, the Milburns had made something like an effort hold out. (48)

Yet the Milburn foibles are accepted (or at least tolerated) by the people of Elgin (it is considered an honour to be invited to the Milburn parties):

Crossing the Atlantic they doubtless suffered some dilution; but all that was possible to conserve them under very adverse conditions Mrs Milburn and Miss Filkin made it their duty to do. Nor were these ideas opposed, contested, or much traversed in Elgin. It was recognized that there was "something about" Mrs Milburn and her sister – vaguely felt – that you did not come upon that thinness of nostril, and slope of shoulder, and set of elbow at every corner. They must have got it somewhere. (48)

Duncan's opinion of the Milburns is expressed with subtlety. It becomes apparent throughout the above passage that even though Elgin chooses not to censure the Milburn attitude, the Milburn family is guilty of pretence and deceit. The attitude of social superiority assumed by the Milburn family is as false and as incongruous as their carefully planned pose in the drawing-room.

Other pioneer families learned to change their preconceived social views when they moved to Canada. Faced with an overwhelming sense of dislocation in Canada, many emigrants held on to their social values for as long as possible, but, as Duncan points out, most of them changed to suit the situation. Of the original social élite Duncan says:

Such persons would bring their lines of demarcation with them, and in their new *milieu* of backwoods settlers and small traders would find no difficulty in drawing them again. But it was a very long time ago. The little knot of gentry-folk soon found the limitations of their new conditions; years went by in decades, aggrandizing none of them. They took, perforce, to the ways of the country ... Trade flourished, education improved, politics changed ... The original dignified group broke, dissolved, scattered. Prosperous traders foreclosed them, the spirit of the times defeated them, young Liberals succeeded them in office. Their grandsons married the daughters of well-to-do persons who came from the north of Ireland, the east of Scotland, and the Lord knows where. It was a sorry tale of disintegration with a cheerful sequel of rebuilding, leading to a little unavoidable confusion as the edifice went up. Any process of blending implies confusion to begin with; we are here at the making of a nation. (47)

Here Duncan has provided a brief summary of one inevitable consequence of the participation in the pioneering process in Canada – the initial levelling, and the subsequent restructuring of society.[21] The Murchisons have followed the common pattern; the Milburns have clung to their old ways.[22] Mrs Murchison is the product of a Canadian pioneer environment. Her children, specifically Lorne and Advena, are members of a new social élite, a meritocracy based on intelligence and ability rather than on ancestry and material wealth.[23]

Dora has inherited the artificial posturing of her mother. Both generations of Milburn women cling tenaciously to the remnants of the life of an English lady, and, as far as she is able, Dora mimics an English gentlewoman. She assumes a primarily decorative role at home; she is pampered by her parents; she has cultivated various leisure activities (for example, she is first seen playing the piano); and she speaks with an unnatural "English" (49) accent. Moreover, in her relationship with Lorne Murchison, Dora plays the part of a coquette, a role which is compatible with the artificiality which she demonstrates elsewhere in her life but not with Canadian social conditions.[24] Dora's coquetry and misleading behaviour clash with Lorne's straightforward approach to romance. Dora ignores the more recent traditions of the Canadian pioneer woman as an ideal and turns to the past for her role model, making herself an unsuitable mate for Lorne. For, despite his reverence for Britain, the Empire, and the concept of imperialism, Lorne is definitely the product of a pioneer environment. Hard-working, forthright, and honest, he epitomizes the virtues of young people in a frontier society:

Youth in a young country is a symbol wearing all its value. It stands not only for what it is. The trick of augury invests it, at a glance, with the sum of its possibilities, the augurs all sincere, confident, and exulting. They have been justified so often; they know, in their wide fair fields of opportunity, just what qualities will produce what results. (80)

Dora suffers a fate suitable for a coquette: she jilts Lorne to marry Hesketh. This is a surprise and a disappointment to no one but Lorne; others, including Lorne's sister Stella, are of the opinion that "Mr Hesketh's engagement to Miss Milburn was the most suitable thing that could be imagined or desired" (268). Lorne has failed to notice that Dora is not in love with him, and that much of her life is based on pretence and affectation. She chooses Hesketh primarily because she considers him, with his English background, his money, and his accent, to be superior to Lorne. But, in Duncan's view, Lorne is the better man. He is more intelligent, a visionary, and a leader of men rather than a follower. He certainly deserves a better destiny than marriage to Dora Milburn.

It is ironic that the man chosen by Dora fails to recognize the effort that the Milburn family has made to remain aloof from other families in Elgin. In fact, Hesketh perceives the family to the "typically Canadian":

He described them in his letters home as the most typically Canadian family he had met, quite simple and unconventional, but thoroughly warm-hearted, and touchingly devoted to far-away England. (211)

Hesketh condescends to say of Dora that she "will compare with any English girl" (265) he knows. Duncan is not notably sympathetic to either Dora or Hesketh. They are described as somewhat inferior beings, lacking the energy, resolve, intelligence, and vision typical of the other protagonists, who, like Lorne, are more representative products of a Canadian frontier environment.

Advena Murchison is the most problematic of the young female protagonists in *The Imperialist,* less easily defined than either Abby or Dora. She is, first of all, quite different from her sister Abby. While Abby has chosen to emulate Mrs Murchison, the efficient housekeeper who is proud of her role, Advena seem to be the antithesis of her mother. Mrs Murchison, in fact, openly despairs of Advena's matrimonial prospects:

I don't call Advena fitted to be a wife, and last of all a minister's. Abby was a treasure for any man to get, and Stella won't turn out at all badly; she's taking hold very well for her age. But Advena simply hasn't got it in her, and that's all there is to say about it. (104)

Thus, in the eyes of Mrs Murchison, and in the view of Elgin generally, Advena and Abby are quite dissimilar: Abby is accepted and Advena is viewed with suspicion. Advena is also juxtaposed to Dora Milburn, though less directly. On the one hand, Dora is a coquette, distinguished by her pretences, her dishonesty, and her role-playing. The course of Dora's love affair with Lorne is dominated by Dora's inability to tell Lorne the truth about her feelings (or perhaps, more to the point, her inability to admit the truth to herself). Advena, on the other hand, is almost frightening in her direct honesty and lack of pretense. In her love affair with Hugh Finlay, Advena confesses her feelings to herself, and demonstrates them openly to her lover.

From an early age, Advena is considered odd by Elgin's standards: "Advena, bookish and unconventional, was regarded with dubiety" (45). She perfers daydreaming and reading to doing housework. Mrs Murchison is proud of the economy she displays by making soft soap; Advena looks at the bubbles in the sink, and dreams:

Advena poured cupfuls of it from on high to see the foam rise, till her mother told her for mercy's sake to get on with those dishes. She stood before a long low window, looking out into the garden, and the light, filtering through apple branches on her face, showed her strongly featured and intelligent for fourteen. (16)

Nor does Advena prefer to learn any of the more artistic and less practical skills demonstrated by Dora Milburn. Dora is proficient at playing the piano; Advena refuses to take lessons, and announces that it will be a waste of time. Advena, then, would appear to be a unique character type in *The Imperialist*, quite unlike the other women in Elgin. She pursues her own interests; she has an education; she works for a living; she has always ignored rules and social convention; she has an almost total lack of interest or expertise in the most basic household tasks; and she refuses to waste her time in the pursuit of impractical, decorative drawing-room skills. At first glance, Advena seems to be an unfeminine "new woman," the type feared by non-feminists and, indeed, by many Canadian feminists, at the turn of the century.[25]

While Duncan's narrator notes the differences between Advena and those about her, she also defends her young protagonist. In the first family scene in the Murchison house in *The Imperialist*, Advena annoys her mother by playing with the soap; but Duncan balances the maternal criticism by adding a comment about Advena's "strongly featured and intelligent" (16) face. She indicates the general disapproval expressed towards Advena by Elgin residents, but here also she undercuts the opinions of Advena's critics. Mrs Murchison is presented as the representative of an ideal feminine type, yet her views about Advena are subtly refuted by Duncan:

When you have seen your daughter reach and pass the age of twenty-five without having learned properly to make her own bed, you know without being told that she will never be fit for the management of a house – don't you? (32)

On the one hand, Duncan indicates that Mrs Murchison has many worthy qualities, and that she is to be respected and emulated – to a point. On the other hand, although Duncan admits that Advena is hopeless as a housekeeper, she points out that when Advena is judged by other standards, she too is worthy of respect and emulation.

Upon closer examination, Advena's superiority as a character asserts itself in a number of ways. She does not need the intercession and defence of Duncan's narrator. For example, it becomes apparent that in her criticism of her daughter, Mrs Murchison is ignoring the many ways in which Advena actually resembles her. In fact, Advena more nearly approximates Catharine Traill's definitions of an ideal pioneer woman than does her sister Abby. Like the majority of early Canadian feminists, Duncan tends to be cautious in her expression of new ideas.[26] Nevertheless, Advena undoubtedly is a "new woman":

Advena justified her existence by taking the university course for women at Toronto, and afterward teaching the English branches to the junior forms in the Collegiate Institute, which placed her arbitrarily outside the sphere of domestic criticism. (32–3)

In spite of this relatively bold step into the depiction of an alternative feminine lifestyle, Duncan adheres to previous definitions of femininity in her characterization of Advena. Although Advena creates a new life for herself outside the home, she is not unfeminine, and Duncan establishes links between Advena and more traditional female roles so that she may display many of the traits essential to the woman on the frontier. Furthermore, Duncan justifies Advena's departure from tradition by defining it as a natural response to the Canadian social environment of the period at the end of the nineteenth century. Advena is both a "new woman" in the feminist sense of the word, and a "New World" woman, meaning that she is a new type of pioneer, a woman who inhabits a far different frontier environment from that confronted by her mother, perhaps, but still recognizable as a frontier. Skills which are not essential to the woman on the new frontier (such as making soft soap) are ignored and left undeveloped as Advena learns new skills more compatible with the frontier environment which surrounds her. Advena has not inherited the housekeeping skills of her mother, since, unlike her mother, she has not needed to learn and to practice the various pioneer economies familiar to her mother and to her mother's generation. Despite her mother's low opinion of this, Advena represents an ideal of sorts in *The Imperialist*. She has her faults; none of Duncan's protagonists is without flaw. But she demonstrates many of the mental strengths of the pioneer. She is a readily recognizable version of the pioneer woman, once the common perception of the frontier as a place has been revised to include a social background and a sociological orientation. As Duncan develops the characterization of Advena as a modern pioneer, Advena's likeness to her mother becomes more pronounced.

It will be remembered that the maternal role is a vital element in Traill's vision of the pioneer woman; her youthful protagonist, Catharine Maxwell of *Canadian Crusoes* (1852), assumes the role of the mother in the small group of lost children and becomes the emotional centre of the family unit. Advena's position as a teacher, a role which involves the control and the instruction of others, can be perceived as compatible with this role. Duncan does not show Advena at work in her classroom, however, and her maternal qualities, her ability to provide emotional strength to those around her, are more readily demonstrated in her relationship with Hugh Finlay. Like Abby and Dora, Advena reveals many of her character traits through her handling of a love affair. She loves Hugh, accepts his decisions, and is proud of his work and his intelligence; but underlying this devotion is more than a hint of maternal indulgence, and Advena emerges as the stronger character:

She watched his academic awkwardness in church with the inward tender smile of the eternal habile feminine, and when they met she could have laughed and wept over his straightened sentences and his difficult manner, knowing how little significant they were. With his eyes upon her and his words offered to her intelligence, she found herself treating his shy formality as the convention it was, a kind of make-believe which she would politely and kindly play up to until he should happily forget it and they could enter upon simpler relations. She had to play up to it for a long time, but her love made her wonderfully clever and patient; and of course the day came when she had her reward. (70)

The Advena revealed here, the "eternal feminine" of Goethe's *Faust*,[27] is most definitely feminine. Her attitude towards her lover is fiercely protective. This echoes her mother's role within the Murchison family unit and bodes well for Advena's future success as a wife and mother, even if she is inept in the kitchen.

In an earlier demonstration of her maternal instincts Advena brings home an Indian baby for her family to adopt. Although her mother dismisses this gesture as one of Advena's "queer satisfactions and enthusiasms" (45), it actually shows a generalized love of humanity and a desire to change the world about her. Thomas Tausky has said, of Duncan's work in general, "'Woman's World,' then, in Sara's definition of it, was not the traditional 'woman's sphere' but rather the enlarged possibilities suggested by full participation in the wider, public world."[28] In fact, many of the early feminist crusaders in Canada perceived their social role as a mothering one.[29] Women could make improvements in the world because their maternal orientation made them ideal agents for social progress and amelioration. Advena's "queer" humanitarian ideas about her responsibility to those less fortunate are evidence of her maternal sensibilities and of her related desire to improve these people's living conditions. Mrs Murchison,

unfortunately, does not assess Advena's gesture correctly, and criticizes it rather than defending it.

The maternal streak in Advena's personality demonstrates her
adherence to a traditional female role, traditional in a Canadian sense
of the pioneer woman as feminine ideal. Advena's latent maternal
instincts are among the traits which identify her as a pioneer; but
Advena shows other qualities of the pioneer woman as well. For example, the two vital elements in the creation of the ideal female pioneer,
as the pioneer is defined by Traill in *The Backwoods of Canada* and
The Canadian Settler's Guide, are the woman's acceptance of the adverse
circumstances inherent to a frontier landscape[30] and an immediate,
active response to that adversity.[31] In these two aspects Advena clearly
shows her superior worth and indicates that she, like her mother, is
a version of the pioneer woman.

Advena ignores her mother's opinions and the attitude of the town
of Elgin in general. She refuses to be ruled by others and she redefines her role to suit her own circumstances. She copes with social
hostility by ignoring it and by following her own inclinations. Advena's
ability to act decisively is demonstrated constantly; she is seldom passive despite her propensity to daydream. She announces to her parents that she will not take piano lessons and makes good her
statement by escaping to the roof of the house. Later she pursues a
career in the face of real opposition from those who see her choice
as a refutation of a proper female role. Advena never acknowledges
the criticism; she goes her own way.

Many of Advena's personality traits, specifically those traits which
mark her as a pioneer woman, are revealed throughout the course
of her love affair with Hugh Finlay. Advena accepts the bad news of
Hugh's engagement to Christie Cameron with cheerful resignation.
She accepts an undesirable situation and gives Hugh no hint of her
anguish, continuing instead to be his good friend. But Advena's original acceptance of Hugh's engagement comes into conflict with her
active energy, her seemingly innate, idealistic desire to change an
undesirable situation by positive action. This conflict echoes back to
the essential dichotomy of Traill's blueprint for pioneering: the pioneer woman accepts her lot in life, then attempts, through her active
participation in the pioneering process, to change her fate. Advena
challenges her fate when she confronts Christie Cameron. This confrontation is perhaps the most important example of Advena's behaviour as a "New-World" woman. The honesty and personal sense of
freedom shown by Advena in this case are part of her inheritance as
the daughter of pioneers; they are traits which link her to her mother,

and are evidence of Advena's own pioneering spirit. The Old World, as represented by Christie, the refined gentlewoman, meets the New World, as represented by Advena, the pioneer spirit. Advena's courage, conviction, freedom of speech and movement confuse Christie and her companion Mrs Kilbannon. The Scottish ladies' actions are still influenced by social rules, propriety, and class definitions:

Their special virtues, of dignity and solidity and frugality, stood out saliently against the ease and unconstraint about them; in the profusion of the table it was little less than edifying to hear Mrs Kilbannon invited to preserves, say, "Thank you, I have butter." (216)

Advena's actions come as a shock to the Old-World women. They cannot define her social status, for her actions and her speech defy classification, and they look at each other in "blank astonishment" (219):

"When she sat down," as Mrs Kilbannon said afterward, "she seemed to untie and fling herself as you might a parcel." Neither Mrs Kilbannon nor Christie Cameron could possibly be untied or flung, so perhaps they gave this capacity in Advena more importance than it had. But it was only a part of what was to them a new human demonstration, something to inspect very carefully and accept very cautiously – the product, lile themselves, yet so suspiciously different, of these free airs and these astonishingly large ideas. (218)

To Advena, it seems natural that she, as Hugh Finlay's best friend, should welcome his fiancée in spite of her personal feelings about his marriage. To Christie Cameron, this action is lacking in propriety and is, therefore, quite wrong.

One positive result of the pioneering process had been a sense of freedom from the restraint of social rules. Traill comments on this feeling in her work, most notably in her discussion of Grundyism in *The Backwoods of Canada*.[32] The feeling of freedom and its companion, pride in accomplishment, is a direct result of the pioneer woman's active participation in the process of pioneering. The awareness that women are not limited by physical or mental frailty to the performance of one particular social role, and the knowledge that, on a frontier, women are not constricted by rules of social propriety and social convention, result in a welcome sense of freedom, felt by the majority of emigrant women.[33] In helping to change the frontier, the pioneer woman changes as well: the frontier and its inhabitants interact to create change. In his Introduction to *The Imperialist*, Claude

Bissell comments on one aspect of this interaction when he notes that the New World is an "active agent"[34] and that the Old World is "subjected to a refining influence."[35]

Advena, as a pioneer's daughter, and as a pioneer herself, has become part of this process of discovering independence. Indeed, it is worth noting that Hugh defines the freedom which is an essential element of the inhabitant of the New World in a discussion with Advena:

I sometimes think that the human spirit, as it is set free in these wide unblemished spaces, may be something more pure and sensitive, more sincerely curious about what is good and beautiful. (111)

At this point Advena blushes, and Hugh recognizes her as "his idea incarnate" (111). As a more recent emigrant, Christie Cameron can also discover the freedom inherent in the New World. She has two options: to accept the spirit of change and freedom which is typified by Advena, or, like Dora, to hold on to an old way of life which is outmoded in Canada and not suited to Canadian social conditions. She can choose to interact with the frontier, and to accept change within herself, or she can attempt to deny the possibilities of the frontier.

Advena's pioneer spirit leads her to challenge her fate when she confronts Hugh after his trip to the West. Her visit to Christie has obviously been somewhat of a failure and she tries an even more direct approach. When Hugh expresses his uncertainty – "I don't know ... how we are to bear this" (249) – Advena immediately asserts her opinion:

"We are not to bear it," she said eagerly. "The rose is to tell you that. I didn't mean it, when I left it, to be anything more – more than a rose; but now I do. I didn't even know when I came out tonight. But now I do. We aren't to bear it, Hugh. I don't want it so – now. I can't – can't have it so." (249)

The conflict is a central one between these two young people. Hugh, the recent emigrant, stands "helplessly, clinging to the sound and the form of the words" (250). Advena, "so greatly the more confident and daring" (250), is also the more pragmatic of the two. She tries to convince Hugh that their ideal of platonic friendship is impossible to achieve, that they must act: "Indeed I know now what is possible and what is not" (250). But Hugh, holding to his words, his promises, and his sense of propriety, dominates the discussion to the extent that Advena again accepts an undesirable fate, this time in a spirit of "hapless defeat" (250). Advena eventually proves to have been the wiser, and Hugh's stubborn insistence on form and his renunciation of Advena have been pointless. Hugh discovers that Christie Cameron has decided to marry Dr Drummond, who, unlike Hugh, has acted quickly and decisively to gain his matrimonial objective, ignoring in the process the conventions which dictate that Christie must marry Hugh.

Advena, alone among the younger women of *The Imperialist,* takes full advantage of the choices available to the women of the period. She seizes the opportunity to redefine a woman's role in the changing social background of the early twentieth century in Ontario. Lacking the adventurous spirit, and perhaps also the confidence of the pioneer, Abby and Dora have chosen to follow safe, established patterns of behaviour. Advena, however, has inherited the pioneer traits of her mother and has put them to work on a new frontier, a frontier of her own choosing. It seems appropriate that Hugh and Advena will be moving to western Canada when Hugh goes to his new charge of the White Water Mission Station in Alberta, since the West represents the last physical frontier in Canada at this period. In Alberta, Advena will have an opportunity to prove her worth on a physical frontier, having already proved it on a social one.

In *The Imperialist,* Duncan has confronted some of the major social issues facing Canadian women at the beginning of the twentieth century. Although the West was still being settled, Ontario had passed through its pioneer era. The greater prosperity which had resulted from a longer period of settlement was giving women in eastern Canada an increased amount of leisure time. Social problems rather than personal survival had begun to assume an increased importance in the lives of many women. Duncan herself was a pioneer feminist; she was, for example, a newspaper reporter at a time when such jobs were not generally available for women. Rights for women, education, and career options are issues she addresses in *The Imperialist,* chiefly through her depiction of her protagonist Advena Murchison. Like the majority of Canadian feminists of the period,[36] however, Duncan is sympathetic to the more traditional perceptions of a feminine ideal, traditional, of course, in a Canadian context. Her portrayal of Advena places this young female character within the tradition of the pioneer woman as fictional heroine, in spite of the new definition of the pioneer woman's frontier surroundings.

It is important to view Duncan within the context of other writers of fiction as well. She is a representative feminist of her era; she is also representative (to a certain extent) of the writers of "feminist" fiction. The female protagonists of L.M. Montgomery, Nellie

McClung, and Robert Stead face some of the same social issues as
Advena Murchison. Montgomery treats of a post-frontier Prince
Edward Island, and McClung of a post-frontier Manitoba. The protagonists of Robert Stead's *The Homesteaders* move westward in search
of the quickly disappearing frontier. The young female protagonists
of each writer conform to traditional perceptions of an ideal, or are
attempting, in the course of the novel, to achieve that ideal. Moreover,
each is clearly a pioneer woman in transition, as is Duncan's Advena,
a pioneer woman defining a new frontier for herself.

Despite their sentimentality, Lucy Maud Montgomery's *Anne of
Green Gables* and *Emily of New Moon* are much like Duncan's *The Imperialist* in the author's examination of the concerns of Canadian feminists of the early twentieth century, specifically in the treatment of
a "generation gap" between two women. Moreover, while there is no
demonstrable link between Traill and Montgomery, Montgomery, like
Duncan, evidently has accepted the myth of the pioneer woman as
a Canadian ideal and has incorporated this ideal into her fiction.
Montgomery (again like Duncan) was the descendant of pioneers and
undoubtedly heard and assimilated stories of the active pioneer
woman who could cheerfully cope with a wide variety of tasks. Thus,
Montgomery's heroines, Anne and Emily, display many of the qualities of the ideal Canadian woman. Finally, Montgomery also adapts
her portrayal of the pioneer to suit the social and economic conditions
of early twentieth-century Canada so that her work reflects a woman's
changing role in Canadian society.

The confrontation between two women forms the basis for much
of the plot development in Montgomery's *Anne of Green Gables* and
Emily of New Moon. As in Duncan's *The Imperialist,* a woman from an
earlier era – here Duncan's Mrs Murchison compares with Montgomery's Marilla Cuthbert and Elizabeth Murray – and the "new
woman" who seeks to carve out a new way of life for herself – Duncan's
Advena, Montgomery's Anne and Emily – meet and interact.
Although both the old-fashioned woman and the new woman are
connected thematically to the pioneer woman, neither is a perfect
embodiment of the type at the outset of the action. Clearly, Anne
and Emily are given a more sympathetic portrayal than are Marilla
and Aunt Elizabeth; yet all characters grow and develop to become
closer approximations of an ideal.

Marilla Cuthbert of Montgomery's *Anne of Green Gables* possesses
many of the practical skills of the pioneer. She can cook; she helps
Matthew in the barn when necessary; she keeps her house orderly
and spotless; she can sew (for example, she makes new clothes for
Anne). What is initially lacking in Marilla, however, is an appreciation

for beauty and things of the spirit. The clothes for Anne are serviceable but plain; and the house is barren:

The whole apartment was of a rigidity not to be described in words, but which sent a shiver to the very marrow of Anne's bones.[37]

Like Marilla, Elizabeth Murray of *Emily of New Moon* is an active, capable woman who runs her house well. The New Moon kitchen floor is "spotlessly white";[38] Elizabeth prides herself on the New Moon home-made sausages; moreover, it is a New Moon tradition that "the jam pots must never be empty" (108). Despite her many evident strengths, though, Elizabeth is suspicious of beauty and frivolity: Emily must not read novels; she disapproves of Emily's writing, and Emily must hide her "letter-bills" from her aunt.

Another shortcoming of these two women, Elizabeth and Marilla, is that they continue to emphasize the importance of their domestic skills long after the time of pioneering. At best they are old-fashioned; at worst they are rigid and narrow-minded. Elizabeth Murray is perhaps the worse offender here. Things are done at New Moon as they have always been done, regardless of change in the outside world. For example, New Moon uses homemade candles long after everyone else has stopped. Cousin Jimmy says to Emily, "Your Aunt Elizabeth doesn't like new-fangled things. In the house, we belong to fifty years ago" (62). Nor does Elizabeth want Emily to change with the times. Accordingly, she initially disapproves of the suggestion that Emily be trained as a teacher, since, in her view, "A girl's place was at home" (316). These, then, are women who have inherited some of the skills of their pioneer ancestors, but who are moribund, lacking a frontier upon which to test their skills, and refusing to recognize change. The arrival of the younger women provides this frontier (a frontier of the spirit), and it is through their interaction with Anne and Emily that the older women become "better" women, more perfect representations of Traill's definition of the ideal pioneer.

Like Advena Murchison, Anne Shirley and Emily Starr initially are virtually useless in the house. They are creative, intelligent, imaginative, eccentric, and bookish, rather than domestic in their inclinations. Anne's imagination, for example, is a powerful one. Shortly after Anne's arrival at Green Gables, Marilla notes the child's inclination to daydream:

while this odd child's body might be there at the table her spirit was far away in some remote airy cloudland, borne aloft on the wings of imagination. (36)

Emily too is ethereal: she writes poetry; she experiences the "flash"
– a physical reaction to beauty. Her Aunt Elizabeth Murray views
these tendencies with grave suspicion – and sometimes with active
opposition. She takes down and burns a picture Emily has hung on
the bedroom wall (105).

Both girls can and do learn housework, however. Marilla, in fact,
notices Anne's quickness shortly after the girl's arrival:

Anne was smart and obedient, willing to work and quick to learn; her most
serious shortcoming seemed to be a tendency to fall into daydreams in the
middle of a task and forget all about it until such time as she was sharply
recalled to earth by a reprimand or a catastrophe. (57)

Despite a series of catastrophes, such as the day she gives Diana Barry
currant wine instead of raspberry cordial, Anne continues to learn
from Marilla. Finally Marilla says of her, "I wouldn't be afraid to trust
her in anything now" (264). Thus, Anne becomes an ideal: she unites
practical ability with aesthetic sensitivity. Moreover, through her ambi-
tions to become independent, to get an education, and to become a
teacher, Anne, like Duncan's Advena Murchison, clearly belongs to
the generation of "new women" pioneers whose frontier is social
rather than physical in nature.

But Marilla has changed as well. For example, her house now contains things of beauty – Anne brings in flowers – and she appreciates
the spiritual side of Anne. In addition, Marilla has become less rigid
and has learned to love Anne. This development of a maternal
instinct in Marilla comes late in her life; nevertheless, it is an important part of the change in her and is directly caused by her interaction
with the younger woman.

The relationship between Emily Starr and Elizabeth Murray in
Montgomery's *Emily of New Moon* has similar results. While Elizabeth
never understand or approves of Emily's writing, she begins, grudg-
ingly, to accept that it is inevitable. And Emily learns the ways and
the traditions of New Moon. In a letter to her dead father, Emily
says, "Aunt Laura is teaching me to sew. She says I must learn to make
a hem on muslin that can't be seen" (193). One day when both aunts
are away, Emily receives unexpected company, and is able to entertain
correctly, even baking a cake that does not disgrace the reputation
of New Moon. Like Anne Shirley and Marilla Cuthbert, then, Emily
Starr and Elizabeth Murray are teaching each other valuable lessons.

Thus, while Montgomery, like Duncan, moves forward in her presentation of the pioneer woman to indicate that pioneering includes
more than settlement on a physical frontier, she continues to reinforce

the traditional role of women. Her protagonists do not inhabit a traditional pioneer landscape: they are writers, poets, and teachers; they
pursue an education; they can and do earn a living for themselves.
Yet they, like Duncan's Advena Murchison, and like Canadian feminists in general, remain within the tradition of the capable pioneer
woman, never denying the old values. The frontier environment is
social rather than physical in nature, but like Traill's pioneer, the
typical Montgomery protagonist works to effect change in that environment. Here the change is most apparent in the evolution of the
attitudes of the older women, Marilla and Elizabeth.

Nellie McClung must be included in any list of feminist writers in
Canada. McClung was more assertive in voicing her feminist views
than were either Montgomery or Duncan. Consequently, her fiction,
such as for example *Purple Springs*, presents her personal concerns
and theories, and in fact, Pearl Watson, the heroine of the three
Watson family books, *Sowing Seeds in Danny* (1908), *The Second Chance*
(1910), and *Purple Springs*, is McClung's chief representative in her
fiction which includes the Canadian new woman. Pearl's views tend
to be those of McClung herself, and Pearl (like her creator) owes a
debt to the tradition of the pioneer woman.

In the first novel of the Watson series, *Sowing Seeds in Danny*,
McClung establishes many of Pearl's admirable traits. At twelve years
of age, Pearl is the surrogate mother for the large Watson family.
(Mrs Watson does laundry for women in the town and is often away
from home.) Far from resenting this burden of responsibility, Pearl
is cheerful and conscientious in the performance of her duties – a
reaction which echoes back to Traill's advice to women on the nineteenth-century Ontario frontier. The Watson house shows evidence
of poverty, but also of much happiness, for in the Watson family the
home life is rich: Pearl is imaginative and creates visions and stories
for the younger children. Later, in *The Second Chance*, it is Pearl who
attends to the moral upbringing of her siblings. When Danny comes
"swaggering home one night feeling deliciously wicked smoking a
licorice pipe,"[39] Pearl is faced with irrefutable evidence of the moral
decline of the family, and she suggests that they move to a farm, away
from the evil influence of town-dwellers. In addition, it is Pearl who
ensures that the children attend school. In the first two novels of the
Watson series, then, Pearl displays homemaking and maternal abilities. She is also courageous, imaginative, cheerful, and pragmatic.
These are all appropriate traits for a pioneer heroine.

The final phase of Pearl's development occurs in *Purple Springs*
when she, apparently quite naturally, becomes an active supporter of
women's rights. She is now a teacher, an independent young woman

with a decided mind of her own. At this point, Pearl represents the new pioneer woman, of the same type as Duncan's Advena Murchison, a crusader in what is often a hostile environment. But the sweetness and basic goodness of her character have been reaffirmed throughout the three works, and Pearl's new activities are carried out with the cheerfulness and the strength of conviction which marked her pioneer ancestors.

Throughout *Purple Springs* Pearl is a spokeswoman for McClung. Indeed, McClung includes an account of a political play, performed by a group of Winnipeg women and starring Pearl, which is based on a similar event described in McClung's autobiography, *The Stream Runs Fast* (1945). Evidently then, although the settling of her fiction is predominantly rural, McClung is concerned with the lives of women in a post-pioneer period. In McClung's opinion, as expressed in *The Stream Runs Fast,* women should be looking elsewhere for fulfilment, seeking new frontiers to conquer:

The first part of life here, the pioneer period, is closing, and a new era is about to break. Some day, before long, there will be electric light in all these houses and new machines to lift the burden of drudgery. Co-operative movements are coming too, but to bring all this about the people must develop a new mentality. The people of mother's generation were great people in their own way. They took great pride in their endurance ... But these feats of endurance sound foolish now, for the angle of life is changing.[40]

The image of the "angle of life" can be applied to the rearrangement of the frontier to suit new social conditions. McClung uses her writing to point out the possibilities for change, the way that women can move on. She includes the pathetic story of an overworked farm woman, Mrs Paine, in *Purple Springs* (Pearl of course helps Mrs Paine) in order to protest a woman's lack of legal right to her fair share of a farm on which she has performed an equal, not to say superior, role in homesteading. Romantic, idealistic, and sentimental, *Purple Springs* is, nevertheless, a strong feminist treatise. Even as McClung reaffirms traditional values – Pearl marries Dr Clay – she explores other avenues open to women – Pearl campaigns for women's rights. And in *The Canadian West in Fiction,* Edward McCourt comments that Pearl "embodies in her own small person all of the orthodox pioneer virtues, together with an appreciation of 'the better things of life' which sets her apart from most of her acquaintances."[41]

The McClung heroines are, generally speaking, notable for their ability to speak their minds and for their sturdy independence. In the tradition of the pioneer heroine, they are also capable, practical women who are happiest when they are working in a kitchen or managing a large family. Helmi, the Finnish emigrant who is the protagonist of *Painted Fires* (1925), is a new woman in her assertion of independence: she hits and knocks over a "fresh" man; she throws soup at another; she chastises a slovenly girl for washing dishes incorrectly by hitting her over the head with a tray. But Helmi is hardworking and capable: work melts away in front of her, and she can never get enough to do. She is maternal and, in a sense, visionary in her ability to see beyond and through her kitchen walls. Finally, she is connected with beauty and things of the spirit; her spirit is soothed by nature. These are all traits which place Helmi within the continuum of pioneer women in Canadian fiction. Moreover, Helmi can be viewed as a pioneer on two levels: as a new Canadian, and also as a "new woman."

Whereas Duncan, Montgomery, and McClung describe post-pioneer days in their fiction, Robert Stead's *The Homesteaders* is a work which bridges the gap between frontier and civilization, or rather, the gap between an earlier physical frontier and a later social and spiritual frontier, and which furthermore demonstrates the importance of the pioneer woman on both frontier settings. At the beginning of *The Homesteaders,* John and Mary Harris leave Ontario to become prairie homesteaders. Mary, a "heroine,"[42] is the daughter of Ontario pioneers and has inherited the pioneer spirit from her mother. Mary's mother shows her courage when she says goodbye to her daughter:

The breed that had not feared, a generation back, to cross the seas and carve a province and a future from the forest, was not a breed to withhold its most beautiful and noble from the ventures of the greater West. (9)

Mary's contribution to the pioneering process in the West echoes back to Traill's analysis of the pioneer woman's role in Upper Canada when she had insisted that an emigrant must be pragmatic and accept her fate:

[Mary] was going to be brave. She had talked with the other women on the train and in the town. They were women from Ontario farms, some of them well into middle life, women who had known the drudge of unremitting toil since childhood. Their speech was faulty; their manners would not have passed muster amid her old associations; but their quiet optimism was unbounded, their courage was an inspiration. She too would be brave! (33–4)

Up to the time of her departure for western Canada, Mary has obviously been sheltered from hard work, but, as the daughter of pioneers, she has inherited the requisite courage to face her new life bravely. When she reaches the West, Mary immediately begins to work. In the tradition of the pioneer woman, her most important contribution is her management of household concerns. Her home is her true domain, and, like Traill's pioneer, she is concerned with the inclusion of beauty in her home:

In the interior of the little house an extraordinary change was wrought; simple draperies and pictures relieved the bareness of the walls; shelves were built for the accommodation of many trinkets dear to the feminine heart; a rag carpet covered the centre of the floor; plain but appetizing dishes peeked enticingly from behind the paper curtain that now clothed the bare ribs of the cupboard; and a sense of homeliness pervaded the atmosphere. (46)

Mary appears to be the ideal pioneer: pragmatic, idealistic, capable, active, courageous, equally concerned with things of the spirit and with practical matters. The first section of *The Homesteaders* closes with the birth of her son Allan.

Stead does not leave the story at this point; he resumes the narrative at a time twenty-five years later. The original pioneering period has ended. The Harris family has prospered but appears to have lost something of value:

The pioneer days had passed away, and civilization and prosperity were rampant in the land. There were those, too, who thought that perhaps the country had lost something in all its gaining; that perhaps there was less idealism and less unreckoning hospitality in the brick house on the hill than there once had been in the sod shack in the hollow. (86)

"Mammonism" (97) has replaced the ideals of the pioneer:

the old sense of oneness, the old community interest which had held the little band of pioneers together amid their privations and their poverty, began to weaken and dissolve, and in its place came an individualism and a materialism that measure progress only in dollars and cents. (96)

In spite of the increased prosperity of the Harris family, Mrs Harris is overworked and careworn. Browbeaten by her husband, she continues to perform a never-ending series of tasks. In effect, a new frontier has emerged to take the place of the old one. Ironically, it is the very success of the early pioneers which has sparked the need for new effort on a largely spiritual frontier. The skills of Mary Harris do not serve on this frontier and she is struggling to survive. Like

Mrs Murchison of Duncan's *The Imperialist,* Mary is locked into a role which is no longer appropriate given the improved fortunes of the family. Yet salvation is at hand. Beulah, Mary's daughter, is a pioneer woman who can cope with the new frontier and who can effect change and improvement on that frontier. Beulah has inherited the pioneer skills and the feminine spirit of her mother along with what Stead defines as a freer, more masculine attitude:

with her mother's beauty and fine sensibility she had inherited the indomi-table spirit which had made John Harris one of the most prosperous farmers in the district. She moved in an easy, unconscious grace of self-reliance – a reliance that must be just a little irritating to men of old-fashioned notions concerning woman's dependence on the sterner sex – (87–8)

The sense of feminine independence and a freer spirit is, in fact, typical of the ideal Canadian feminist of the period, and Beulah resembles McClung's Pearl Watson, Duncan's Advena Murchison, and Montgomery's Anne Shirley in her recognition of new possibilities for women. Beulah leaves home, significantly moving farther west in a recreation of the original pioneer movement. Through the efforts of Beulah, the Harris family's conflicts are resolved, an emotional balance is restored, and the perils of Mammonism are averted.

Thus, Duncan's concerns as a writer, and as a feminist, are mirrored in the work of her contemporaries. Duncan (like Traill before her) is not so much innovative as she is expressive of a general feeling – a social atmosphere, as it were. Just as Traill's views on pioneering are echoed (albeit unconsciously) by many other pioneer women (as for example Anne Langton, Mary O'Brien, and, to some extent, Susanna Moodie), so too Duncan's adaptations of the pioneer myth to late nineteenth- and early twentieth-century feminist social theories are echoed by Canadian feminists and writers of fiction alike. Duncan's use of the pioneer woman in fiction is, perhaps, more realistic and less idealistic than the others mentioned. Her Advena never achieves the standard of perfection attained by Montgomery's Anne or Emily, McClung's Pearl, or Stead's Beulah. Though no direct link between Traill and subsequent writers can be established, it is evident that by Duncan's time, the pioneer woman had become a Canadian archetype.

CHAPTER FOUR

Ralph Connor's
Pioneer Heroine

On a superficial level, the fiction of Ralph Connor (Charles Gordon) treats of the heroic struggles of men and women on a Canadian frontier landscape, whether that landscape is the Glengarry backwoods of Ontario, as in *The Man from Glengarry* (1901) and *Glengarry School Days* (1902), or the Canadian North-West and prairie foothill country as in *Black Rock* (1898) and *The Sky Pilot* (1899). At a deeper level, Connor's use of metaphor, specifically of religious metaphor, adds a spiritual dimension to his depiction of the Canadian frontier. When account is taken of both these levels, it can be argued that in his fiction Connor redefines the process of settling the frontier so that it becomes the metaphoric equivalent of a Christian struggle for salvation. In "Ralph Connor and the Canadian Identity," J. Lee Thompson and John H. Thompson define the spiritual dimension to Connor's fiction as "the playing out of a morality in a magnificent natural setting, with colourful characterizations and vivid descriptive passages to put flesh on the archetypal confrontation of men with their unruly souls."[1] Connor's female protagonists, such as the Mrs Murray of the Glengarry books, who inhabit the frontier landscapes, are brave and competent pioneers. Yet these women perform an equally important, possibly a more important function: they are pioneers on a spiritual frontier. Like Sara Jeannette Duncan in *The Imperialist*, Connor in *The Man from Glengarry* seems to accept and treat the pioneer woman as a genuine Canadian social type, and, like Duncan, he transfers this type into fiction. Both Duncan and Connor continue to develop this character type beyond the original model advanced by Catharine Parr Traill in *The Backwoods of Canada* (1836) and *The Canadian Settler's Guide* (1855) into a female character type which is more compatible with post-frontier Canadian social conditions and attitudes than is Traill's emigrant woman in the backwoods.

Again, the fact that no direct link can be established between Traill and a later writer provides evidence that the pioneer woman had moved quickly from her origins in historical reality to become a Canadian archetype, one which could be adapted to inhabit a wide variety of frontier landscapes. Whereas Duncan's Advena Murchison of *The Imperialist* is a pioneer woman who moves into a primarily social frontier, Connor's Mrs Murray of the Glengarry books seeks to improve conditions on a spiritual one. In Connor's interpretation, the frontier becomes a concept, as well as a real place, and the pioneer woman becomes an abstract ideal, as well as a real woman.

At a time when many godly persons "regarded novel reading as a doubtful indulgence for Christian people,"[2] Connor's fiction enjoyed great popularity[3] even among the more religious segment of society. One reason for this popularity was undoubtedly the "truthful" or realistic portrayal of characters, places, and events in his fiction.[4] Another was the strong religious bias which characterizes Connor's writing, a bias common to much of the Canadian fiction of the period.[5] Indeed, the number of "religious" novels produced during the latter part of the nineteenth century and the early years of the twentieth is almost overwhelming. Some other writers who added a large portion of moral fibre to their fiction included Mack Cloie in *The Old Orchard* (1903), H.A. Cody in *The Frontiersman, A Tale of the Yukon* (1910), Robert Knowles in *The Singer of the Kootenay, A Tale of Today* (1911), Marian Keith in *Duncan Polite* (1905), *The Silver Maple* (1906), and *'Lizbeth of the Dale* (1910), R. and K.M. Lizars in *Committed to His Charge* (1900), and W.H. Withrow in *Barbara Heck, A Tale of Early Methodism* (1895) and *The King's Messenger; or, Laurence Temple's Probation. A Story of Canadian Life* (1879). While a few of these works feature urban, post-pioneer settings (Lizars), others use northern or western frontiers (Cody), or, at the least, a rural setting (Keith). Thus, while some works may paint an accurate and valuable picture of pioneer life in several parts of Canada (Withrow, Connor), the authors' major purposes are most commonly moral ones. For the main part, these authors are now forgotten, largely because the moral messages which shape the narratives are no longer popular, and, of the writers listed above, Connor alone is published today. Despite their current disfavour, however, these writers are important in an historical survey of Canadian literature. For example, their use in fiction of the pioneer woman as a heroine indicates the general acceptance of this figure as a literary character type.

Of this group, Connor merits special attention: he is, arguably, one of the better writers; certainly, he is better known today than the others. Nevertheless, it is important to note that Connor is representative of his era. His adaptation of the pioneer woman to suit a religious or moral purpose is not unique. As has been shown in the work of Traill and Duncan and their contemporaries, the pioneer woman seems to appeal to some common perception of women and their role in Canadian society. Writers merely rearrange or redefine the frontier and adapt the pioneer to fit that frontier.

Given the demands of popular taste during the late nineteenth and early twentieth centuries, it is not surprising that in his fiction Connor uses what is essentially a sermon method of writing: "Paradoxically the secret of Ralph Connor's astonishing vitality may lie in the fact that he was a novelist second, a man with a message first. Like the preacher of all ages he tells a tale to point a moral."[6] The typical narrative structure of a Connor novel consists of a series of anecdotes strung together, following a loose plot line and illustrating a specific moral precept. Every story has an obvious point so that the narrative and the religious message are inseparable. The protagonists are chosen to demonstrate either a particular character weakness or to represent human virtue. In the best of Connor's writing, as for example *The Man from Glengarry* and *Glengarry School Days*, his adherence to historical accuracy and his recreation of real life through the perspective of the Presbyterian moralist work together to produce a cohesive moral and historic view of pioneer life in the Glengarry backwoods.

Connor's pioneers are the western rancher, the backwoods farmer, the itinerant preacher, and, most important for present purposes, the frontier wife and mother. Each character confronts a personal spiritual dilemma, a frontier of the mind; the frontier and pioneering become metaphors for Christian struggle.[7] Difficulties and moral dilemmas are conquered by faith in a manner comparable to the process of pioneering on a real, physical frontier. Furthermore, the crusading Christian pioneers prove to be adept on either frontier and the traits which ensure success on the one are readily transferable to the other. Finally, in Connor's view, the non-Christian will probably not be as successful as the Christian on a frontier landscape; he or she must reform to become a better person and a better pioneer.

The fact that the underlying structure of Connor's works is always a moral one means that there is always a clear differentiation made between right and wrong actions and between good and bad characters. One "good" character who moves easily through both the physical and the spiritual frontier is the Connor heroine. There is, in fact, only one female character type in Connor's fiction, perhaps only one female character who merely assumes a variety of different names. There are no bad women, and all of Connor's female protagonists are approximations of one particular idealized interpretation of the frontier woman. As Edward McCourt puts it:

The women of Ralph Connor's novels are even more limited in range than the men. The men at least fall into two broad divisions – good and bad. But Ralph Connor created no "bad" women. One suspects that he found it hard to acknowledge the fact of their existence. And yet his stereotyped heroines, like so many of his heroes, carry a kind of conviction because their creator never doubts their reality. To him Mrs. Mavor of *Black Rock*, Lady Charlotte Ashley of *The Sky Pilot*, and Mrs. Murray of the Glengarry books are living persons because they are idealizations of his own mother.[8]

In *Postscript to Adventure*, Connor acknowledges his literary debt to his mother, Mary Robertson Gordon. His memory of her certainly influenced his fiction, and he says of *The Man from Glengarry:*

the soul of the book ... its response to the appeal of beauty whether of the woods and wild flowers or of the things of the spirit and all that is best in it Ralph Connor had from the Lady of the Manse. (153)

Both Mrs Murray of *The Man from Glengarry* and *Glengarry School Days* and Connor's mother come from wealthy, cultivated backgrounds. Both marry Highland Presbyterian ministers and move to the backwoods settlement of Glengarry where they serve the needs of their families and their parishioners with the untiring devotion of saints. It is important to note, however, that while Connor claimed to have based his version of the saintly pioneer woman on his mother, other writers of the period produced similar heroines in their fiction. The Jessie Hamilton of Marian Keith's *Duncan Polite* and the Constance Radhurst of H.A. Cody's *The Frontiersman* are, in most respects, reproductions of the same ideal.

If Connor's fictional character seems at times to be unbelievable – too saintly, too capable – one needs only to examine Connor's *Postscript to Adventure* to see that he perceived his mother as an ideal woman, a woman "with the soul of the saints of old" (412). Although Connor used an ideal as the basis for his development of female characters, he genuinely believed in the existence of such women:

And even those who deny everything that Ralph Connor preached, who detest his crudities and flinch from his breaches of good taste, who deride the simplicity of his character and the genial optimism of his faith, must recognize that intense spiritual awareness, which, however distorted in the presentation, gives his novels a passionate sincerity rare in Canadian literature.[9]

Connor's heroine was, in his eyes, a real person, an ideal of femininity which could be realized in a living woman.

Fictional recreations of Mary Robertson Gordon, the original Lady of the Manse, reappear throughout Connor's work. Whether she appears as Mrs Mavor, Mrs Murray, or any of a dozen others, she is always the heart and soul of the narrative. A practical, capable, active pioneer woman, often a wife and mother, responsible for the care of a large family, she is also linked with ideals of truth and beauty, to things of the spirit, and to a feminine religious principle.[10] The use of a dual focus in the description of the Canadian pioneer woman was not new in Canadian literary history at the time that Connor was writing his novels. As has been seen, Catharine Parr Traill, in her handbooks of advice to emigrant women, *The Backwoods of Canada* and *The Canadian Settler's Guide*, had defined the role of the female pioneer in much the same fashion. She described the many diverse household tasks which a pioneer woman must perform. But she also insisted that a primary function of the woman in the backwoods home was to add beauty and elegance, whenever and wherever possible, to even the rudest backwoods dwelling.[11] But, while Traill and Connor both idealize the pioneer woman and her role, they do so to achieve quite different ends. Traill created and published a picture of the woman who was most suited to backwoods life. For the benefit of her fellow emigrants, Traill developed a theory of pioneering, a method of coping with the strange new world and the many hitherto distasteful household tasks which were the lot of pioneer women in Canada. Connor was writing his fiction near the end of the pioneer era in Canada. While Traill had to prove that the pioneer woman could be a heroine, Connor was able simply to accept the theory that the ordinary pioneer woman was one. In *Postscript to Adventure,* he refers to the women of Glengarry:

It is one of the tragedies of literature that historians fill their pages with the doings of men and leave unsung the lives of the heroines of the race. Less colorful doubtless are the lives of mothers, wives, sisters, but more truly heroic and more fruitful in the upbuilding of human character and in the shaping of a nation's history. At the very foundation of a people's greatness is the home. Splendid and hazardous as are the deeds of men in the battle of life, nothing they endure in the way of suffering can compare with what the mothers of a pioneer colony, remote from civilization, are called upon to suffer in the bearing and reading of children. The loneliness, the dangers, the hardships of fathers and sons in the remote lumber camps or in the rafts down the river are as nothing to the appalling loneliness, the dangers, the hardships that mothers and daughters have to meet and endure in the little log houses in the clearing with children to clothe and care for in health and in sickness, and to keep regularly at school, to train and discipline, with beasts to water and feed, with fires to keep alight when snowdrifts pile round the little house to the eaves, shutting them off for days and nights from their neighbors, with no one but God available for their help. All this is a part of my experience, and at times when I begin to lose my faith in the nobler qualities of the race I let my mind wander back to the wives, mothers and sisters of the pioneer-settlers of Glengarry and find my faith revive. (14)

Connor's work, as illustrated by the above passage, often assumes an elegiac as well as an historical role. As F.W. Watt says:

The world of Ralph Connor, in so far as it existed at all, lasted for only a short period. It was already passing as he wrote about it. And indeed, he was well aware of this, for he set himself in part the task of recording it before it was entirely lost.[12]

In Connor's fiction, pioneers and their exploits are romanticized; the pioneer, like the frontier, exists in an historical rather than a real, physical context.

The highly idealized central female figure in Connor's fiction, the Lady of the Manse, is a mentor and a guide for the men and women around her: she serves as a role model for other women and as a ministering angel to all who need her. Even among a race of "heroines," she becomes a leader in both a practical and a religious sense. In such Connor novels as *The Man from Glengarry* and *Glengarry School Days,* the faith and personal nobility of the female protagonist seem to thrive in a frontier atmosphere of hard work, and the occasional digressions of the frontier men from the straight and narrow, as for example the blasphemy and drunkenness of the shantymen, only serve to strengthen the resolve of heroines like Mrs Murray of the Glengarry books and Mrs Mavor of *Black Rock*. The Connor heroine is both an exemplary figure and a catalyst to good deeds. Consequently, other female characters, such as Kate Raymond of *The Man from Glengarry,* either mirror the central character's goodness or try to emulate her. The Connor heroine brings about changes in the men and the women around her without changing her own essential goodness. Moreover, she is a frontier woman who tackles bravely the adverse circumstances of frontier living and who lives up to Traill's high standards of excellence. She is, therefore, an active agent on both a physical and a spiritual frontier – a force for order and good in a lawless and sometimes amoral society. Connor says of Mrs Murray: "She lived to serve, and the where and how were not hers to determine. So, with bright face and brave heart, she met her days and faced the battle."[13] This statement serves as a definition of the driving force behind the lives of any of Connor's female protagonists.

One primary function of the central female character in Connor's fiction is that she serves as a role model for other women. She is an excellent homemaker and teaches her skills to others. Mrs Murray is equally at home in a kitchen and a sick-room, as she proves during her first visit to Macdonald Dubh's home in *The Man from Glengarry*. Macdonald's sister Kirsty is kind-hearted but she is neither a good housekeeper nor a good nurse, and Mrs Murray tries to help her. Among other things, Mrs Murray convinces Kirsty that gruel will be good food for Macdonald Dubh during his illness:

Kirsty took the pot from the bench, with the remains of the porridge that had been made for supper still in it, set it on the fire, and pouring some water in it, began to stir it vigorously. It was thick and slimy, and altogether a most repulsive looking mixture, and Mrs. Murray no longer wondered at Macdonald Dubh's distaste for gruel. (34)

Mrs Murray is as tactful as she is capable. Before she leaves, she has washed and fed Macdonald Dubh without hurting Kirsty's feelings and has taught Kirsty some basic nursing and housekeeping skills.

In the R. and K. Lizars novel, *Committed to His Charge*, the chief female protagonist, Helen Huntley, performs an interesting version of this female role. Since *Committed to His Charge* has a primarily satiric rather than religious purpose, the heroine is less saintly and more real. Yet, Helen Huntley is, as is typical of this type of character, both beautiful and approachable – a minister's wife with kind words for everyone. While Helen is much admired, however, she lacks the devoted slaves which throng around the saintly pioneers in other works. But this novel, like Duncan's *The Imperialist*, is, at best, cautiously realistic, for Helen displays few faults for the other women to discuss – with one notable lapse when she forgets the words of the Lord's Prayer. "I could as easily have said the Lord's prayer in Greek as in English,"[14] she says to her husband. A few women learn from Helen Huntley, but, by and large, it is after Helen's death that the majority of the women in the parish discover her true worth.

In his *Postscript to Adventure* Connor refers to a woman's role in the home as "the greatest in the world" (16), indicating his belief that a good homemaker is living up to her fullest potential as a woman. Mrs Murray's home reflects the personality of the homemaker. Duncan, in *The Imperialist*, also uses the motif of the house as a mirror of the housekeeper's personality, but Connor moves into religious metaphor with his use of the house and the garden as evidence of the state of the woman's soul and of her proximity to salvation. Mrs Murray's home, therefore, is described as a place of refuge where people find comfort. The central rooms are those in which the family congregates: the kitchen and the living-room. In *Glengarry School Days*, when Hughie is troubled by events at school, he finds his mother at work:

He found his mother, not at the door, but in the large, pleasant living-room, which did for all kinds of rooms in the manse. It was dining-room and sewing-room, nursery and play-room, but it was always a good room to enter, and in spite of playthings strewn about, or snippings of cloth, or other stour, it was always a place of brightness and of peace, for it was there the mother was most frequently to be found. This evening she was at the sewing-machine busy with Hughie's Sunday clothes, with the baby asleep in the cradle beside her in spite of the din of the flying wheels, and little Robbie helping to pull through the long seam.[15]

Since Hughie has a guilty conscience about his behaviour (he has stolen money from his mother to buy a pistol), he feels like an intruder in his mother's domain, and he is "glad of the chance to get away" (171) as quickly as possible:

Hughie ran away, glad to get out of her presence, and seizing the pie, carried it out to the barn and hurled it far into the snow. He felt sure that a single bite of it would choke him. (172)

Hughie has sinned; until he repents, he cannot feel at ease in his mother's presence. He cannot accept her loving gift of food; nor can he benefit from the aura of peace which surrounds Mrs Murray when she is working in her home.

A young man in Robert E. Knowles's *The Singer of the Kootenay* suffers a similar fate. Murray McLean (who is a rather "wild" young man) is saying goodbye to his mother when she begs him to be "good" in the Kootenay country:

"And Murray, Murray," as she released him once again and poured her soul into his eyes, "promise me you'll keep your heart pure and good, for me, unstained, my darling, for your mother, from all the temptations that I know will beset you there. Promise me, won't you promise me, my son?"[16]

As a "good" woman, Mrs McLean would be a powerful force any-where. When she is ensconced in her own home, however, no man can withstand her entreaties, and Murray must yield to his mother's wishes. Any danger to Murray's soul has been averted; he keeps his promise.

In H.A. Cody's *The Frontiersman*, the heroine, Constance Radford, seems to have an aura about her – particularly when she is in her cabin. She is perceived by Keith Steadman, the hero, to be a "sweet, patient woman, adorning the humble cabin with a true and gentle grace."[17] Cody's Constance, like Connor's Mrs Murray and Knowles's Mrs McLean, becomes a powerful figure when set against the back-drop of her own home.

This theme – that the appearance of the good woman's home mir-rors the beauty of her soul – is reiterated in the description of the Finch home in Connor's *Glengarry School Days*. In spite of the poten-tially disruptive male forces in the family (Mr Finch is a zealous, Old-World Presbyterian who clashes with the independent, New-World sons), the saintly presence of the mother prevails and makes her home a happy refuge:

The usual beautiful order pervaded the house and its surroundings. The back yard, through which the boys came from the barn, was free of litter; the chips were raked into neat little piles close to the woodpile, for summer use. On a bench beside the "stoop" door was a row of milk-pans, lapping each other like scales on a fish, glittering in the sun. The large summer kitchen, with its spotless floor and white-washed walls, stood with both its doors open to the sweet air that came in from the fields above, and was as pleasant a room to look in upon as one could desire. On the still of the open window stood a sweet-scented geranium and a tall fuschia with white and crimson blossoms hanging in clusters. Bunches of wild flowers stood on the table, on the dresser, and up beside the clock, and the whole room breathed of sweet scents of fields and flowers, and "the name of the chamber was peace."

Beside the open window sat the little mother in an arm-chair, the embod-iment of all the peaceful beauty and sweet fragrance of the room. (203–4)

Mrs Finch is enough like Mrs Murray to be her sister. And through the suffering and eventual death of Mrs Finch, Connor allows his reader to enjoy the pathos of a good woman's death without having his major female character, Mrs Murray, suffer any serious hurt.

Helen Huntley of the Lizars' *Committed to His Charge* is a similarly warm and welcoming person. Her home and the things in her home serve to illuminate this point:

the things originally had been ... good ... but some of them were much the worse for wear. There were easy chairs, used many times by a heavy figure; vases to hold flowers, and large, strange things for ferns; soft cushions everywhere, and many other articles hitherto unknown in Slowford. (88)

The comforting, welcoming aspect of Helen's home acts as a reflection of her personality: "one clear look from Helen's gentle eyes ... disarmed all fears" (70–1).

A clue to the personality of Lawrence Temple's saintly mother in W.H. Withrow's *The King's Messenger* can be found in the books she reads. Here, the items in the house indicate the state of the woman's soul, and, in her own chamber, Mrs Temple surrounds herself with instructional and uplifting works:

the well used Bible which was the daily food of her spiritual life; "Wesley's Hymns," with which, singing as she worked, she beguiled her daily household tasks; Bunyan's Pilgrim's Progress, the Lives of Mrs. Fletcher, Hester Ann Rogers, and other religious biographies and devotional works.[18]

Evidently, the reading material is functional as well as illustrative of the woman's pious mind. It serves its purpose – Mrs Temple sings as she works.

Later in the same narrative, Lawrence Temple meets Edith Norris (who will become his wife) and discovers in her a woman who is able to add a touch of grace to the backwoods shanty of her schoolteacher father:

His abode was humble, but bore evidence of refinement. Flowers without and within, snowy curtains, spirited pencil and crayon sketches on the wall, and the thousand nameless indications of female taste – felt rather than seen – made the little cottage seem to Lawrence like an oasis in the wilderness. (152)

The cabin's furnishings denote the hand and the soul of a woman at work. The state of the cabin provides clear evidence that Edith is a suitable mate for Lawrence, the pioneer preacher.

While Connor's female protagonist is always concerned with the important task of homemaking, and her home reflects this aspect of her personality, Mrs Murray also influences and instructs those outside her immediate family circle. Kirsty Macdonald is given a helping hand when she proves to be inadequate as a nurse and as a housekeeper. Among a race of backwoods heroines, there are apparently some women who need assistance. Even the task of teaching other women basic household skills becomes, in *The Man from Glengarry*, saintly and Christian:

Eight years ago the minister had brought his wife from a home of gentle culture, from a life of intellectual and artistic pursuits, and from a circle of loving friends of which she was the pride and joy, to this home in the forest. There, isolated from all congenial companionship with her own kind, deprived of all the luxuries and of many of the comforts of her young days, and of the mental stimulus of that conflict of minds without which few can maintain intellectual life, she gave herself without stint to her husband's people, with never a thought of self-pity or self-praise. By day and by night she laboured for her husband and family and for her people, for she thought them hers. She taught the women how to adorn their rude homes, gathered them into Bible classes and sewing circles, where she read and talked and wrought and prayed with them till they grew to adore her as a saint, and to trust her as a leader and friend, and to be a little like her. (23)

Mrs Murray assumes a leadership role, and instructs the other Glengarry women in the noble art of homemaking. More important, and as illustrated by the concluding sentence of the passage just quoted, Mrs Murray assumes the role of a moral leader, specifically in her relationship with other women. In *The Man from Glengarry*, Mrs Murray influences two younger women – Maimie St Clair and Kate Raymond. These two women are not identical, however, either in their character or their development. Maimie, who figures much more prominently in the narrative, is one of Connor's few female characters to fall short of ideal femininity. Despite the example set by her aunt, Mrs Murray, Maimie is neither a good Christian nor a suitable candidate for frontier living. As a result, she loses Ranald, the muscular Christian frontiersman, to Kate, the woman who emulates Mrs Murray and who has the qualities of the good Christian and the potential to be a successful pioneer.

Maimie St Clair has been more strongly influenced by the opinions of her Aunt St Clair than by those of her Aunt Murray. The St Clair home life, like the Murray home life, reflects, for good or ill, the attitudes and the standards of the feminine leader and homemaker. The St Clair home is "a place of cultured elegance and a centre of fashionable pleasure" (51). Unfortunately, the standards set by Miss

St Clair are false and shallow, and, as a result, Maimie's education has been sadly lacking, suited more to the role of an English lady than to the life of a young Canadian woman:

> She was a gentle girl, with an affectionate, yielding disposition, tending towards indolence and self-indulgence. Her aunt's chief concern about her was that she should be frocked and mannered as became her position. Her education was committed to a very select young ladies' school, where only the daughters of the first families ever entered ... Hence Maimie came to have a smattering of the English poets, could talk in conversation-book French, and could dash off most of the notes of a few waltzes and marches from the best composers, her *pièce de résistance*, however, being "La Prière d'une Vierge." She carried with her from school a portfolio of crayons of apparently very ancient and very battered castles; and watercolours of land-scapes, where the water was quite as solid as the land. True, she was quite unable to keep her own small accounts. (52)

Maimie has acquired a few decorative skills, more suited to the draw-ing-room than to the kitchen. (Maimie's acquisition of the accomplish-ments of the English lady in a select school for young women resembles Hagar Shipley's acquisition of similar skills in Margaret Laurence's 1964 novel *The Stone Angel*.)

When Maimie visits her Aunt Murray, she finds the Glengarry people and their customs strange. She makes fun of Ranald when she meets him, basing her mockery on his odd clothing and on his manners. In other words, she judges the man by his appearance and does not perceive his real worth. Later, at the sugaring-off party, Maimie further sets herself apart from the Glengarry young people by refusing to play forfeits with them. To her surprise Mrs Murray defends the game. In Mrs Murray's opinion, it is a simple and honest pastime, and, as Mrs Cameron says, "They that kiss in the light will not kiss in the dark" (62). Maimie's refusal to play forfeits is ironic because she is, in fact, playing a much more harmful and deceitful game with Ranald. Ranald is straightforward and honest in his emo-tions; it never occurs to him that Maimie is a flirt, and is therefore dishonest. Maimie's refusal to enter the social world of Glengarry indicates her general inability to fit into a pioneer world. She lacks the emotional strength and the moral fortitude of the backwoods settlers of Glengarry. The final, damning, evidence of Maimie's fail-ure to cope with the backwoods is her getting too close to the fire (in spite of Ranald's warning) and setting herself alight. She resorts to a fit of hysterics; Ranald acts quickly and competently to extinguish the blaze. There can be little doubt that, at this point in her life, Maimie is not cut out to be a pioneer. In Connor's terms, this also means that she is far from being an ideal, or even a good, woman.

Maimie's Aunt Murray, unlike her Aunt St Clair, is a strong, positive force in Maimie's life. Maimie herself notices the difference when she is near Mrs Murray and says to her aunt:

Oh, I will never forget you! You have taught me so much that I never knew before. I see everything so differently. It seems easy to be good here, and, oh! I wish you were not so far away from me, Auntie. I am afraid – afraid – (144)

Yet even Mrs Murray cannot change Maimie. Maimie continues to follow the patters of behaviour set by her Aunt St Clair. When she meets Ranald again several years later, she is embarrassed by Ranald's colourful shantyman attire. Kate Raymond is proud to be seen with Ranald, since, unlike her friend Maimie, she can discern and value the quality of the man despite the quality of his clothes. Although Ranald is perceptive enough to notice the difference in the greetings of the two girls, he is as yet unable to believe that Maimie might be an insincere and shallow flirt:

Something was wrong. Was it this fop of a soldier, or had Maimie changed? Ranald glanced at her face. No, she was the same, only more beautiful than he had dreamed.

But while she was shaking hands with him, there flashed across his mind the memory of the first time he had seen her, and the look of amusement upon her face then, that had given him such deadly offence. There was no amusement now, but there was embarrassment and something else. Ranald could not define it, but it chilled his heart, and at once he began to feel how badly dressed he was. (173–4)

Ranald knows that something is wrong, but he blames himself rather than Maimie. For her part, Maimie has decided that "Ranald was not of her world" (184). The wealthy upper-class society in which she is "the toast of all the clubs and the belle of all the balls" (168) has no use for a poorly dressed shantyman. Maimie much prefers to be seen with Lieutenant De Lacy, a son of "one of the oldest English families of Quebec" (168). She values his name, his wealth, his education, his appearance, and his ancestry (this is what her brother scornfully refers to as her "ancestor worship" [187]). De Lacy is neither as honest nor as moral as Ranald, but he is not a bad man. He joins in a fight in Quebec to defend Le Noir and his friends, and, in Connor's world of muscular Christian heroes, bravery and loyalty to one's friends are qualities to be valued. Yet De Lacy has certain weaknesses. Like Maimie, for example, he values appearances and is anxious to maintain his status as a De Lacy and as a member of the upper class. The qualities that De Lacy cherishes would be quite foreign to Ranald. De Lacy is

handsome, tall, well made, with a high-bred if somewhat dissipated face, an air of *blasé* indifference a little overdone, and an accent which he had brought back with him from Oxford, and which he was anxious not to lose. Indeed, the bare thought of the possibility of his dropping into the flat, semi-nasal tones of his native land filled the lieutenant with unspeakable horror. (169)

De Lacy is a Canadian, but he turns to the Old World for his standards of speech, dress, and status. Even Maimie admits that Ranald is the better man, and indicates to Mrs Murray that she could marry Ranald if his name was De Lacy.

Maimie's choice of a husband is reminiscent of a similar decision made by Dora Milburn in Duncan's *The Imperialist,* and in many ways the two girls, Maimie and Dora, are quite similar. Both come from wealthy, pretentious homes; both have been taught decorative skills; both are coquettes who refuse the love of a good man, choosing instead a man with more money and a more prestigious family background. In any event, in her selection of a mate, as in her earlier actions in *The Man from Glengarry,* Maimie falls short of the exacting standards set by the ideal woman, Mrs Murray. She chooses De Lacy as her husband for reasons of wealth and prestige, and ignores the Christian and pioneer values of hard work, activity, and honesty.

When Ranald visits Maimie after her marriage to De Lacy, he finally sees her flirtatious manner and notices the shallow tone of her conversation:

How brilliantly she talked, finding it quite within her powers to keep several men busy at the same time; and as Ranald listened to her gay frivolous talk, more and more he became conscious of an unpleasantness in her tone. It was thin, shallow, and heartless. (278)

Once again, the woman's home and the way in which she entertains her friends indicate her inner qualities. Maimie's party reflects the type of person she is. Whereas Mrs Murray's gatherings feature uplifting conversation and the singing of hymns, Maimie's party is fashionable and frivolous. The implication is, of course, that Maimie does not possess the spiritual strength of the Lady of the Manse.

Maimie escapes very lightly in Connor's *The Man from Glengarry;* perhaps Connor is leaving the inevitable punishment for ungodliness and frivolity to a higher authority. A more common fate is reformation. Some other writers were not as benevolent as Connor, and the inadequate or evil women in their novels were not as lucky as Connor's Maimie. For example, in Mack Cloie's *The Old Orchard* (which is in the main a temperance treatise), several drunkards die terrible deaths. A Mrs Martin dies in a fire; the local tavern owner's son dies trying to rescue her; Mrs Stenson, the wife of the tavern owner, drinks herself to death in a sordid slum; her husband burns to death in his own tavern. The tavern is hell; the tavern owner is the devil; those who drink are evil – the devil's accomplices – and are doomed to die a horrible death, with no chance for reformation. Cloie is perhaps a bit harsh; more often, the writers of religious and moral novels permitted women to reform and to follow the good example set by the saintly pioneer woman.

Kate Raymond, of Connor's *The Man from Glengarry,* is Maimie's friend and serves a narrative function as Maimie's opposite or her foil. Unlike Maimie, who aspires to the life of an idle English lady, Kate is completely of the New World. She looks for the real worth of the men she meets, disreagarding appearance. Kate is much closer in spirit to Mrs Murray than is Maimie. She is a true Christian, and is a candidate suitable for frontier life. It is appropriate that she and Ranald will move to western Canada (this echoes back to a similar situation in Duncan's *The Imperialist* as Hugh Finlay and Advena Murchison also plan to move to the West after their marriage), where she will have an opportunity to prove her worth on a real, physical frontier. One of Kate's most valuable moral virtues is her honesty. She likes Ranald immediately and shows her feelings openly by welcoming him with a "frank smile" (173). Ranald has been vaguely troubled by Maimie but is reassured by Kate. Later, when Kate admits to herself that she is in love with Ranald, she acts with the courage of Mrs Murray and "the saints of old."[19] After an honest assessment of her love for Ranald, Kate faces an intolerable situation with patience, humility, and self-denying courage:

Then, from her room, Kate came down with face serene, and, but for the eyes that somehow made one think of tears, without a sign of the storm that had swept her soul. She did not go home. She was too brave for that. She would stay and fight her battle to the end. (208)

Kate is ennobled by the suffering that she feels as a result of her unrequited love for Ranald. She learns to be patient, and to endure difficulties with a brave smile. Like the Lady of the Manse, she begins to help others less fortunate than herself, and when Ranald leaves for the West, she takes over many of his duties at the boys' club he has founded. Thus, Kate faces her own personal frontier, a frontier which is largely spiritual in nature, and begins to acquire the traits of the pioneer woman.

Jessie Hamilton in Marian Keith's *Duncan Polite* faces a frontier similar to that confronted by Kate Raymond. Jessie's trials begin when she is faced with the possibility of losing the man she loves to another woman:

It was the first real trial of the girl's bright, easy life. But she came of a stock of pioneers, hardy folk, accustomed to shoulder the adversities of life, and she bore her burden bravely.[20]

Jessie, like Kate, learns to become a better woman through the process of struggling with her frontier. The girl turns to Duncan Polite for spiritual guidance as well. By the end of the narrative, she is fit to become a minister's wife, and accordingly, she is reunited with Don Neil (who is, appropriately enough, headed for the ministry).

As Kate becomes more like her model and mentor, Mrs Murray, Ranald becomes increasingly aware of her inner worth. He begins to love Kate and to value her good judgment. While Maimie chooses a lesser man and turns Ranald down, Kate earns his love and is suitably rewarded. The moral strength which has allowed Kate to conquer her personal frontier of suffering will undoubtedly stand her in good stead when she moves to the frontier lands of western Canada with Ranald. At the close of *The Man from Glengarry*, Kate is a good Christian, a leader of both men and women, capable, active, decisive, self-sacrificing, and honest. She is thus a close approximation of Mrs Murray in all but one respect: she does not inhabit a manse.

A rather odd and somewhat whimsical use of this motif – the "good" woman acting as role model for other women – occurs in the Lizars' *Committed to His Charge*. When Helen Huntley (the minister's wife) dies, her husband in desperation marries an elderly spinster, Dulcie, in order to have a caretaker for his children. Dulcie is considerably older than Helen; nevertheless, she uses Helen as her model and imitates her – to the the dismay of the minister:

Dulcie made some mistakes. One that tended to drive him towards madness was a laudable attempt to imitate her predecessor as faithfully as memory would allow. It was all too faithfully. The same terms of endearment came from her lips, the same small attentions, even Helen's habits, were reproduced; and to the husband such work was hideous travesty. (276–7)

More conventional in this respect is Marian Keith's *'Lizbeth of the Dale*. At the outset of the narrative, the chief protagonist, Elizabeth, is a madcap, careless, forgetful child. Only a neighbour, "Mother" MacAllister, listens to Elizabeth and understands her. Mrs MacAllister teaches Elizabeth household skills and counsels her in religious matters. When the adult Elizabeth has a crisis of the soul, she turns to Mrs MacAllister for advice. At the end of the novel, by now clearly a good woman herself, Elizabeth marries Mrs MacAllister's son.

While Mrs Murray serves simply as a guide and a mentor for the other female protagonists in the two Glengarry books, her relationship with the male protagonists is more complex. To begin with, she has a mothering, nurturing function which extends beyond the boundaries of her own immediate family circle. In addition, she personifies the qualities of beauty, goodness, truth, virtue, and Christian love. She has a great deal of influence on the men around her, and in *The Man from Glengarry*, her nephew Harry St Clair refers to her as a "rare woman" (189) who has "a hundred men ... ready to die for her" (189). Ranald agrees with Harry: "They would just die for her, and why not? She is a great woman and a good" (189). Others of Mrs Murray's admirers include the schoolmaster Craven and his uncle, Professor Gray, of *Glengarry School Days*, who believe that "for love of her men would attempt great things" (334). The source of Mrs Murray's power over men seems to be her Christianity. Her brand of gentle, trusting, all-encompassing Christian love differs markedly from the sectarian Presbyterian creed espoused by her husband and the elders of his church and is specifically mentioned in *The Man from Glengarry*: "with the minister's wife religion was a part of her every-day living, and seemed to be as easily associated with her pleasure as with anything else about her" (64). Mrs Murray's power can be defined as a feminine religious influence. She represents a sweet, gentle, persuasive force who sets an example of Christian excellence and who wins souls by trust and love. The male religious figure in Connor's novels, as for example, Mr Murray, tends to be a crusader, an active man who is hasty to make decisions. He is a fiery leader of men who by his words can incite men to great things, and who by his superb physique can dominate all physical opposition.[21] The Lady of the Manse, who is more subtle in her methods, reaches out to and helps the more hopeless cases, those persons who cannot be helped by the minister. For example, in *Black Rock*, Mrs Mavor profoundly affects the degenerate Billy Breen, and Billy attempts to reform his life of alcoholism.

This partnership of the strong, untiring, muscular Christian and the gentle, sweetly persuasive, usually female soul occurs regularly in the moral fiction of the turn of the century. There is seldom a clash between the two divergent types (despite their evident differences), and the division into masculine and feminine Christianity is a split which is often resolved by marriage, as in the Murray marriage in Connor's Glengarry books, or by close friendship. The spirit of compromise and unity in Christ is achieved metaphorically in the novels when the two figures are united in love. In Marian Keith's *Duncan Polite*, the polarization of Christian endeavour is clear in the close friendship of two devout and dissimilar old men, Duncan Polite and Andrew Johnstone. Duncan Polite is the self-appointed spiritual watchman of Glenoro, who, despite the fact that he is male, is a gentle, "feminine" Christian. He watches over the Oro as a mother watches her children:

everything that brought discredit upon it gave him deepest pain, everything that tended to raise its moral tone was, to him, a personal favour and joy. (14)

Keith tends to describe Duncan in feminine terms, both in his physical appearance and in his personality. Gentleness and self-sacrifice are his main features. Like Connor's Lady of the Manse, he is an agent for good; he brings people to Christ by means of personal example and through loving words. Duncan's oldest and dearest friend, Andrew Johnstone, is quite different; like Mr Murray in Connor's Glengarry books, he is forceful and opinionated, an elder of the church, "a terror to evil-doers and so prone to carry out the law and the prophets by physical force that he had earned, among the irreverent youth of the community, the name of 'Splinterin' Andra'" (15). Yet the stronger force is often the feminine one, and Duncan helps those who cannot turn to Andrew. The way in which Duncan helps Jessie Hamilton, the "good" woman of *Duncan Polite*, reminds us of the relationship between Mrs Murray and Kate Raymond of Connor's *The Man from Glengarry*, and Jessie comes to epitomize Keith's version of the Lady of the Manse. (She will eventually marry a minister.) Ultimately, Duncan is the cause of change in his friend Splinterin' Andra as well; when Duncan dies, sacrificing himself for the good of the community, Andrew becomes less fiery and more subdued – in other words, more like Duncan.

Another pairing of the two religious types can be found in R. and K.M. Lizars' *Committed to His Charge*. The Anglican minister, Tom Huntley, tends to be somewhat distant, and his wife, Helen, says to him, "I always think you lock your heart behind you when you close the hall door" (44). The implication is that Helen is the heart. Arguably, Helen's most important role in the novel is to act as her husband's emotional prop. The larger than life dimensions of the contrast between the two religious types are missing in this novel, however. The qualities of leadership, strength, health, and the tendency to inspire fear are less pronounced in Tom than in the other masculine Christians; Mrs Huntley is not as sweet or as saintly as Connor's Mrs Murray. Yet, the Huntleys adhere to roles similar to Connor's husband-and-wife pairings. Helen is clearly a descendant of the pioneer woman; her frontier is the socially stagnant town of Slowford-on-the-Sluggard.

A third example can be found in W.H. Withrow's *The King's Messenger*. Lawrence Temple, Withrow's hero, attacks evil in the rough lumber camps of northern Ontario. Lawrence is an eloquent and "strong-limbed warrior" (43) who saves souls while he conquers the forest. Near the end of the narrative, Lawrence meets the girl he will marry. Edith Norris's character is not clearly defined, but she is intelligent, pretty, and devoted to her parents. It is indicated that she will not shrink from hard work. If she marries Lawrence, she is certain to have these qualities tested, for she will perform a pioneer's role on two frontiers – the physical frontier of nineteenth-century Ontario, and a spiritual frontier as well, helping Lawrence with his ministry.

In Connor's Glengarry books, Mrs Murray's sweet, gentle influence changes a number of men, some of whom have turned away from her husband and his church. The stolid Thomas Finch of *Glengarry School Days* seems an unlikely candidate for falling victim to Mrs Murray's charms; however, at the school examinations in the novel, the usually unmovable Thomas goes to great lengths to please Mrs Murray when she begs him to add feeling to his reading of a poem. Thomas's odd delivery of the passage reduces the majority of his audience to helpless laughter, but he is aware that he has done his best and that Mrs Murray is pleased:

Thomas was surprised to find himself trying to swallow a lump in his throat, and to keep his eyes from blinking; and in his face, stolid and heavy, a new expression was struggling for utterance. "Here, take me," it said; "all that I have is thine," and later days brought the opportunity to prove it. (61)

Mrs Murray's ability to evoke this type of response in her male acquaintances, to appeal to their best qualities, is one of her most salient traits. On at least one occasion she serves as her son Hughie's conscience. Hughie's sense of wrongdoing in *Glengarry School Days* when he steals from his family in order to buy a gun and ammunition from his friend Foxy is heightened by his anticipation of his mother's disappointment and disillusionment. This fear of her reaction to his misbehaviour is a greater deterrent to Hughie than is his own conscience. Like Thomas Finch, he wishes to do his best at all times to please Mrs Murray. Mrs Murray's greatest triumph in *Glengarry School Days*, however, is her reformation of the schoolmaster John Craven. She makes it clear to Craven that she trusts him, even though she knows about his faults – he apparently drinks too much on occasion. Like Hughie and Thomas, Craven is reluctant, or even unable, to betray her trust. He leaves Glengarry a better man for having met Mrs Murray. He has renounced the evils of drinking and is ready to enter the ministry. Furthermore, he attributes his reformation to the power of Mrs Murray.

In *The Man from Glengarry*, several similar projects are tackled by Mrs Murray. All meet with similar success. It is her power over Ranald and his father Macdonald Dubh that transforms the two men from troubled, revenge-seeking shantymen into peaceful, forgiving Christians. Under her instruction, the men learn to forgive their sworn enemy, Le Noir. This in itself is no small task, since it is Le Noir's savage beating of Macdonald Dubh that eventually causes the Highlander's death. But Macdonald Dubh forgives his enemy, and, for the first time in his life, begins to attend church regularly. This is a great surprise to Mr Murray because he had given up on Macdonald Dubh. On his deathbed, Macdonald Dubh thanks Mrs Murray for her help and inspiration:

Then he turned to Mrs. Murray, and said, with a great light of joy in his eyes: "It is you that came to me as the angel of God with a word of salvation, and forever more I will be blessing you." (161)

Ranald finds it more difficult to forgive Le Noir than does his father. But, like a knight in a medieval romance, he pledges himself to Mrs Murray's service: "Ranald could not speak, but he looked steadily into Mrs Murray's eyes as he took the hand she offered, and she knew he was pledging himself to her" (48). The task she asks him to perform is a difficult one. She demands nothing less than his absolute forgiveness of his father's murderer. Eventually Ranald succeeds in his quest and even defends Le Noir in a fight in Quebec. Mrs Murray becomes an ideal of femininity to Ranald, and she represents a standard by which he will measure all other women. He idolizes and idealizes her:

Mrs Murray's high courage in the bush, her skill in the sick-room, and that fine spiritual air she carried with her made for her a place in his imagination where men set their divinities. The hero and the saint in her stirred his poetic and fervent soul and set it aglow with a feeling near to adoration. (40)

Mrs Murray possesses all the traits of the ideal pioneer. She is brave, skilful, and active, and she is a heroine in Ranald's eyes because of these qualities that he perceives in her. But she is not an ordinary pioneer. Her "fine spiritual air" (40), her Christianity, her ability to influence the men who meet her, her high ideals, raise her to the level of a saint to be worshipped and obeyed.

Similarly, the women in the other novels of this era support and influence the men around them. In Marian Keith's *The Silver Maple,* the child Scottie is strongly affected by his grandmother's reactions: "a look of grief on Granny's face could move him quicker than the sternest command of his grandfather."[22] Granny MacDonald teaches Scottie the twenty-third Psalm, and the reciting of "the Lord is my Shepherd" comforts Scottie when, as a child, he first crosses the swamp alone. It also comforts him as an adult when he is at war. Mrs MacDonald influences others as well, including a young girl, Isabel Herbert; Isabel, who marries Scottie, has learned her scriptures from Granny.

Barbara Heck, the Methodist heroine of W.H. Withrow's novel of the same name, leads by example and convinces the ungodly to reform. Not only does Barbara help to subdue the wild frontier environment of Upper Canada (she is a United Empire Loyalist), but she also attacks energetically and effectively the more difficult frontier of sin and riotous living. To cite one example, when she enters a home and discovers that the inhabitants are playing a game of cards, she is horrified. As Withrow notes, playing cards was "a device of the devil for killing time in an age when books and intellectual occupations were few."[23] Barbara acts accordingly. She throws the cards into the fire and lectures the sinners, evidently to good effect:

The little company dispersed, seemingly saddened and sobered by the fearless reproof of an honest and God-fearing woman, faithful to her convictions of duty and her intuitions of right. No more cards were played in that house, and deep religious convictions settled upon not a few minds of the company. (29)

Connor's heroine, the Lady of the Manse, the pioneer saint, obviously sets a high standard for other women to follow. She is an ideal figure, Connor's interpretation in fiction of the Christian Canadian pioneer woman at her best. H.A. Cody's Constance Radhurst of *The Frontiersman* is typical of the "Mrs Murray school" of Canadian frontier Christian women: she is good, sweet, brave, intelligent, and comes from a good family. Like Connor's Mrs Murray, Cody's Constance charms uncouth frontiersmen into Christianity by the sweetness and sincerity of her personality. Also like Mrs Murray, Constance has a religious counterpart. Her sweetheart, Keith Steadman, is a crusading missionary minister, saving souls in northern Canada. He is young, manly, physically strong and handsome, intelligent and dedicated, fearless in his physical and mental battles with the forces of evil. His physical attributes inspire respect in the rough men about him; and his manly personality invites their emulation. When Keith is offered a church in Toronto, he considers accepting for the sake of Constance. Constance reproaches him, however; she is definitely a lady, but she is not afraid of hard work:

And would a woman be worthy of your love unless she were willing to share your lot wherever it might be? A true, loving wife would rather be with her husband in the midst of the fight, by his side to sustain and comfort him in his trial. Then, where love reigned, the little log cabin would be a more blessed spot than a palace where love was not. (341)

Here Constance speaks for self-denying Christian pioneer women; indeed, the speech echoes back to the sentiments expressed by Traill in *The Backwoods of Canada* and *The Canadian Settler's Guide*.

In *The King's Messenger*, W.H. Withrow describes the saintly Mrs Temple in similar terms. She is married to an itinerant Methodist preacher, and despite her suffering, she has remained a worthy and loyal mate:

the noble wife who had been such a faithful help mate during the years of his itinerant toil never flinching, ever cheering and supporting his own somewhat despondent spirit by her buoyancy of soul, her cheerful courage, her saintly piety, and her unfaltering faith. (4)

Through his creation of this character, Withrow, like Cody in his *The Frontiersman*, pays tribute to the legend of the Canadian pioneer woman – albeit one redefined in religious terms.

Often in Connor's work the figure of the pioneer woman comes closer to metaphor and even to myth than to reality. Indeed, the inclusion of motifs of Christian endeavour on a spiritual frontier transforms Connor's fiction from romantic social history into works of myth-making proportions. As Watt notes, for Connor, and for his readers, the real, physical frontier becomes a place which is ideal for self-examination, revelation, and reformation:

The West had become a mythical land, a place where such revelations were forced upon one. Men went there to escape the old life and in search of a new life, and there the faith in conversion and re-birth took on a new meaning. It was a place where biblical parables easily merged with actuality.[24]

In such a setting, Connor's heroine, who is also produced by merging parable with actuality, seems an appropriate, even inevitable, figure.

The appreciation and idealization of a woman's role in the home, and the related theory that a woman, because of her primary function as a mother, is ideally suited to perform a leadership role outside the home, were both central aspects of the woman's movement in Canada during the early twentieth century.[25] The National Council of Women of Canada claimed to represent the majority of Canadian women,[26] and the speeches made by the delegates to the first annual meeting of the council in 1894 indicate that Connor's sentiments were very much a part of the spirit of the times, and that Canadian women generally accepted definitions of the ideal woman very similar to Connor's. To cite one example, the president of the council, Lady Aberdeen, refers to "our grand women's mission" as a mission which is related to "mothering,"[27] not only within the family unit, but in a global context as well:

Can we not best describe it as "mothering" in one sense one [sic] another? We are not all called upon to be mothers of little children, but every woman is called upon to "mother" in some way or another; and it is impossible to be in this country, even for a little while, and not be impressed with a sense of what a great work of "mothering" is in a special sense committed to the women of Canada.[28]

Canadian reformers were ever traditional, ever cautious, always concluding that:

home will ever be our chosen kingdom, but we shall order our homes with greater wisdom and truer love and more steadfast principle by far, from taking a woman's part in helping the great world out of the sins and distresses which make the day of its redemption seem to us still a vision that tarries and a day afar off.[29]

This statement of a global view of the maternal duties of the Canadian feminist indicates that the definitions of the frontier, and, therefore, of the frontier woman as well, shifted and changed to suit the changing social conditions in Canada. While women's suffrage theories and concerns are not a major part of Connor's fiction, his female protagonists adhere to the Canadian feminist perception of the ideal woman. He portrayed women as in his day they evidently preferred to see themselves: maternal, independent, vigorous, courageous, intelligent, and visionary pioneer women. Connor's heroines inhabit wild frontier lands – the Glengarry backwoods and the Canadian North-West – but they are also pioneer women on a new frontier as they help to change the hearts and the souls of the men and the women around them. They are strongly family oriented, the centre of their own family unit, and, in addition, they perform a larger mothering function as they influence an extended group of people outside the family. Finally, and most important, Connor's heroines serve as models of perfection for his female readers. Connor defined Canadian women as they wished to be perceived; he presented ideals that both men and women were apparently willing to accept. This vision of women and women's role may not have lasted for any great length of time,[30] but it was an essential part of Canadian social life, and an important ingredient in fiction during the early years of the twentieth century.

The Appearance of the Pioneer Woman as Character Type in the Fiction of Margaret Laurence

In "My Final Hour," an address given to the Trent University Philosophy Society in 1983, Margaret Laurence repeated one of Catharine Parr Traill's maxims:

So the basic message of My Final Hour would have to be – do not despair. Act. Speak out. In the words of one of my heroines, Catharine Parr Traill, "In cases of emergency, it is folly to fold one's hands and sit down to bewail in abject terror. It is better to be up and doing."[1]

Not only does Laurence define Traill as one of her personal "heroines" in this speech, but she also quotes a passage from Traill's *The Canadian Settler's Guide* (1855), obviously feeling that Traill's advice to emigrant women of the nineteenth century has continued relevance today. By quoting Traill, Laurence makes evident a link between, on the one hand, herself and the problems of twentieth-century society, and, on the other, Traill and the nineteenth-century pioneer society of Upper Canada. Laurence's portrayal of women in her Canadian novels, specifically Hagar Shipley in *The Stone Angel* (1964), Rachel Cameron in *A Jest of God* (1966), and Morag Gunn in *The Diviners* (1974), provides further evidence of a similarity of outlook between these two writers. And, in fact, Laurence's protagonists become contemporary versions of the pioneer woman, the character type created by Traill in *The Backwoods of Canada* (1836) and *The Canadian Settler's Guide* and transposed by her into fiction such as *Canadian Crusoes* (1852). As has been demonstrated by her appearance in the fiction of later writers such as Sara Jeannette Duncan's *The Imperialist* (1904) and Ralph Connor's *The Man from Glengarry* (1901) and *Glengarry School Days* (1902), this character type can be adapted to various definitions of the frontier, specifically to recreations of the frontier as a state of mind rather than as a place. The traits which identify the pioneer woman remain unchanged despite the shifting nature of her frontier environment, and can be quickly summarized: courage, resourcefulness, pragmatism, an ability to accept adverse circumstances with equanimity, and the strength to act decisively in the face of discomfort or danger. These lasting traits of the pioneer woman as character type in fiction and as an ideal of femininity are evident once again in the female protagonists of Margaret Laurence.

Laurence's Hagar, Rachel, and Morag, drawing upon this tradition of characterization confront a frontier landscape which is often hostile, disorienting, and confusing. In Laurence's work the frontier is chiefly an internal one. Consequently, the difficulties faced by the pioneer woman are not external objects and physical hazards but internal, personal problems, often created by the pioneer herself – as they are, for example, in the case of Rachel Cameron, who creates her own dilemmas and imaginary obstacles in *A Jest of God*. Occasionally, however, the problems encountered by the protagonist can be traced to social conditions and attitudes which have influenced her thoughts and actions. An example of this is the way in which the adverse opinions expressed by Manawaka residents towards Morag Gunn and her guardians in *The Diviners* shape Morag's decisions. Unlike examples of the pioneer woman as character type discussed previously (notably Mrs Murray, the pioneer woman in the Glengarry fiction of Ralph Connor), Morag cannot change or influence the attitudes of those about her except through her fiction; she must make her own decisions; the onus is on her to make changes in her own life, rather than to make changes in the society around her. In effect, the social and the personal frontiers become inextricably linked in Laurence's fiction: the personal crisis may have its origin in a social situation, and the protagonist's actions may affect the people around her, but the changes only occur when the protagonist acts for herself.

Just as Connor and Duncan were not alone in their use in fiction of a pioneer woman who faces a social frontier, so too Margaret Laurence is not alone in her use in fiction of a pioneer woman who confronts an internal, personal one. Hagar Shipley and Morag Gunn are by no means the only representatives of the Canadian pioneer woman in twentieth-century fiction. Works such as L.M. Montgomery's *The Blue Castle* (1926), Ethel Wilson's *Swamp Angel* (1954), Constance Beresford-Howe's *The Book of Eve* (1973), Joan Barfoot's *Abra* (1978), Aritha van Herk's *Judith* (1978), and Katherine Govier's *Between Men* (1987), to name only a few, include contemporary versions of the pioneer woman. Laurence's use of the pioneer woman in her fiction merits intensive literary analysis; however, brief critical allusions to the work of some other writers serve to set Laurence and her work within a more extensive contemporary context. As in previous chapters, an in-depth analysis of one writer's work will be set within both an historical and a contemporary literary context.

Although the frontier domain of the contemporary pioneer woman is largely an internal one, quite different from the physical frontier of Upper Canada which was the setting for Traill's *Canadian Crusoes,* these modern women, like Laurence's protagonists, are clearly the literary descendents of Traill's Catharine Maxwell. It may be useful to point out at this juncture that perhaps none of these writers has read Traill's work; indeed, no such direct relationship needs to be established. The pioneer woman is accepted both as a literary character and as a social ideal, certainly owing a debt to Traill, but having gone far beyond Traill's original conception. It is interesting, for example, to know that by the time of writing *The Diviners,* Margaret Laurence had read Traill and had recognized an affinity between the pioneer woman created by Traill and Laurence's own fictional characters. Yet, surely this affinity is evidence of Laurence's adaptation of a commonly accepted and widespread use of the pioneer woman as a character type rather than evidence of a direct causal relationship between Traill's writing and Laurence.

While the frontier environment of the contemporary pioneer would be unfamiliar territory to Traill, the actual process of pioneering would be clearly recognizable, as would be the pioneer woman's discovery of her own intrinsic worth during the course of her pioneering efforts. In "Ivory Tower or Grassroots? The Novelist as Socio-political Being," Margaret Laurence has indicated her awareness of certain interconnected themes which appear throughout her fiction:

The quest for physical and spiritual freedom, the quest for relationships of equality and communication – these themes run through my fiction and are connected with the theme of survival, not mere physical survival, but a survival of the spirit, with human dignity and the ability to give and receive love ... The themes of freedom and survival relate both to the social/external world and to the spiritual/inner one, and they are themes which I see as both political and religious. If freedom is, in part, the ability to act out of one's own self-definition, with some confidence and with compassion, uncompelled by fear or by the authority of others, it is also a celebration of life and of the mystery at life's core. In their varying ways, all these characters experience a form of grace.[2]

It would not be far-fetched to see this as essentially a restatement of Traill's views of the dichotomy of pioneering, as these views are expressed in *The Backwoods of Canada* and *The Canadian Settler's Guide*. More specifically, Laurence's statements echo back to Traill's concept of the dual nature of the interaction between the frontier and the frontier woman: although, for Traill, the pioneer woman must accept adversity with equanimity, humility, and pragmatism, she must also begin immediately to improve her situation.[3] The positive results of the successful tackling of the frontier (whether that frontier is expressed in the physical context of Traill's nineteenth-century Ontario backwoods or in the metaphoric context of Laurence's twentieth-century existential angst) are numerous. The pioneer woman may discover a previously hidden or unexpressed sense of independence, a feeling of freedom from fear, restraint, and social criticism (Catharine Traill's "Mrs. Grundy"),[4] a sense of pride in her accomplishment of distasteful or difficult new tasks. While none of Laurence's protagonists is an ideal character, there is an awareness of some elusive ideal towards which each is working. Similarly, Montgomery's Valancy of *The Blue Castle*, Wilson's Maggie of *Swamp Angel*, Beresford-Howe's Eva of *The Book of Eve*, Barfoot's Abra of *Abra*, van Herk's Judith of *Judith*, and Govier's Suzanne of *Between Men* are involved in a process of self-amelioration. The recognition of the frontier (be it external or internal) and the successful tackling of the process of pioneering on that frontier lead to the protagonist's discovery of her own strengths, and help her to more closely approximate that ideal of femininity defined as the pioneer woman. As she pursues her new activities, each of these contemporary pioneers, like Traill's original model of the pioneer, discover hitherto unguessed reserves of strength and courage.

The protagonist of the first of Laurence's Manawaka novels, Hagar Shipley of *The Stone Angel*, is the daughter of Manitoba pioneers. She grows up during the last years of the Canadian pioneer era in western Canada – the latter part of the nineteenth century and the early twentieth century. Consequently, the pioneer era, as it had been encountered by Hagar's parents, no longer exists in her adult lifetime. At a time when many women began to define themselves as pioneers in a new sense,[5] Hagar appears to be lost, unable to develop her own personal and unique role. This is a problem that lasts through most of her life, being resolved only in the weeks preceding her death when Hagar finally understands and accepts her own self, a self that inevitably includes a pioneer legacy.

Initially, Hagar is torn between two opposing views of her self and her social role, and she is unable to reconcile them. On the one hand, Jason Currie wishes to recreate in his daughter the image of the English lady, a model of femininity which is inappropriate to a Canadian frontier context, whether that frontier territory is the physical wasteland encountered by Hagar's mother or the emotional wasteland that Hagar creates for herself.[6] On the other hand, following the example set by her pioneer father, Hagar epitomizes the New-World freedom and strength of mind which is common to Canadian pioneers. Unfortunately, she is unable to identify or to understand the nature of her dilemma until the end of her life. During the period in which she cannot see her frontier, Hagar behaves inappropriately, and cannot begin the pioneering process. When she is dying, she finally identifies her frontier: "Pride was my wilderness."[7] Although she has spent most of her life lost in a frontier wilderness, unable to respond as a capable pioneer woman, from this moment of recognition she begins to demonstrate the qualities of a pioneer as defined by Traill in *The Backwoods of Canada* and *The Canadian Settler's Guide*. Hagar's achievements as a pioneer during the last days of her life are few in number but are monumental in scope.

Similarly, Beresford-Howe's Eva in *The Book of Eve* is trapped in a loveless marriage. She has conformed to social expectations and is playing an unrewarding role. Like Laurence's Hagar, Eva recognizes her dilemma relatively late. Eva leaves her husband to start a new and more rewarding life as a pioneer woman. Eva's pioneering period will last longer than Hagar's; it is by no means finished at the end of the narrative.

One source of Hagar's initial problem is her lack of a proper role model. Her mother was evidently, if Hagar's assumptions are to be trusted, the type of the Old-World lady who came to grief on the frontier.[8] Although Hagar does not remember her mother, she despises her weaknesses. For example, Hagar regards her mother's death in childbirth not as an unfortunate and inevitable consequence of the difficulties faced by women on the frontier but rather as a proof of her mother's inherent weakness. Accordingly, Hagar perceives her mother as an inadequate and unsuitable role model. In a photograph she sees

a spindly and anxious girl, rather plain, ringleted stiffly. She looks so worried that she will not know what to do, although she came of good family and ought not to have had a moment's hesitation about the propriety of her ways. But still she peers perplexed out of her little frame, wondering how on earth to please ... I used to wonder what she'd been like, that docile woman, and wonder at her weakness and my awful strength. (59)

As Traill pointed out in *The Backwoods of Canada* and *The Canadian Settler's Guide*, coming from a "good" family was irrelevant if the emigrant lady could not adapt to frontier conditions. Throughout her life Hagar continues to think of her mother with some contempt. She is disdainful of her mother's image as a fragile, "graceful unspirited" (7) woman; she despises her mother's evident physical weakness, equating it with an inability to cope with the stresses of frontier living. When her brother Matt asks her to wear her mother's shawl to comfort their sick brother Dan, she retreats from the situation in confusion:

But all I could think of was that meek woman I'd never seen, the woman Dan was said to resemble so much and from whom he'd inherited a frailty I could not help but detest, however much a part of me wanted to sympathize. To play at being her – it was beyond me. (25)

It is ironic – but also revealing of the affinity between physical and mental frontiers – that while Hagar disavows any similarity between herself and her mother, she, like Mrs Currie, has difficulty understanding and coming to terms with her frontier.

It is also ironic that Hagar rejects her mother's image and accepts her father's version of ideal femininity by allowing herself to be shipped off to Toronto to learn "how to dress and behave like a lady" (42). Hagar refers to herself as "the dark-maned colt off to the training ring, the young ladies' academy in Toronto" (42). Despite her contempt for her mother, she accepts her father's decision; she learns decorative, ladylike skills, accomplishments which are reminiscent of an earlier, Old-World way of life that is irrelevant on the Canadian prairie farm lands:

When I returned after two years, I knew embroidery, and French, and menu-planning for a five-course meal, and poetry, and how to take a firm hand with servants, and the most becoming way of dressing my hair. Hardly ideal accomplishments for the kind of life I'd ultimately find myself leading, but I had no notion of that then. I was Pharaoh's daughter reluctantly returning to his roof, the square brick palace so oddly antimacassared in the wilderness. (42–3)

Hagar's continued resentment of her mother is at odds with the role that she is assuming here; she is to be the lady of the house, and she is to assume a primarily decorative and passive role.

In spite of her apparent acceptance of her father's wishes, however, it is always clear that Hagar cannot be dominated or disciplined. She has inherited a fiercely independent spirit, a legacy which comes partly from her father and partly, surely, from the pioneer environment from which she has sprung. Her marriage to Bram Shipley is an early, misguided, and ultimately doomed attempt to escape the confines of Grundyism and the restraints imposed on her by Jason Currie's social value – misguided because Hagar initially does not understand her own motives, and doomed because she later fails to clarify or to express her feelings. She acts decisively but does not understand her action. She is attracted sexually to Bram but cannot admit this attraction – a saddening indication of the extent to which she is a victim of what can broadly be called Victorian attitudes. Furthermore, she remains chained by the laws of polite Victorian society which dictate that a lady must suffer and be silent in sexual relations. Despite her enjoyment of sex, she follows the dictates of propriety and ladylike behaviour:

It was not so very long after we wed, when first I felt my blood and vitals rise to meet his. He never knew. I never let him know. I never spoke aloud, and I made certain that the trembling was all inner ... I prided myself upon keeping my pride intact, like some maidenhead. (81)

In addition, although she is drawn by Bram's evident disregard of Grundyism, she seeks to change him to fit into her father's world:

I fancied I heard in his laughter the bravery of battalions. I thought he looked a bearded Indian, so brown and beaked a face. The black hair thrusting from his chin was rough as thistles. The next instant, though, I imagined him rigged out in a suit of gray soft as a dove's breast-feathers. (45)

Hagar defies her father by marrying Bram; then, ironically, she tries to reshape Bram in her father's image, an attempt which will never succeed. From the perspective of old age, Hagar can admit her love for Bram, but she remains confused about her reactions to him: "His banner over me was only his own skin, and now I no longer know why it should have shamed me" (81).

Even before her growth towards understanding, Hagar possesses many of the traits of Traill's pioneer woman. For example, Hagar is always able to make decisions and to act on her decisions; she is a capable woman who refuses to sit still in an emergency. While many of her actions are inappropriate to her particular frontier and although she has been trained to assume a decorative rather than a functional role in a home, she begins to take care of Bram's house as soon as she moves in:

The next day I got to work and scrubbed the house out. I planned to get a hired girl in the fall, when we had the cash. But in the meantime I had no intention of living in squalor. I had never scrubbed a floor in my life, but I worked that day as though I'd been driven by a whip. (52)

Hagar never does obtain hired help. She does the work by herself and, like the original pioneers, even begins to take an unhappy pride in her domestic accomplishments:

Work filled the time. I worked like a dray horse, thinking: *At least nobody will ever be able to say I didn't keep a clean house.* I used to black the stove until it glowed like new-polished boots, and wipe the kitchen floor clean no matter how many times a day the mud or slush or dust, according to season, was tracked in upon it. (112)

When faced with adversity, then, Hagar is capable of taking immediate and decisive action. Unfortunately, because of her lack of understanding, her attempts at action fail to satisfy her. Her flight from her father and from the Grundyism which he represents fails when she takes her father's values with her. Her assumption of the role of the housewife is equally unsatisfactory because she continues to resent the role: "I felt something else must happen – this couldn't be all" (112). Hagar's later flight from an intolerable marriage is further proof of her ability to take action in an emergency. Yet this action is also doomed. Hagar takes with her a memory of Bram's physical presence which haunts her at night. Her departure is precipitated by her desire to recreate the image of her father in her son John: "Jason Currie never saw my second son or knew at all that the sort of boy he'd wanted had waited a generation to appear" (64). This effort also fails, since Hagar has not understood her son; he returns to Manawaka and to his father.

Barfoot's Abra takes similar action to escape an unsatisfactory role. She, like Hagar, is a housewife, trapped in what has become, for her at any rate, a loveless, intolerable marriage. She too is relatively inarticulate at the time of her flight, knowing only that she must go if she is to survive. Fortunately for Abra, however, flight is the right action to take. Much later, when her daughter (now grown up) comes to visit her, Abra realizes that her need for escape was caused by her madness and that life on her solitary farm has permitted her survival. Acting instinctively, Abra (unlike Hagar) has acted wisely.

Although Hagar has the pioneer woman's ability to act, she lacks the judgment and self-knowledge necessary to act properly, and her way of coping with stresses and emergencies is misguided. She can neither change the frontier nor be changed by it until she identifies the nature of her problem. The changes which occur during the last weeks of Hagar's life represent the process of a pioneer woman squarely facing her frontier, and choosing the activities appropriate to that frontier. At the last, Hagar's innate strengths combine with her recognition of her frontier to produce changes in herself.

Hagar's first genuinely positive action – her flight to Shadow Point – succeeds where other attempted escapes have failed simply because it corresponds with (or, more accurately, leads to) a change in her perspective: an increased awareness of herself and her needs, and of others and their needs. This is the beginning of an improvement in Hagar's personal wilderness.[9] At the beach Hagar meets Murray F. Lees, another fugitive, and when Murray tells her his life story, she is moved by compassion, by her illness, and by her need for companionship to reach out to him emotionally and to say: "No one's to blame" (234). For the first time Hagar has compromised her own beliefs to help another person. The result is that Lees helps her in return, although she is too ill to recognize his gesture. She tells him the story of John's death, then, in a delirium, mistakes Lees for John and asks for John's forgiveness. Lees, like Hagar, is able to give absolution to a fellow fugitive. Later, when Hagar considers that Lees has betrayed her by bringing Marvin and Doris to get her, she is able to forgive him: "I didn't mean to speak crossly. I–I'm sorry about your boy" (253). And, once again, she finds that by speaking this way, she is rewarded: "Having spoken so, I feel lightened and eased. He looks surprised and shaken, yet somehow restored" (253). A feeling of freedom from constraint thus accompanies Hagar's first true confrontation with her as yet unidentified wilderness of pride.

A similar linking of physical escape into a wilderness with a change in perspective is found in Wilson's *Swamp Angel*. Maggie escapes from her husband and heads north into the mountains:

For three days Maggie stayed at the Similkameen cabins. She slept long, walked and watched in the woods, and fished the river. Spring was pouring in over the whole countryside, and she knew that she could not stay any longer. She was refreshed now ...

These days had been for Maggie like the respite that perhaps comes to the soul after death. This soul (perhaps, we say) is tired from slavery or from its own folly or just from the journey and from the struggle of departure and arrival, alone, and for a time – or what we used to call time – must stay still and accustom the ages of the soul and its multiplied senses to something new ... So Maggie, after her slavery, and her journey, and her last effort – made alone – stayed still, and accustomed herself to something new.[10]

Maggie, however, has more clearly articulated her needs than has Hagar at this point. She has already identified her frontier, and has begun to act decisively and correctly on that frontier.

Hagar identifies her frontier when she forces the minister, Mr Troy, to sing the hymn "All people that on earth do dwell." At this point, she suddenly recognizes the name and the nature of her personal frontier:

Every good joy I might have held, in my man or any child of mine or even the plain light of morning, of walking the earth, all were forced to a standstill by some brake of proper appearances – oh, proper to whom? When did I ever speak the heart's truth? Pride was my wilderness, and the demon that led me there was fear. I was alone, never anything else, and never free, for I carried my chains within me, and they spread out from me and shackled all I touched. (292)

Significantly, Hagar uses the past tense, indicating that her recognition and acceptance of the frontier – pride – and of the conditions inherent to it – she has been ruled by fear – have facilitated the conquering of that frontier.

Like Hagar, other pioneer women in twentieth-century novels experience a moment of truth in which they recognize their personal frontier environment. Valancy Stirling of Montgomery's *The Blue Castle* awakens on the morning of her twenty-ninth birthday to a sense of hopelessness and futility:

Reality pressed on her too hardly, barking at her heels like a maddening little dog. She was twenty-nine, lonely, undesired, ill-favoured – the only homely girl in a handsome clan, with no past and no future. As far as she could look back, life was drab and colourless, with not one single crimson or purple spot anywhere. As far as she could look forward it seemed certain to be just the same until she was nothing but a solitary, little withered leaf clinging to a wintry bough. The moment when a woman realises that she has nothing to live for – neither love, duty, purpose nor hope – holds for her the bitterness of death.[11]

Beresford-Howe's Eva also has an epiphany of sorts. She stops midway up the stairs one day, suddenly aware that she feels like a prisoner in her own home:

But what chiefly stopped me was the cold white autumn light pouring through the landing window ... It seemed to bleach the stairway into something like a high white cell.[12]

Eva says, "there I was ... Under bars" (2), and she prepares to leave home, to escape this confinement.

What begins as a "furtive idea" which has "brushed through her mind"[13] for the protagonist in van Herk's *Judith* becomes "the implacable truth she was looking for" (116) when she is interrupted by her boss/lover in the midst of daydreaming:

She stared up at him for a moment, uncomprehending, then instantly perceived his arrogance, so casual and confident and unaware of her privateness, felt her face whiten and a sickening flood of black, pitted rage against him. Suddenly saw the clear outlines of the vague, sluggish thought she had been half-heartedly pursuing in her helplessness against him, and knew just as suddenly what she had to do ... and she was suddenly perfectly sure. (116–17)

Armed with this knowledge, Judith begins her preparations to buy a farm.

Like so many discontented Abby Murchisons (if Abby Murchison of Duncan's *The Imperialist* were to awaken to the knowledge that she lacks a frontier upon which to demonstrate her talents as a pioneer), these women realize that something is lacking. Either they lack a frontier, or they are acting incorrectly upon an individual, personal frontier. Each woman escapes to find independence and self-sufficiency, and survives with courage and dignity. Through a recognition of the frontier and of the conditions inherent to that frontier, each begins to act appropriately upon the frontier to effect change, moving from what is, in effect, an emotional wasteland to achieve a measure of self-understanding. In the course of the pioneering process, Valancy, Maggie, Eva, Judith, Abra, and Suzanne leave behind the forces of Grundyism and relearn a more vital, valid role, a role which is linked to their common pioneer origins.

Even though Hagar's pioneering efforts in Laurence's *The Stone Angel* last for only a few days, through the naming of her frontier she is able to choose the activities which are both suitable and appropriate to the frontier environment. For example, Hagar tries to combat her false pride and begins to reach out to others, seeking to end her solitude. She reassures Mr Troy and thanks him for singing to her: "Thank you. That wasn't easy – to sing aloud alone" (292). In a manner typical of her past actions, Hagar tells Doris that Troy has done no good, then, ashamed, she admits the "heart's truth": "Doris – I didn't speak the truth. He sang for me, and it did me good" (293). But her most important gesture occurs later when she gets out of bed, ignoring her own discomfort and pain, to help Sandra Wong with a bedpan. The nurse catches Hagar in the act of carrying the bedpan to Sandra, and Hagar and Sandra laugh together at the look on the nurse's face. This is Hagar's reward for selfless action – the first moment of shared laughter for Hagar in the narrative. By helping Sandra, Hagar has denied her own needs and has been rewarded for her positive confrontation of her wilderness of pride.

It is during her final interaction with her son Marvin that Hagar makes the greatest step in improving conditions in her personal wilderness. Uncharacteristically, she tells Marvin that she is frightened, surprising both herself and her son: "What possessed me? I think it's the first time in my life I've ever said such a thing. Shameful. Yet somehow it is a relief to speak it" (303–4). Hagar is shaking off the chains of Grundyism; she begins to speak the "heart's truth" rather than the expected platitudes. As in her encounter with Lees, she feels a welcome sense of relief at her admission of weakness. It is at this point that Hagar suddenly perceives Marvin in a new way:

Now it seems to me he is truly Jacob, gripping with all his strength, and bargaining. *I will not let thee go, except thou bless me.* And I see I am thus strangely cast, and perhaps have been so from the beginning, and can only release myself by releasing him. (304)

The Jacob role was the one into which Hagar had tried unsuccessfully to place John (179). Her changing perspective leads her to tell Marvin what he has always wanted to hear: "You've been good to me, always. A better son than John" (304). The fact that Hagar does not fully mean this is irrelevant; she has learned to reach out of her isolation in order to help someone else. She hears Marvin tell the nurse that his mother is a "holy terror" (304) and realizes that she has been rewarded for her unselfish action: "Listening, I feel like it is more than I could now reasonably have expected out of life, for he has spoken with such anger and such tenderness" (305). Hagar's reward may seem momentary and fleeting, but to her it is a priceless, albeit unexpected, gift.

Hagar has achieved much in the last weeks of her life. Though she spends her last days immobilized in a hospital bed, she follows the tradition of the active pioneer woman by struggling to abandon her false pride and to ignore her fears. Moreover, in confronting and attempting to change the frontier, she is granted a certain freedom from Grundyism, and feels true pride in the accomplishment of difficult or distasteful tasks:

I lie here and try to recall something truly free that I've done in ninety years. I can think of only two acts that might be so, both recent. One was a joke – yet a joke only as all victories are, the paraphernalia being unequal to the event's reach. The other was a lie – yet not a lie, for it was spoken at least and at last with what may perhaps be a kind of love. (307)

Hagar retains her stubborn independence to the last. Her final action is to wrestle the water glass from the nurse so that she can drink unaided. Despite the short-lived nature of her pioneering efforts, and despite the fact that her victory may be only a partial one, the conclusion is nonetheless triumphant. Hagar discovers the "inner freedom" which defines the pioneer woman in fiction.

Eva in Beresford-Howe's *The Book of Eve* is also a senior citizen when she begins to examine her frontier. Almost immediately upon leaving her husband, Eva feels a sense of freedom: "I felt excited as a girl, and happy enough to fly" (4). She goes on to say:

And who would believe it possible to wake up in these circumstances as happy as a birthday child? I opened my eyes into a perfect, self-centred bliss without past or future, and rejoiced in everything I saw. (6–7)

These feelings of euphoria disappear when Eva has doubts about her decision (the self-centredness must disappear, for example), but nevertheless, her mood is a determinedly optimistic one. Other pioneers experience similar feelings of euphoria, although in vastly dissimilar situations. In both Aritha van Herk's *Judith* and Joan Barfoot's *Abra*, the pioneering process is closely connected with the protagonists' farming efforts: Judith manages a pig farm; Abra moves to a farm where she grows vegetables and survives on her own. Yet, like Hagar and Eva, Judith and Abra achieve a measure of independence and feel the pride that comes with the successful accomplishment of difficult, occasionally distasteful tasks. For example, Judith refuses to let anyone help her in the barn; she castrates her pigs when her neighbour Jim cannot:

now she knew why he never touched her, why there was always the distance between them. That sudden knowledge flashed on her. I wanted too much, she thought. I have always wanted too much and not enough, and why can I not just let things go, let them be and allow them to go on? (165–6)

Judith is now "sure and fearless, so perfectly knowing" (166); and after she has castrated the pigs, she feels "the lightness of relief"

(170). A further reference to Judith's acquisition of pride occurs in the bar scene where she starts a fight defending her pigs; at this point she refers to herself as "the Amazon woman of Norberg" (140).

Abra, too, learns to survive in a hostile environment. When she first moves into her cabin, Abra realizes that she must plant a garden: she will need the produce in order to survive through the winter. Although she does not like the idea of working in a garden, she is pragmatic and accepts the demands of necessity:

The idea did not attract me particularly then, but I was beginning to understand that there would be many things I would have to do to survive that I might not enjoy.[14]

This might be one of Traill's protagonists speaking here. There is also pride in the accomplishment of difficult tasks, tasks similar to those faced by the original pioneers:

there had been so many things that I did not know, so many simpler ways there must have been to make curtains, refinish furniture, cut wood, but I didn't know any of them, and so I learned alone, by trial. There were times when I was annoyed, impatient with my ignorance, but still there was pleasure in doing things slowly, even if I was clumsy, and knowing when they were finished, satisfied, that however they had turned out, they were mine. (116)

Abra's conclusion is that "It was pleasing to feel strong" (110). The diversity of frontier landscapes inhabited by women in contemporary Canadian fiction demonstrates the widespread acceptance of (and the adaptability of) the pioneer woman as protagonist.

Rachel Cameron of *A Jest of God* would appear to be the antithesis of Hagar Shipley. As Laurence points out in "Gadgetry or Growing: Form and Voice in the Novel":

Rachel was self-perceptive, indeed a compulsive pulse-taker. She saw things about herself which Hagar did not see about herself, although Rachel tended to exaggerate vastly her own inadequacies and shortcomings.[15]

Rachel has the introspective power that Hagar must learn, but she lacks Hagar's ability to act, to speak out, and to make decisions. Furthermore, Rachel's introspection, as Laurence has noted, does not always help her to reach accurate conclusions. Hagar's wilderness is her false pride; she must learn humility, and with humility comes freedom and, paradoxically, a true sense of pride in her actions.

Rachel's wilderness is her uncertainty, her lack of pride and self-confidence; she must learn to act decisively, and with the ability to act comes a sense of true humility:

> I was always afraid that I might become a fool. Yet I could almost smile with some grotesque lightheadedness at that fool of a fear, that poor fear of fools, now that I really am one.[16]

Like Hagar (and other pioneer protagonists), Rachel must identify and name her wilderness – "that fool of a fear"; she must face her inner conflict and begin to resolve it. Again, the recognition of the frontier leads to the protagonist's ability to act correctly on the frontier; she learns to act decisively and competently in order to effect change and improvement. The benefits which result from her action are familiar ones in a pioneer context: freedom from Grundyism (in Rachel's case Grundyism is represented both by her own fears and by the social values espoused by her mother and her mother's friends) and pride in the accomplishment of hitherto unthinkable or distasteful tasks. An important related theme, one which appears throughout Laurence's fiction, is the protagonist's fulfilment of a maternal role. Finally, like Hagar, Rachel achieves a measure of success, which, although it is not, and perhaps never will be, a total one, allows Rachel to approximate closely the ideal of the pioneer woman as proposed by Traill in her backwoods writing.

Initially, Rachel is a passive, lonely woman. A spinster and a virgin, she lives with and obeys her mother, having denied herself the one role that all Laurence's protagonists have in common – a maternal role.[17] Nor is her literal mother the only me who dominates her. Calla calls her "child" (9), and Willard makes her feel like "a naughty child" (43). Rachel is, in fact, still acting as a child, resenting the demands and the interference of others, perhaps, but unable to assert her own independence. That she neither acts nor admits her resentment of such domination is shown by her ambivalent response to her mother's bridge party:

> It's her only outlet, her only entertainment. I can't begrudge her. Anyone decent would be only too glad.
> As I am, really, at heart. I'll feel better, more fortified, when I've had dinner. I don't begrudge it to her, this one evening of bridge with the only three long long friends. How could I? No one decent would. (15)

This evasion is followed by Rachel's sigh of relief when the evening is over: "Thank God, thank God. They are finally gone" (15). Introspective but dishonest, Rachel refuses to identify correctly her frontier of suffering.

Montgomery's Valancy of *The Blue Castle* resembles Laurence's Rachel; a browbeaten, subdued, shy, and passive spinster, Valancy is treated like a child by her relatives. She is "cowed and subdued and overridden in real life" (4). On the rare occasions when she disagrees with her domineering mother, she quickly backs down: "Valancy did not persist. Valancy never persisted. She was afraid to. Her mother could not brook opposition" (4). Valancy's relatives even make sarcastic jokes at her expense. Thus, since her family sees her as childlike and helpless, when Valancy announces her intention of leaving home, all family members are aghast and assume that she is mad, even sending the minister to scold her.

Although Rachel is a public school teacher, a role which is related in a peripheral way to a maternal role, her maternal needs are not being met. Her relationship with her students is hampered by the short time that she spends with them, and also by her emotional distance from them. Not only is Rachel unable to show her feelings; she cannot admit these feelings, even to herself: "Quickly, I have to gather my children in. I must stop referring to them as my children, even to myself. It won't do" (2). Rachel cannot, for example, demonstrate her feelings for her favourite student, James; nor is she merely passive in this instance. She actively retreats from the admission or the demonstration of her maternal feelings towards him. Rachel's denial of partiality leads ultimately to her betrayal of James to Willard; after his punishment, James returns to the classroom and Rachel sees "his face like bone, his eyes staring my betrayal at me" (25). Then, when Rachel does finally act decisively in the classroom, she acts inappropriately, and strikes James too hard: "From his nose, the thin blood river traces its course down to his mouth. I can't have. I can't have done it" (52–3). Until Rachel can admit her frustration and anger, she will be unable to act to effect change.

Govier's Suzanne of *Between Men* has a similar problem. Unlike Laurence's Rachel, however, Suzanne has been pregnant and has lost a child. We are given to understand that the "loss" is actually an abortion which Suzanne has tried to deny and to forget. Until she can face her earlier decision and define her need to become a mother, she too is unable to act effectively.

Related to Rachel's thwarted maternal needs are her unfulfilled sexual needs. (Here also one is reminded of Montogmery's Valancy of *The Blue Castle;* Valancy achieves happiness when she flouts her family's morals and marries Barney Snaith.) Again Rachel is initially unable to act because she cannot identify or admit the nature of her problem. When she realizes that she feels an urge to touch Willard Siddley's "spotted furry hands" (9), she reacts in panic: "I didn't. I won't. I didn't feel that way. I'm only imagining things again" (9). In the same fashion, she attempts to deny her need for the sexual gratification afforded to her by her fantasy at night:

I didn't. I didn't. It was only to be able to sleep. The shadow prince. Am I unbalanced? Or only laughable. That's worse, much worse. (19)

Rachel's release from captivity is occasioned by her recognition of the true nature of her personal frontier, by her open admission of her sexuality, and by her affair with Nick Kazlik. The decision to have an affair with Nick is an important one for Rachel, since she learns to act courageously in the face of her fears, ignoring her mother's (and her own) emotional sabotage. After Rachel makes love with Nick, the voices within her begin to panic. She berates herself for her timidity, for her lack of experience, and for admitting her inexperience to Nick:

He believes I was lying to him, out of some false concern for – what? ... I want to laugh, to rage at him for thinking me a liar, to – Hush. Hush, Rachel. This won't do. Not now. Not here. (92)

The initial love-making episode with Nick has enormous significance in Rachel's life; she has acted instinctively, decisively, and appropriately in the face of her fear, and, furthermore, she begins to identify her fear as inappropriate and irrelevant. For the first time in the narrative Rachel refuses to allow her uncertainty and timidity to dominate her, and her previously ignored maternal voice speaks, soothing her anger and confusion. From this point on, Rachel begins to act, and her actions demonstrate her growing awareness of her own needs. She starts to move towards people, to verbalize her resentments, and to express her needs. The initial actions are small and tentative; nevertheless, they are crucial to her development and growth. On the way home with Nick, for example, she frets in a manner consistent with her usual avoidance of confrontation:

But I must not move closer to him. He's driving. It would be dangerous. What if we were in an accident, and I were found with my hair all disarranged and my lipstick gone and my dress creased and crumpled? (93)

But Rachel, as has been noted, has begun to change. When Nick stops the car, she moves towards him: "Without thinking, I've put my arms around him, held my face to his, asking to be kissed" (93).

Sexual roles are understated in *The Blue Castle;* even Montgomery's most realistic fiction avoids direct mention of sex. Yet, Valancy's attraction to Barney Snaith is clearly a physical one. He is her prince-lover in the imaginary "Blue Castle" (a character somewhat similar to Rachel's imaginary lover): "recently ... her hero had had reddish, tawny hair, a twisted smile and a mysterious past" (5). When she first meets Barney, Valancy finds herself "trembling from head to foot" (110). Valancy likes everything about Barney, and to a great degree, this liking is physical:

She liked his nice voice which sounded as if it might become caressing or wooing with very little provocation. She was at times almost afraid to let herself think these thoughts. They were so vivid that she felt as if the others must know what she was thinking. (114)

Like Rachel, Valancy can be the aggressor in the relationship – she proposes to Barney, for example. And it is through her relationship with Barney that she changes and develops. Indeed, Barney has given her strength long before she meets him, since he is the author of the books she reads for comfort. Ironically, on Valancy's first visit home after her marriage, she discovers that another man also wants her: Edward Beck, a widower with nine children, needs a wife and has asked for Valancy. To the horror of her family, Valancy is no longer available for Mr Beck. To their further consternation, she arrives at home stronger, more assertive and "so oddly, improperly young-looking" (171). Moreover, the change is not merely an external one; her happiness has taught her understanding:

Valancy was so happy she didn't hate her people any more. She could even see a number of good qualities in them that she had never seen before. And she was sorry for them. Her pity made her quite gentle. (171)

Valancy gains a measure of freedom by leaving her family; then by marrying Barney, she achieves understanding.

There is also a strong sexual component in Beresford-Howe's *The Book of Eve.* Eva has considered herself to be old and sexless. Her encounter with Johnny Horvath, however, forces her to reconsider both her newly discovered independent life and her assessment of herself as sexless: "He was drowning me then in a sweet, familiar pleasure I thought I'd forgotten all about" (101). Then, at the end of the narrative, Eva, like Valancy and Rachel, assumes an active role in furthering the relationship. She says to her son, "Got something to do that's irrational, so it can't wait" (170), and she goes to find Johnny, seeking to continue their relationship. It seems paradoxical that although the protagonist has escaped a former stifling life to achieve understanding and independence, part of her new understanding is the knowledge that she cannot (or does not want to) live alone.

It is clear that Rachel has begun to free herself from Grundyism and fear, and she continues to move towards other people. She visits Hector Jones at night when she need someone to talk to, saying simply, "Let me come in" (119), and surprising herself by her lack of pride in making this plea. She realizes that "It doesn't matter. Suddenly it doesn't matter at all to me" (119). For the first time in the narrative, Rachel has an honest emotional exchange with another person, admitting her need for human contact. Hector assumes the role of "comic prophet, dwarf seer" (124), sharing his own problems with Rachel, comforting her, and teaching her the truth about her father. Rachel realizes that her father (like herself) had other options and could have chosen differently: "If my father had wanted otherwise, it would have been otherwise. Not necessarily better, but at least different" (124–5). As she is leaving, Rachel apologizes to Hector for disturbing him. Then she stops herself and thanks him instead: "No – listen, Hector – what I mean is, thanks" (128). This is symptomatic of Rachel's continuing metamorphosis: she realizes that an honest exchange has taken place and that an apology is inappropriate.

From a passive role as a virgin, spinster, and child, Rachel moves into an active adult role and towards maternity (of a sort). This transformation is seen most clearly in her changing attitude towards teaching and in the reversal of her role with her mother. Initially, Rachel is a teacher of small children, unable to admit that they are a temporary, unsatisfactory substitute for her own children. In the course of her brief relationship with Nick she begins to recognize and to verbalize her need for children, in effect to face another aspect of her personal frontier. When Rachel gets her period, she starts, in the old way, to ignore and to deny her real feelings. This time, however, her newly discovered assertive and truthful self dominates the conversation:

I was terribly relieved. It was a release, a reprieve.

That is a lie, Rachel. That is really a lie, in the deepest way possible for anyone to lie.

No. Yes. Both are true. Does one have to choose between two realities? (133)

And Rachel concludes, "If I had to choose between feelings, I know which it would be" (133). In addition, because she identifies her

thwarted maternal instincts, she recognizes that teaching is an unsatisfactory substitute. She faces her new class in September, looking for
another student like James, the next surrogate son, only to discover
that this evasion no longer works for her:

I wonder who will be the one or ones, as it was James last year? All at once
I know there will be no one like that, not now, not any more. This unwanted
revelation fills me with the sense of an ending, as though there were nothing
to look forward to. (155)

Rachel has begun to face the problems which constitute her frontier;
here she is being honest about her needs.

Because she has correctly identified her desire to have children,
Rachel is able to move one step closer to the achievement of personal
freedom. When she thinks she is pregnant, she decides to keep the
baby: "Look – it's my child, mine. And so I will have it. I will have
it because I want it and because I cannot do anything else" (171).
Ironically, she finds that she is not pregnant, and that her admission
of personal need has been in vain. Nevertheless, she has made a
positive step in the amelioration of her frontier condition. Consequently, she receives one of the rewards for active participation in the
pioneering process. She experiences a sense of freedom – freedom
from the constraint of social opinion and from her own brand of
Grundyism:

All that. And this at the end of it. I was always afraid that I might become
a fool. Yet I could almost smile with some grotesque light-headedness at that
fool of a fear, that poor fear of fools, now that I really am one. (181)

By identifying, confronting, and admitting this fear of appearing
foolish, and by refusing to be dominated by it, she has begun to
liberate herself. This echoes back to Montgomery's Valancy Stirling,
who begins to change when she reads a phrase from a book and
applies that phrase to herself: "Fear is the original sin" (30).

Despite the fact that she has identified her problems, Rachel cannot
easily conquer her frontier. She has admitted her need to bear children, but she does not have the baby she wants; she has become more
self-confident, but she will continue to make mistakes:

I will be different. I will remain the same. I will still go parchment-faced
with embarrassment, and clench my pencil between fingers like pencils. I
will quite frequently push the doors marked *Pull* and pull the ones marked
Push. (201–2)

The identification of the frontier and the problems inherent in that frontier is an important first step in pioneering, a necessary first step in the pioneer woman's quest to improve conditions on the frontier. Although Rachel has admitted her weaknesses, she has also discovered her personal strength. She has, for example, learned to act decisively, to move towards people rather than away from them. In addition, she realizes that her mother is weak rather than tyrannical, and that her mother too has fears:

So that's it. I ought to have seen. She's wondering – *what will become of me?* That's what everyone goes through life wondering, probably, the one absorbing anguish. What will become of me? Me. (114)

As a result of this discovery of her mother's fear and weakness, Rachel discards the role of the daughter and assumes the role of the mother. Under anaesthetic she says, *"I am the mother now"* (184). When the nurse repeats these words to her, Rachel accepts her new role, and she begins to make decisions which affect her mother. As she and Mrs Cameron move west – that is, move in the direction traditionally associated with the frontier – Rachel watches over the "elderly child" (201) sleeping beside her. Rachel has learned to act; she has also assumed a leadership role within her small family unit.

Govier's Suzanne Vail of *Between Men* identifies her need to have children when she admits to herself that she is lonely:

How could she be lonely? It came to her suddenly what kind of company she wanted. She wanted another life inside her, a child.[18]

This is the relevation for which she has been searching throughout the narrative. Her historical research into the murder of an Indian girl, Rosalie New Grass, has helped to direct Suzanne towards this knowledge: for example, Suzanne rewrites history so that Rosalie has been looking for an abortionist; therefore, Rosalie too has lost a child. And Suzanne, like Laurence's Rachel, begins to define herself as a mother:

She, Suzanne, was a childless mother. She must have a child to be complete. She sat in the dark, and looked inside herself. She thought she knew herself before, but now the eyepiece of the kaleidoscope had been turned. All the little pieces were the same, but they made a different design. (191)

Finally, then, after she identifies her need to have children, Suzanne begins actively to pursue men in order to achieve her goal.

Initially, Maggie Lloyd of Wilson's *Swamp Angel* is in an undesirable situation. Her unhappiness is due (in some measure) to thwarted maternity: her daughter has died. This is only part of the problem, however, since Maggie has also lost her husband and her father. In short, her family has been torn apart. She marries Edward Vardoe to escape her loneliness, only to discover that she has made a mistake. Although she has acted, she has acted incorrectly because she has not defined her needs. Maggie's happiness, or at least, her contentment, is largely restored when she leaves Vardoe – in a dramatic, middle-of-the-night flight – and assumes a maternal role within the Gunnarson family. The Gunnarsons need Maggie as much as she needs them:

When Mrs Lloyd came to the lake, she brought with her a source of fresh happiness which flowed from her and reached and encompassed the little boy. It reached Haldar and his wife, too, and, insensibly, life was relaxed and easy for a time. (95)

Maggie has one again acted, this time correctly:

Her tormented nights of humiliations between four small walls and in the compass of a double bed were gone, washed away by this air, this freedom, this joy, this singleness and forgetfulness. (96)

Paradoxically, Maggie's flight to freedom has brought new responsibilities. Her escape is complete only when she takes on a maternal role in the Gunnarson family and becomes responsible for them. For example, even though she is angry with Vera, she helps the other woman after Vera's unsuccessful suicide attempt.

By the end of *A Jest of God*, Rachel's liberation from fear has begun, but as Laurence points out in "Ten Years' Sentences," a total victory has not been and may never be achieved:

She tries to break the handcuffs of her own past, but she is self-perceptive enough to recognize that for her no freedom from the shackledom of the ancestors can be total. Her emergence from the tomb-like atmosphere of her extended childhood is a partial defeat – or, looked at in another way, a partial victory. She is no longer so much afraid of herself as she was. She is beginning to learn the rules of survival.[19]

The rules for survival on the physical frontier of nineteenth-century Ontario were clearly delineated by Traill in *The Backwwods of Canada* and *The Canadian Settler's Guide*. There are no such guidebooks for pioneers like Rachel; she faces her own, unique circumstances. Like Hagar of Laurence's *The Stone Angel*, Rachel of *A Jest of God* learns to cope with the problems of her frontier. Rachel's pride in her accomplishment and her sense of relief at her freedom from social constraint bode well for her continued success in combating the frontier. When she hears the rumours of her pregnancy, for example, Rachel refuses to acknowledge or to deny them:

For an instant I'm tempted to deny the rumours, to explain, to say to Hector, so he can pass on the message, let them ask Doctor Raven if they don't believe me. But no. I like it better this way. It's more fitting. (200)

No longer dominated by her fears, with her last words Rachel demonstrates an acceptance of an uncertain fate combined with a newly acquired strength of mind: "God's mercy on reluctant jesters. God's grace on fools. God's pity on God" (202). Significantly, these words are spoken as Rachel moves west. Pioneer days have ended, but Rachel's re-enactment of the original pioneer movement towards the West is symbolic of her personal movement towards freedom.

Montgomery, Wilson, Beresford-Howe, Barfoot, van Herk, and Govier also recreate the pattern used by Laurence, in which the female protagonist, stifled by her family and by the forces of Grundyism associated with the family, leaves the original family unit in order to create a new one. In fact, this echoes back to the pattern used by Stead in *The Homesteaders*, and by Traill in *Canadian Crusoes* when Catharine Maxwell, her brother, her cousin, and an Indian girl form a family group while they are lost in the bush. *The Blue Castle's* Valancy, *Swamp Angel's* Maggie, *The Book of Eve's* Eva, *Abra's* Abra, and *Judith's* Judith are initially trapped in an unrewarding domestic life. *Between Men's* Suzanne is dissatisfied with her personal life; she has already fled from her marriage, becomes trapped in another unsatisfactory relationship, and is also caught in an unrewarding work environment. Drudgery, confinement, and petty rules (Grundyisms) govern the days of these women.

As has been noted, the pioneer process is an internal one in contemporary fiction. Typically, however, the protagonist's flight involves a physical movement from a city towards an open space. Rachel of *A Jest of God* makes love to Nick outside of the town; later she moves farther west with her mother. Hagar of *The Stone Angel* tries unsuccessfully several times to escape the confinement of her life; the marriage to Bram is an early, failed attempt to escape the constriction of her father's world. Maggie of *Swamp Angel* goes north in British Columbia into the mountains to work at a fishing camp. Valancy of

The Blue Castle leaves a small town to keep house for Roaring Abel (a genial drunkard) and his daughter Cissy. Eva of *The Book of Eve* does not leave the city, but she discovers a whole new aspect of urban life; she frequents the parks, and she becomes a scavenger, surviving by selling what she finds in the street. Abra of *Abra* moves to a farm and becomes self-sufficient, as does Judith in van Herk's novel. Suzanne moves west in *Between Men;* then, near the end of the narrative, she leaves the city to walk along the Bow River; it is here that she meets and talks to the ghost of Rosalie New Grass, thereby gaining insight into her own problems.

Yet, despite a rejection of her original living arrangement, each protagonist moves to form new domestic attachments, to create a new family structure, and to endorse new rules. The strain of maternal feminism which links Traill's work with Duncan's, Connor's, and Laurence's is strongly evident in the works of Montgomery, Wilson, Beresford-Howe, van Herk, Barfoot, and Govier. Their protagonists have a spiritual function; personal survival is always a primary concern, but they have also a duty to perform in their relationships with others, and this duty is most clearly expressed in the formation of new family attachments or in the clarification of existing relationships. Rachel Cameron of *A Jest of God* redefines her role with respect to her mother; Maggie assumes a maternal role with the Gunnarson family of *Swamp Angel*; Abra rediscovers her daughter in *Abra*; Judith reaffirms her ties with her father by choosing in *Judith* to become a pig farmer; Eva has a love affair with Johnny Horvath and strengthens her relationship with her son in *The Book of Eve*; Suzanne is reunited with her husband in *Between Men* and decides to have a baby; and in the "Memorybank Movies" of "The Halls of Sion" in Laurence's *The Diviners,* Morag Gunn becomes pregnant, and, in the present time sequences, resolves current conflicts with her daughter.

Morag is a twentieth-century version of the pioneer woman in fiction. Like the other Laurence protagonists mentioned, Morag faces a personal, unique frontier, a frontier created partly by the protagonist herself, and partly by the protagonist's social environment. Morag is typical of Laurence's pioneer women, and typical of contemporary pioneer women generally, in her internalization of the process of pioneering. Like Hagar and Rachel, Morag learns to recognize and to accept her limitations in order to begin to effect change and improvement on the frontier. In Laurence's terms, as she defines them in "A Place to Stand On," Morag learns the rules of survival:

The theme of survival – not just physical survival, but the preservation of some human dignity and in the end some human warmth and ability to reach out and touch others – this is, I have come to think, an almost inevitable theme for a writer such as I, who came from a Scots-Irish background of stern values and hard work and puritanism, and who grew up during the drought and depression of the thirties and then the war.[20]

Laurence's definition of survival is, in effect, a reworking of the definition of successful pioneering as proposed by Traill in *The Backwoods of Canada* and *The Canadian Settler's Guide*, and, not fortuitously, Laurence notes her sense of a legacy, inherited from her own pioneer ancestors, which influenced her ideas. Morag is undoubtedly a more successful pioneer than is either Hagar or Rachel; at any rate, she is closer to achieving the ideal of survival as stated here by Laurence. Hagar becomes able to "reach out and touch others," but she is cut short by her death at the end of *The Stone Angel;* Rachel, too, has merely begun to reach out of her self-imposed isolation at the end of *A Jest of God.* In both of these works, the narrative ends with the triumphant beginning of the pioneering process.

In contrast, as Morag reviews her life in *The Diviners*, it becomes apparent that this protagonist has achieved a level of self-awareness and self-determining activity that is denied to Hagar and Rachel. On the one hand, Morag faces a personal crisis which causes confusion; the departure of her daughter Pique is the event which forces Morag to re-examine her past decisions and actions in an attempt to understand her present confusion. On the other hand, Morag is evidently capable of defining her frontier and of choosing the activities which are appropriate to that frontier. Her current problem does not occasion anything more than a temporary stasis in Morag's life:

Morag comes to us then as perforce a watcher, first by the terms of her life, in the present stage of her relationship with Pique, and also by the terms of her profession. She is far from calm, but she is becalmed. She is not powerless to act, but at this point in her life the opportunities for dynamic action do not exist in her relationships with others. They only exist when her work is going well, in the act of writing her fiction.[21]

Nor does any major change, any change comparable to those that take place in the lives and attitudes of Hagar and Rachel, occur in Morag's life through the present time sequence of *The Diviners.* Major changes have taken place in the past and are reviewed by Morag in her "Memorybank Movies." Rather, in the present time of the novel, Morag learns to perceive herself differently; she learns to define herself as a pioneer – the descendant of pioneers like the Cooper and the Traill families. She also gains added insight into her roles as a mother and as a writer of fiction (a creator of myth). Suzanne of Govier's *Between Men* is also concerned with these three things. Throughout the course of the narrative she, like Morag, redefines her role as a wife, as a mother, and as a writer; moreover, she examines her relationship to earlier residents of Calgary, specifically through her research into the death of Rosalie New Grass.

In the first section of *The Diviners,* "The River of Now and Then," Morag's crisis is introduced; Pique's abrupt departure for the West has caused a mixed reaction in Morag:

Something about Pique's going, apart from the actual departure itself, was unresolved in Morag's mind. The fact that Pique was going west? Yes. Morag was both glad and uncertain ... Would Pique go to Manawaka? If she did, would she find anything there which would have meaning for her?[22]

Reduced to a basic level, that unresolved "something" in Morag's mind is composed of three related concerns: Morag's ambivalent feelings about her past, specifically her Manawaka past; her as yet unresolved definition of her role as a writer; and her anxiety about her changing relationship with her daughter.[23] In "The River of Now and Then" Morag begins to review her past in an effort to identify and to resolve her present confusion, indicating by this immediate respose that she is neither unaware nor inactive. Although she does not yet understand her confusion, she begins, in the manner of the competent pioneer woman, to deal actively with an emergency. The second section of *The Diviners,* "The Nuisance Grounds," continues to juxtapose past and present events. Here, the flashback sequences deal with Morag's childhood in Manawaka, and culminate in her decision to leave. The present events develop more fully the extent of Morag's anxiety and confusion. Both narrative sequences – past and present – contain a protagonist who is, to some extent, unable to define her frontier and unable, therefore, to improve conditions on that frontier.

The "Memorybank Movies" of "The Nuisance Grounds" show the social rejection endured by Morag as a ward of Prin and Christie Logan. The section ends with Morag's determination to escape from Manawaka: "And I'm never coming back" (165). At this point in her life, Morag lacks the self-knowledge to understand that such an escape will fail – that, as Christie later predicts, "It'll all go along with you, too. That goes without saying" (207). This section of the novel contains many of Christie's stories, his "myths"; at this time Morag cannot appreciate the validity of the stories and she questions their truth. Much later in her life Morag discovers that Christie's stories are valuable and "true," and, at this point, she begins to recognize that his interweaving of fact and fiction is a process which is analogous to her own production of fiction – a process which Suzanne learns in Govier's *Between Men*. Suzanne, a history professor, breaks with academic tradition to reinvent and to rewrite the history of Rosalie New Grass. Suzanne knows that her so-called research is actually "breaking the rules of her kind of scholarship" (41). She further realizes that, to achieve her goals, she will "have to make assumptions, to invent" (41). Yet, Suzanne, who also teaches a course called "Reinventing the West" (100), is able to understand the death of Rosalie only when she rewrites history. Just as Laurence's Morag eventually discovers the "truth" in Christie's stories, so, too, Govier's Suzanne reinvents history in order to get at some essential "truth."

Because Morag does not initially understand this type of "truth," and because she tries to deny her past, her initial flight (which is as misguided as is Hagar's marriage to Bram in *The Stone Angel*) cannot succeed. And in the following sections of *The Diviners*, the extent of her failure becomes more apparent.

In the present time sequence of "The Nuisance Grounds," Morag is also avoiding the truth about herself and her relationship to the people around her. More specifically, perhaps, the truth is not immediately apparent to her. Morag's confrontation of the A-Okay Smith family demonstrates her uncertainty about her role in society – just as, to a greater extent, she could not understand her relationship to others in Manawaka. In the past, she tried to run away; in the present, she faces her confusion. The Smith family is a group of "back-to-the-land" former city dwellers. Morag perceives the Smiths as "new pioneers" (170), comparing herself to them in a unfavourable light, envying the fact that they have so clearly defined their role and are dedicated to the pursuit of their dream. Morag is not certain of her role, and, as a result, she feels a sense of inadequacy when she is with them. Yet, even as Morag envies A-Okay and Maudie Smith, she mocks them, evidently aware (even if only on a subconscious level) that the pioneer way of life which they are emulating – a way of life known to such pioneer families as the Coopers and the Traills – is no longer applicable or appropriate in a post-pioneer, twentieth-century environment. Consequently, when Morag enumerates Maudie's many virtues, she also points out the underlying absurdity of Maudie's determined efforts to go back in time:

Maudie herself was slender and small and would probably look young at fifty, a plain scrubbed face, blonde hair worn long or in a plait, her dress nearly always ankle-length, granny-type, in gingham she sewed determinedly herself on a hand-cranker sewing machine. A wonder she didn't sew by hand with needle, thread and tiny silver thimble. At night. By coal-oil lamp. (55)

The major argument between Morag and the Smiths in "The Nuisance Grounds" concerns the fate of Morag's garden. Maudie Smith, true to her attempts to recreate the experiences of an earlier era, has cultivated a large garden. She tells Morag, "I put in six packets of seeds yesterday" (56). Morag comments, defensively and not very convincingly, that she has other work to do, work which precludes gardening:

If I spent all my time gardening, how in hell could I get any writing done? No great loss, you may say, but it'd be a loss to *me*, and also I need a minimal income, even here. Whatever Susanna Moodie may have said in *Roughing It in the Bush*, I am not about to make coffee out of roasted dandelion roots. (57)

Morag lacks the strength of conviction to believe that her own efforts are of equal validity and, when the Smiths also remain unconvinced, she changes from a defence of herself to a direct attack on them:

I approve of your efforts, God only knows ... I applaud. I think it is great. I cannot help feeling, however, that like it or not the concrete jungle will not be halted by a couple of farms and a vegetable garden. (57)

Morag is ashamed of her outburst, but she has, in fact, spoken the truth and has exposed the flaw in the pioneering efforts of the Smiths. A-Okay is generous enough to recognize this and he identifies Morag's "real work" as her writing: "'Your writing is your real work,' A-Okay said, with embarrassing loyalty and evident belief. 'It's there you have to make your statement'" (58). Just as the Smiths, through their farming attempts, are making a statement of belief, a belief that the rural way of life experienced by past generations was inherently better than contemporary urban life, Morag makes a personal statement in her writing, and engages in a parallel, albeit different type of pioneering.

Morag greets A-Okay's defence of her work with scepticism and a noted lack of conviction, and thinks, "Or not make it. You can't write a novel in that way, in any event" (58). Again Morag confronts one aspect of her central dilemma: she cannot recognize the intrinsic validity of her writing. She has defined her writing as "work," as a means to earn money; A-Okay has defined it as a statement of belief.

Morag retreats from this latter definition in confusion. Like the mental and physical retreat from Manawaka which is juxtaposed to this section in the narrative, Morag's evasion of her worth as a writer cannot help her.

In "The Nuisance Grounds," Morag also compares herself unfavourably to Royland, the water diviner. She perceives that there is a similarity between them, but she questions the value of her gift:

Morag had once tried divining with the willow wand. Nothing at all had happened. Royland had said she didn't have the gift. She wasn't surprised. Her area was elsewhere. He was divining for water. What is hell was she divining for? You couldn't doubt the value of water. (102)

Morag's continued doubt of the validity of her work is juxtaposed with Christie's stories, and Morag's adolescent scepticism about these stories is contrasted with her adult scepticism in the juxtaposition of present and past sequences of "The Nuisance Grounds."

The first appearance in *The Diviners* of Catharine Parr Traill, in "The Nuisance Grounds," provides further evidence of Morag's initial confusion and temporary stasis. In her imaginary conversation with Traill, Morag compares her life unfavourably with the early Ontario pioneers, the Coopers and the Traills. As in her comparison of herself to the "new pioneers," Morag's comparison of herself to the "old pioneers" demonstrates her uncertainly about the value of her own role, positioned as she is between them:

Was it better or worse now? Both. Both. At least *their* children did not wander to God knows where. Unknown destinies, far and probably lethal places. If any *did,* though, there were no telephones and the mail services could hardly have been very snappy. Well, then, *they* did not have to wrench up their guts and hearts etcetera and set these carefully down on paper, in order to live. Clever of them, one might say. Anyway, some of them did. Including women. Catharine Parr Traill, mid-1800s, botanist, drawing and naming wildflowers, writing a guide for settlers with one hand, whilst rearing a brace of young and working like a galley slave with the other. (95)

Morag, like Traill, has faced hardship and has managed to cope. In addition, Morag has identified another similarity between herself and Traill: both are creative writers. Yet Morag is left feeling not only that Traill's problems were greater but also, and more important, that Traill's abilities far exceeded her own, that Traill accomplished a greater amount under more strenuous conditions. In this preliminary examination of the lives of the pioneers, Morag feels herself to be lacking:

Catharine Parr Traill, one could be quite certain, would not have been found of an early morning, sitting over a fourth cup of coffee, mulling, approaching the day in a gingerly fashion, trying to size it up. No. No such sloth for Catharine P. T. (96)

Despite her lack of confidence (does she really "do" anything?), however, Morag defines her concern about Pique as an "emergency," less in scope than an emergency faced by Traill in the backwoods, but an emergency nonetheless, and she consults *The Canadian Settler's Guide*, Traill's manual of instruction for nineteenth-century emigrants, for advice on the proper handling of emergency situations. Traill's advice is the axiom, quoted earlier: "In cases of emergency, it is folly to fold one's hands and sit down to bewail in abject terror. It is better to be up and doing."[24] Typically, Morag goes on to contradict this early acknowledgment of affinity with Traill, and she imagines Traill's emergencies to have been more difficult to handle than her own. The pioneer ghost says to Morag:

That, my dear, was when we were at one time surrounded by forest fires which threatened the crops, fences, stock, stable, cabin, furniture and, of course, children. Your situation, if I may say so, can scarcely be termed comparable. (97)

Once again Morag counters criticism with a tentative defence: "Hold on, though. *You* try having your only child disappear you know where, Mrs. Traill" (97). This dilemma – the relative importance of her life and her problems – remains unresolved in Morag's mind for the present. She is confronting her problem, to be sure, but she cannot yet see that she has a place in the continuum of history; nor can she define the nature of her relationship with Traill.

The second appearance of Traill in *The Diviners* occurs in the third section of the book, "Halls of Sion." The interaction between Morag and Traill in this section indicates Morag's attainment of a more positive, or at least a more balanced, state of mind. Morag is looking at her unworked, unplanted, weedy garden – the despair of the Smiths – and articulates her personal appreciation of it as "a garden of amazing splendours, in which God did all the work" (170). But Morag's uncertainty continues to mitigate her development of a more positive attitude, and she balances her initial approval with a disparaging comment: "Catharine Parr Traill would have profoundly disagreed, likely" (170). Significantly, however, Morag has begun to defend herself, her attitudes, her feelings, and her work. Generally speaking, the present time sequence of "Halls of Sion" balances Morag's remaining doubts with a newly awakened sense of self-worth and self-awareness. Morag thinks that Traill would disapprove of her wild flower garden; this is "likely" but not definitely true. As in her first imaginary encounter with Traill in "The Nuisance Grounds," Morag points out the differences that she perceives between the pioneer Traill and herself:

Now listen here, Catharine, don't bug me today, eh? All right, I know. You knew more about wildflowers than I'll ever know. But you would have said that there were plenty of wildflowers in the woods etcetera, without taking up half the yard with them. You would diligently have grown turnips, carrots, peas, scarlet runner beans and other nourishing plants, as Maudie Smith does. I am caught between the old pioneers and the new pioneers. At least Maudie can't give names to the wildflowers, as you did. Imagine naming flowers which have never been named before. Like the Garden of Eden. Power! Ecstasy! I christen thee Butter-and-Eggs! (170)

Despite her defensive stance, Morag is clearly fascinated by Traill's creative role in the backwoods, and has identified one source of kinship between herself and Traill; Morag, too, has assumed a creative role, even though she is at present unsure of that role's validity. Conversely, Morag has identified a source for the disharmony which she senses between herself and Maudie Smith: Maudie is not creative; she is, rather, imitative in her efforts to reproduce an earlier way of life. Furthermore, although Morag sees herself as "caught between" two generations of pioneers, she has at least placed herself within the continuum.

Morag's conclusions at the end of her conversation with Traill are at once positive (in defending herself and the relative importance of her emergencies) and negative (in her anticipation of a physical wasteland which far surpassed anything encountered by Traill in Upper Canada):

In the Book of Job it says *One generation passeth and another generation cometh, but the earth endureth forever*. That does not any longer strike me as self-evident. I am deficient in faith, although let's face it, Catharine, if I didn't have *some* I would not write at all or even speak to any other person; I would be silent forevermore ... The evidence of my eyes, however, does little to reassure me. I suspect you didn't have that problem, just as I suspect you had problems you never let on about. The evidence of your eyes showed you Jerusalem the Golden with Milk and Honey Blest, at least if a person was willing to expend enough elbow grease. No plastic milk jugs bobbing in the river. No excessive algae, fish-strangling. The silver shiver of the carp crescenting. My grand-children will say *What means Fish?* Peering through the goggle-eyes of their gasmasks. Who will tell old tales to children then? Pique used to say *What is a Buffalo?* How many words and lives will be gone when they say *What means Leaf?* Saint Catharine! Where are you now that we need you? (170–1)

The wasteland described here by Morag surely equals the wasteland faced by Traill in the backwoods of Ontario. Yet, even though Morag identifies more similarities between herself and the pioneer saint (her faith in humanity, her creativity), she remains uncertain of her role as a possible successor to Traill.

The overall sense of balance which is achieved in Morag's encounter with Traill in the opening section of "Halls of Sion" – an encounter in which uncertainty is juxtaposed with positive action – is also apparent in the "Memorybank Movie" part of the narrative. In this particular segment of her life, Morag learns to identify a frontier, to accept and to work within certain limitations. Knowledge of personal limitation, as Laurence notes in "My Final Hour," does not mean personal defeat:

an acceptance of limitations does not mean that one is not constantly trying to extend the boundaries of knowledge and accomplishment. And it certainly does not mean an acceptance of defeat, in whatever fields our endeavours take place.[25]

Like Hagar Shipley in *The Stone Angel,* Morag initially tries to deny her past in order to escape from a situation she feels in intolerable. When she meets Brooke Skelton, she says to him, "I just feel as though I don't have a past. As though it was more or less blank" (194). This, of course, is a lie (or at best, an evasion of the truth), and Christie points out the flaw in her reasoning: "It'll all go along with you, too. That goes without saying" (207). But Morag tries to leave her past behind her: she marries Brooke; she moves east; and she remakes herself in the image deemed appropriate for social acceptance in Brooke's world:

She watches her diet carefully and is slender. She wears lightly tailored suits in the daytime, with pastel blouses, sometimes frilled ... In the evenings, meeting academic friends, she goes in heavily for the little black cocktail dress, not necessarily black, of course. She looks smart.

She is a competent cook ...

She reads a great deal ...

She grows African violets, which are pretty, and potted parsley, which can be used as a garnish on such dishes as tomato jelly.

She writes short stories and tears them up.

One day she throws a Benares brass ashtray through the kitchen window. (220–1)

That this arrangement is not ideal is obvious. Morag is inactive, and is, therefore, frustrated; the result is that she is incapable of writing (she tears up her work), and, eventually her desperation leads her to throw an ashtray through the window. By moving east to marry Brooke, and by developing a number of ladylike accomplishments, Morag has reversed the Canadian trend to move towards the West and towards personal freedom. It comes as no surprise that her attempt to remake herself in the image of a lady cannot last.

Consequently, from a determined embrace of Brooke's world, Morag turns to an equally determined rejection of the social rules – Grundyisms – which govern behaviour in this world and which stifle her creativity. Her change of attitude and her acknowledgment of her needs lead to freedom. Morag's flight from Brooke and her pursuit of maternity flout convention but bring a welcome sense of release and relief. Both actions are positive ones for Morag because they fulfil previously unacknowledged needs as well as reaffirming her Manawaka past – Jules, her "shaman" (273) is also a Manawaka refugee. He is in and of Canada, and, as her shaman, he possesses knowledge which he will pass on to her – he has already broken the chains of Grundyism. Similarly, after she faces her rage at her inactivity and admits her desire to do something, to act rather than to exist as a decorative ornament (a Benares brass ashtray) in Brooke's home, Morag begins to write. The success of her literary career is linked to her growing recognition of her need to accept her past – that is, her Canadian past, her frontier past – and to her ability to act decisively in times of crisis (her assumption of the role of the pioneer). Morag is not meant to be an idle, decorative lady; she is, by virtue of her heritage, meant to be an active, capable pioneer woman.

Thus, Morag eschews the forces of Brooke's Grundyism: she leaves Brooke; she begins to write; she moves west – once again in the direction of the frontier – and she has a child. These positive actions balance the earlier negative and escapist actions taken by Morag in the "Memorybank Movies" of "Halls of Sion." Morag's inactivity, or incorrect activity, and her lack of understanding are balanced with activity and her growing understanding. A similar balance is achieved by Suzanne in Govier's *Between Men*. Like Morag, Suzanne moved east to escape her memories. This, of course, does not work, and she moves west again. Her return to Calgary is connected with her needs: to examine her past; to write; and to have a child. Initially, she does not understand her action; her return is instinctive, though correct. Both sections of "Halls of Sion," in Laurence's *The Diviners* – the "Memorybank Movies" and the present time conversation with Traill – represent the beginning of the pioneer process within the protagonist, and depict the start of her positive, affirmative action. Although Morag cannot clearly articulate her motives in either section (as she moves westward in the "Memorybank Movie," for example, she is determined, but is also confused and frightened), her movements demonstrate her instinct for survival, as well as her ability to work within her own limitations, bringing her a measure of freedom and personal integrity.

The present time sequence of "Halls of Sion" concludes with the return of Pique and with a partial resolution of the mother-daughter conflict. Morag recognizes that Pique, like her mother before her, is examining her role, specifically her role within the family unit, as part of an historical process, and as an artist. To facilitate her search Pique has gone west to her parents' home in Manawaka. She has evidently found part of what she was searching for; she sings a song given to her by her father, affirming by this action her inherited creativity. In addition, in her relationship with Morag, she begins, on occasion, to assume a maternal, comforting role, a role reminiscent of Rachel's role with her mother in *A Jest of God*. She asks Morag, "Why did you *have* me?" (235). This question, or accusation, strikes a nerve, since Morag is unsure of the answer and is also unclear about her current role in Pique's life. The next minute, however, Pique becomes the comforter, saying, "Never mind. It's okay" (235). The accusation is balanced with the affirmation, and Morag's guilt is relieved. Paradoxically, Pique's actions, while stating her need for freedom, also establish a link between mother and daughter. Pique becomes the inheritor of Morag's Manawaka past, of her creativity, and of her maternal role. By assuming a version of her mother's role, she both affirms and recreates that role.

In the fourth section of *The Diviners*, "Rites of Passage," there is a tipping of the scales towards affirmative action and understanding, and towards the successful culmination of Morag's pioneering process. The ending of the pioneer venture in the past is juxtaposed to the achievement of an increased understanding in the present, and in the "Memorybank Movie," Morag begins to examine the issues that she will resolve during the present time sequence of the narrative. Within the "Memorybank Movies," the birth of Pique is balanced by the death of Christie, and Morag's move to Britain is balanced by her move back to Canada and her subsequent settlement at McConnell's Landing. In the present time Morag gains increased understanding of Pique's place in her life and of Christie's contribution to her creativity; she also analyses the reasons for her move to McConnell's Landing, specifically her relationship to its pioneers.

Of central importance in the "Memorybank Movies" is Morag's discovery that Canada, rather than Scotland, is the home of her ancestors. She has gone on a "pilgrimage" (369) to Britain almost instinctively. As she tells Fan, she does not, at first, understand her need for this pilgrimage: "I've known for a long time I had to go there, Fan. I can't explain it, exactly. I guess I've been waiting for the right moment" (347). Morag does indeed learn something in the course of her pilgrimage, but it is not what she had expected to discover. When she is in Scotland, she realizes that she does not need or even want to visit Sutherland, the birthplace of the Gunn family. She is only partially able to explain her decision to her friend Dan McRaith:

I don't know that I can explain. It has to do with Christie. The myths are my reality. Something like that. And also, I don't need to go there because I know now what it was I had to learn here. (390)

Morag has learned that Scotland is not the land of her ancestors. Her "real country" (391), her ancestral home, is, she tells Dan, "Christie's real country. Where I was born" (391).

This discovery facilitates Morag's later move to McConnell's Landing. After Christie's death, Morag is temporarily immobilized, unable to take action, unable to make decisions, until she sees the advertisement of a farm for sale. The relocation of Morag and Pique in McConnell's Landing represents the culmination of a learning process that has been taking place in Morag for a number of years. Her response to the advertisement is immediate: "Land. A river. Log house nearly a century old, built by great pioneering couple, Simon and Sarah Cooper. History. Ancestors" (414).

Before she leaves her family, Barfoot's Abra is in a state of inertia. She says: "My eyes hurt and the day was like all the others. I had given up trying to understand how to act against it" (81). She is helpless and inactive until she sees an advertisement for a cabin. Her reaction to the advertisement, like Morag's reaction to the advertisement for the cabin at McConnell's Landing in *The Diviners*, is immediate and unequivocal:

I saw it and felt a yearning, not even a verbal thought, just a sensation as if a thin string were pulling me toward – what? (81)

Moreover, this advertisement forces Abra to act – instinctively, but as it turns out, correctly. She moves out of her apathy, forced by something she does not understand, to buy the cabin: "I wasn't sure what I wanted to know, but the desire was strong enough to overcome the apathy" (81). Then, when Abra sees the cabin for the first time, she experiences a shock of recognition. "This was my home" (86), she says.

Laurence's Morag has grandiose plans of recreating the pioneer life of the Coopers when she moves into her cabin; she sentimentalizes her prospective country seclusion:

Morag is filled with a sense of well-being. The shed contains enough split wood for the winter. The basement contains shelves and shelves of bottled preserved plums, applesauce, pears, blueberries, chili sauce, crabapple jelly, and so on, the work of Morag's hands, the produce of her garden. All is well. (415)

These schemes are, of course, doomed to fail. Morag discovers that there is a considerable discrepancy between her dreams and the reality of McConnell's Landing: the "nearly new" (415) furnace does not work properly, there is no water heater, the house is dirty. Like Catharine Traill viewing the emigrants on Grosse Isle in *The Backwoods of Canada*, Morag learns that beauty may be deceptive, and that a close-range examination of a picturesque scene will often reveal unexpected, unattractive elements: "The old grey pine barn, so beautiful from a distance, is now seen to be falling down. It also contains bats" (415). But, in the style of the pioneers, Morag perseveres and survives, learning to cope with disappointment and disaster. She writes a book at McConnell's Landing, *Shadow of Eden*. Significantly, she uses the tales she has been told by Christie as the basis for the book. She has begun to accept the truth of Christie's stories: "Piper Gunn, who probably never lived in so-called real life but who lives forever" (418). As she tells her friend Ella, "Christie knew things about inner truths that I am only just beginning to understand" (418).

At the point of her departure for McConnell's Landing, Morag's actions are instinctive. It is only later, after reflection, after she has written her book, that she understands her actions and can recognize her need for a place like McConnell's Landing, and her need for ancestors. At McConnell's Landing she experiences this growth to a greater understanding, a growth which concludes in the present time.

All Morag's moves in the "Memorybank Movies," up to the time of her arrival in McConnell's Landing, have been based on need and instinct, combined with a certain limited amount of understanding. From this point on, however, she begins to look deeper into herself in order to understand and to articulate her needs. For example, in a letter written to Ella in which she talks about her novel, *Shadow of Eden*, she says, "I like the thought of history and fiction interweaving" (418). This is both a statement of her creative process and an affirmation of Christie's legacy.

In addition to this initial attempt to define the creative process in the "Memorybank Movies" of "Halls of Sion," Morag notes the beginning of a change in her relationship with her daughter. At the age of fifteen, Pique calls Morag "Ma" instead of "Mum":

The word in some way is a proclamation of independence, a statement of the fact that the distance between them, in terms of equality, is diminishing, and the relationship must soon become that of two adults. On balance, Morag is glad. But it will take some inner adjustment. (419)

The mother-daughter relationship, like the creative process, is still being reviewed by Morag in the present time of the novel.

In the present time narrative of "Rites of Passage," Morag continues to adjust to the shifting terms of this relationship, and she manages, here, to resolve the dilemma first mentioned in "The River of Now and Then." She perceives the continuity which exists in the relationship; she recognizes their mutual need of support as well as their ability to provide that support. When she wonders, for a moment, if Pique will have a better life, she stops herself, realizing that such a question is unimportant and irrelevant:

Mine hasn't been so bad. Been? Time running out. Is that what is really going on, with me, now, with her? Pique, harbinger of my death, continuer of life. (290)

This statement is, in effect, Morag's confrontation of her immediate crisis. It is, moreover, a statement of what she has learned, her affirmation of a life cycle, a cycle without a clear beginning or end. Morag faces the fact that Pique's approach to adulthood heralds her own approach to death. Yet, by defining Pique as the "continuer of life," Morag indicates her belief that she will continue to live through Pique and Pique's children.

In the present time sequence of Barfoot's *Abra*, the protagonist, like Laurence's Morag, reviews the past to define the present. The event triggering this retrospection is the sudden arrival of her daughter; this contrasts with Laurence's *The Diviners,* in which the protagonist's examination of her past begins when her daughter leaves. Yet, both women are confronted with a problem: they must redefine their roles with respect to their daughters. When the girl, whom Abra has deserted, appears and asks questions, Abra must search for the answers. The result, as Abra notes, is that "something has grown between us, a special affection" (179). And, although she does not leave with Katie at the end, Abra has been given something by the girl: "I keep wondering what the lack has been that Katie has now arrived to point out or to fill" (183). What has been lacking, of course, is Abra's maternal role.

In addition to her relationship with her daughter, Morag also articulates the implications of her move to McConnell's Landing in "Rites of Passage," and places the move within an historical, cyclical process: "Morag Gunn, fleeing Manawaka, finally settling near McConnell's Landing, an equally small town with many of the same characteristics" (354). Morag's life has come full circle; she has returned to a familiar environment, the environment of her ancestors and, as it happens, the birthplace of the Canadian pioneer heroine. She acknowledges this need for familiar surroundings, and admits that she cannot escape or deny her Manawaka heritage. Indeed, she no longer wants to leave her past behind her.

Furthermore, in "Rites of Passage," Morag recognizes that the Cooper family and Catharine Parr Traill are her ancestors, not in a familial sense, but in a more general, social context. They are ancestors by virtue of having inhabited the same space. Morag, like the Coopers and the Traills, has been a pioneer, albeit a pioneer on a new frontier. And Morag, like her ancestors, has survived with dignity; she has come to enjoy the benefits of freedom and has learned to express her feeling of pride in accomplishment:

Morag, terrified of cities, coming out here, making this her place, her island, and still not going swimming because of the monsterweed. But at least she could somehow cope. City friends often asked if she was not afraid to stay in the house alone, away out here. No, she wasn't. She was not lonely and not afraid, when alone here. She did not think that the loghouse was about to be descended upon by deranged marauders. In New York, Morag's agent and his wife had three locks upon their door. (356)

Echoing Traill's comments in *The Backwoods of Canada* and *The Canadian Settler's Guide,* Morag remarks upon her feeling of confidence, the result of successfully coping with frontier life. Morag knows that she belongs in this place.

Part of Suzanne's search in Govier's *Between Men* is for ancestors. This is one reason for her return to the West from Toronto. She recognizes that she cannot escape her past (her marriage, her lost child), and she returns to confront both her personal past and a more collective social and historical one:

If she could throw off her past, she'd run down her porch stairs and through the picket gate, and back to Toronto. But she'd tried already. There she'd had too little weight, no depth; she had passed along the streets like a shadow. (11)

Like Laurence's Morag, Govier's Suzanne looks to a Canadian past. Her real work is not her teaching; rather, her real work is her research into the death of Rosalie New Grass:

"I came back because of work." It was what she always said. People thought she meant her job. But the job was just earning a living. Work was something else, her secret pursuit, her obsession. That was what gave her whatever he chose to call it, this curious autonomy from events. Work was taking the wrapping off these shapes in her mind. Shapes that had been there before she returned to her hometown, that led her here, that she came back to finally see, and make clear. Because of the work, a part of her was always living in an other story. The story that appeared, in layers on the desk in the spare room. The story had to do with an event in this town a hundred years ago. (25)

Suzanne knows that she belongs in the West, that she is doing what she is meant to do. She learns to defend and to take pride in her rather unorthodox approach to historical research. And, as she rewrites the story of Rosalie, she learns something about herself.

All these protagonists, during the course of a wide variety of pioneering endeavours, learn to take pride in their new (and often strange) accomplishments. Morag discovers, among other things, her place in an historical continuum, and understands the validity of her role as a writer of fiction. Valancy of *The Blue Castle* learns to make fun of her relatives – as they have mocked her in the past. Maggie of *Swamp Angel* ties fishing flies and sells them to earn money. Eva of *The Book of Eve* becomes a "bag lady," picking up things from the street and selling them. Abra of *Abra* becomes a survivalist. Judith of *Judith* runs her own farm. Suzanne of *Between Men* rejects the rules and regulations (Grundyisms) of university history department in order to rewrite history.

An additional link between Laurence's Morag and Traill occurs in "Rites of Passage" through a gesture towards the Crusoe theme.

Morag examines her original impulse to move to McConnell's Landing and discovers that her "island" and her isolation are both illusory.
Traill's isolation as a pioneer in Upper Canada was real, tangible, and
physical; her use of the Crusoe theme in *Canadian Crusoes,* in which
she described the adventures of three people lost in the bush, capi-
talized on the sense of isolation experienced by early settlers. Morag's
island, however, is not a physical place, but a state of mind:

*I've made an island. Are islands real? A-Okay and Maudie, and now Dan, are doing
the same ... Islands are unreal. No place is far enough away. Islands exist only in
the head. And yet I stay.* (356)

The actual place becomes irrelevant to a contemporary pioneering
endeavour; the state of mind is the "island," the frontier.

By and large, other protagonists have the same feeling. Beresford-
Howe's Eva comments on "a very odd feeling ... as if I were isolated
on some forgotten island" (17). Eva's initial voluntary isolation ends,
however, when she begins a relationship with Johnny Horvath. The
island is not just a literary metaphor in *The Blue Castle;* Montgomery's
Valancy actually lives on an island with her husband. Yet, for Valancy
the island is "a realm of mystery and enchantment where anything
might happen – anything might be true" (163). Montgomery's use of
the island differs from other examples of this motif, since Valancy is
neither isolated nor forgotten on her island – it is here that she ends
her long isolation from others as Barney becomes not only her husband, but also her best friend. Another character, Barfoot's Abra,
leads a Crusoe-like existence on her farm, discouraging all contact
with others. The arrival of her daughter forces her to re-examine
her voluntary isolation. While she decides in the end that she must
stay on her "island," Abra has, for the first time in years, tried to
communicate with another human being, and in the process, has
come to understand herself better.

Laurence's Morag is still working out various interwoven strands of
thought – her role as a writer, her need of McConnell's Landing, and
her relationship with Pique – in "Rites of Passage" when she and
Royland see a rare bird, the blue heron. The flight of the heron
becomes a symbol for Morag of the resolution of her conflict. She
and Royland watch the bird's movement in awe:

Like a pterodactyl, like an angel, like something out of the world's dawn ...
The sweeping serene wings of the thing, unknowing that it was speeding
not only towards individual death but probably towards the death of its kind.
(357)

The bird is a symbol spanning the time sequence which separates pre-history from the world's demise (in the "death of its kind" Morag anticipates the death of all kind). In the flight of the heron, Morag sees the visual representation of her personal awareness of the continuity of history, and a confirmation of her conviction that she is a part of this sequence, that she is connected to other people and other places – both past and present:

That evening, Morag began to see that here and now was not, after all, an island. Her quest for islands had ended some time ago, and her need to make pilgrimages had led her back here. (357)

Like the heron, Morag is part of an historical process; she is not isolated. She cannot remove herself from other people; nor can she deny her past.

Other writers use symbols to indicate the placement of their protagonists within a larger context. In Wilson's *Swamp Angel*, Maggie Lloyd watches the birds and animals around her, vaguely seeking to learn something from them. For example, shortly after a fight with Vera, Maggie seeks consolation in the natural world:

She was deeply hurt and she was angry, but she knew that she was stronger – and she thought she was wiser, too – than Vera, and that it rested with her to re-establish and maintain relations on which they could all live together. If she could not, her days at Three Loon Lake were over. But, she thought rather bitterly, life is like that – if it's not one thing, it's another; I have not come to a lagoon for my life; one does not stay, ever, in a lagoon. (89–90)

As this point Maggie sees an osprey; as she watches, the osprey catches a fish, is pounced upon by an eagle, and after a short struggle, drops the fish in defeat and flies off. The battle helps Maggie: "Maggie returned to her reality. She had been lifted by this battle of birds with its defeat and its victory" (90). The "defeat" and "victory" are deliberately left vague. Ostensibly, the eagle is the victor because it has the fish. Yet, the osprey too has had its victory, catching the fish. Moreover, the osprey has had the wisdom to admit defeat. At any rate, the scene has "lifted" Maggie's mood. Into the struggle she has read her own situation.

In "Rites of Passage" Morag has her fifth and final encounter with Traill. Morag, like Traill, is fascinated by the world around her, and her final summoning of the pioneer saint occurs as she is examining books of weeds and wildflowers, worrying about poison plants. Morag imagines that Traill would accuse her of seeing "imaginary dangers"

(406) rather than real ones. On this occasion, strengthened by the discoveries she has made, Morag defends herself confidently and competently:

You're darned right I see imaginary dangers, but do you know why? To focus the mind away from the real ones, is why. Leave me to worry peacefully over the Deadly Water Hemlock, sweet Catharine, because it probably doesn't even grow around here. Let me fret over ravening wolves and poison-fanged vipers, as there is a marked scarcity of these, hereabouts. They're my inner demons, that's what they are. One thing I'm going to stop doing, though, Catharine. I'm going to stop feeling guilty that I'll never be as hardworking or knowledgeable or all-round terrific as you were. And I'll never be as willing to let the sweat of hard labour gather on my brow as A-Okay and Maudie, either ... I'm not built like you, Saint C., or these kids either. I stand somewhere in between. And yet in my way I've worked damn hard, and I haven't done all I would've liked to do, but I haven't folded up like a paper fan, either. (406)

Morag knows that she has worked hard, in her own fashion. She realizes that, although she will never work the land, her wild garden is ultimately as important as Maudie's vegetable garden in the face of a future that includes pollution and the threat of nuclear war:

I'll never till those blasted fields, but this place is some kind of a garden, nonetheless, even though it may be only a wildflower garden. It's needed, and not only by me. (406)

Morag says, "farewell, sweet saint" (406) to Traill, in acknowledgment of the fact that Traill is related to her – but as her ancestor, not her superior. Morag knows that her frontier is her own, and that her emergencies are her own. Finally, in the concluding chapter, "The Diviners," Morag even redefines the nature of an active response to the frontier:

Morag sat in her armchair looking out the wide window. Contemplating. Could this be termed an activity? It was to be hoped so. She certainly spent enough time doing it. (452)

Morag's immediate need of Traill disappears; she has defined herself and her role as a modern pioneer.

By recognizing their inexperience as farmers in "Rites of Passage," and by abandoning their imitative, back-to-the-land attempts at farming (A-Okay decides to take practical farming lessons after Royland points out that "any fool" [410] can grow vegetables), the Smiths have acknowledged their limitations. They, like Morag, have faced a real frontier, and have abandoned a former, inappropriate choice of action. They have admitted the futility of their efforts to recreate the process experienced by the original pioneers. Morag perceives a link which connects the old pioneers – the Coopers and the Traills – with the new pioneers – the Smiths:

They came to the land in ignorance, perhaps expecting miracles which would not occur, but at least with caring, seeing it as a gift and not an affliction. (410–11)

The ability to be pragmatic, to adapt to circumstance, and yet to persevere in the pursuit of a dream – these are the secrets of the successful pioneer, secrets that were discovered by Traill and defined in her *The Backwoods of Canada* and *The Canadian Settler's Guide*, secrets that have been rediscovered and redefined by Morag and the A-Okay Smith family. (Unfortunately for the symmetry of the narrative, this growth towards understanding in the Smith family concerns A-Okay more than Maudie; it is A-Okay who will take farming lessons and who will write articles to supplement the family income, while it is assumed that Maudie will continue to emulate the daily life of the earlier pioneers.)

Unlike the other sections of *The Diviners*, the final chapter, "The Diviners," does not contain flashbacks. In "The Diviners," Morag displays a new confidence, demonstrating that she has changed as a result of an introspective analysis of her previous pioneering efforts. For example, although, as in the first chapter, "River of Now and Then," Pique again leaves home, Morag can let her go without confusion. She has identified her concern: Pique is the harbinger of her death. She has, moreover, recognized the corresponding positive aspect of her daughter's growth to maturity: Pique is the continuer of her life. At this point the women have become equals and Pique has learned to assume the maternal role on occasion. After the death of Jules, the two women comfort each other in an equal sharing of the maternal role.

In "The Diviners," Royland tells Morag that he has lost his power to divine water. In spite of Royland's sense of loss, Morag understands that there is an equally strong sense of affirmation involved in the loss of power since the divining skill does not disappear. It is, rather, passed on to someone else. Royland tells Morag that divining is not a skill that is unique to him:

quite a few people can learn to do it. You don't have to have the mark of God between your eyebrows. Or if you do, quite a few people have it. You didn't know that, did you? (452)

A-Okay Smith is the person mentioned by Royland as the possible inheritor of his skill. This triggers a response in Morag. Just as A-Okay will inherit Royland's knowledge, Morag has inherited Christie's stories; A-Okay will find water, and Morag has used Christie's myths in her fiction. Similarly, Pique will inherit the myths of both Jules and Morag. By creating and singing her own song in "The Diviners," Pique demonstrates that she, like her parents, is an inheritor, a creator, who will pass on a gift to others. More generally speaking, there is an historical continuum operating outside the immediate family circle as well. Morag has already noted the legacy of the original pioneers which has been passed on to her and to the Smiths. Each inheritor develops her legacy according to present circumstance – a crisis may be purely personal and subjective in nature but is, nonetheless, equal in scope to the forest fires faced by the pioneer women in the backwoods – and there is a direct line of descent established between Catharine Traill and Morag, a line of descent which will extend into the next generation:

The inheritors. Was this, finally and at last, what Morag had always sensed she had to learn from the old man? She had known it all along, but not really known. The gift, or portion of grace, or whatever it was, was finally withdrawn, to be given to someone else. (452)

Traill and Morag are survivors. They are also creators of myth. They face a hostile environment and survive with dignity, discovering in the process a real sense of self-worth. They create myth through the mingling of fact with fiction, leaving a legacy for following generations to use and to adapt to their own particular frontiers. Although Morag anticipates the advent of a wasteland, a country destroyed by pollution and possibly by war, a place inhabited by humans who peer through masks, she completes the book she is writing, and, in "The Diviners," she gives a name to this book.

Morag Gunn of *The Diviners* is the protagonist in Laurence's fiction (and in contemporary Canadian fiction generally) who, because of her creative gift, and the correspondingly larger sphere of her personal influence, has the greatest affinity with Catharine Parr Traill and Traill's protagonists. Yet all three of Laurence's protagonists examined – Hagar Shipley of *The Stone Angel*, Rachel Cameron of *A*

Jest of God, and Morag Gunn of *The Diviners,* as well as the other protagonists mentioned above – take their place in a tradition of the characterization of women in Canadian literature begun by Traill in *The Backwoods of Canada* and *The Canadian Settler's Guide* and used by her in such fiction as *Canadian Crusoes.* Looking back on the discussion of *The Stone Angel, A Jest of God,* and *The Diviners,* we can see several links between Laurence's protagonists and Traill's ideal backwoodswoman. Given Laurence's own sense of sympathy with Traill – specifically her application of a quotation taken from Traill's *The Canadian Settler's Guide* to the handling of contemporary stresses and emergencies – it is hardly surprising that her most autobiographical novel, *The Diviners,* includes discussions between Traill and the protagonist, Morag Gunn. Moreover, Morag perceives Traill as possessing desirable character traits. Other links with Traill, while less obvious, are, nonetheless, extremely important. For example, each of Laurence's protagonists participates in a contemporary, and internalized, version of the pioneering process, during which she comes closer to a notion of ideal femininity which, if it is not derived from, is certainly related to the descriptions of the ideal pioneer woman which are found in Traill's *The Backwoods of Canada* and *The Canadian Settler's Guide.*

The recognition and acceptance of the frontier, in the contemporary Canadian fiction of Laurence and others, results, as in Traill's work, in the woman's successful handling of the pioneer situation; in her ensuing attempts to deal with the frontier, the woman rejoices in her escape from the confines of Grundyism into freedom and self-sufficiency. A major difference between contemporary writers and Traill, however, is the extent to which the writer is convinced of the possible existence of the ideal in everyday life. Traill was positive that an ideal backwoodswoman could exist, and in *The Backwoods of Canada* and *The Canadian Settler's Guide,* she created a model for other pioneer women to emulate, drawing upon her life in Britain and upon her experiences in Canada to create the pattern. Contemporary writers, such as Laurence, are less direct in their methods, and are certainly less didactic in their approach. Consequently, these narratives, unlike Traill's writing, describe a process (a working towards an ideal) rather than a finished product. Laurence's female protagonists are aware that there is an ideal, and that they lack some important bit of knowledge or experience to achieve this ideal. Hagar, Rachel, and Morag begin their attempts to effect an improvement. While they never reach perfection, their efforts to gain a better life represent an internalized, metaphoric rendering of the pioneering process. Finally, as a result of their pioneering efforts, these protagonists achieve what

Laurence calls, in *The Diviners,* a "gift, or portion of grace" (452). Much has changed in the years which separate Laurence and Traill, but there remains a direct link through the way in which their fictional characters – Traill's Catharine Maxwell, and Laurence's Hagar Shipley, Rachel Cameron, and Morag Gunn – perceive the world around them, and the way in which they define their roles as pioneer women on a harsh frontier.

The contemporary pioneer, like Traill's, interacts with the frontier to effect change, and discovers a measure of happiness in the process. As Traill has pointed out in *The Backwoods of Canada:* "I find, by impartial survey of my present life, that I am to the full as happy, if not really happier, than I was in the old country."[26] Indeed, these contemporary pioneers, like Traill herself, are happier, stronger, better women as a result of their active participation in the pioneering process.

Notes

INTRODUCTION

1 Frye, Conclusion to the *Literary History of Canada*, in *The Bush Garden*, 232.
2 Frye, *Bush Garden*, 232–3.
3 See Burnet, ed., *Looking into My Sister's Eyes* for an explanation of the ways in which emigration to a new country was the same for a wide variety of women, from nineteenth-century English gentlewomen to twentieth-century Italian women.
4 Rouslin, "The Intelligent Woman's Guide to Pioneering in Canada," 319.
5 Rouslin, "Pioneering," 328.
6 See also Langton, *A Gentlewoman in Upper Canada*, and Tivy, ed., *Your Loving Anna*.
7 Rouslin, "Pioneering," 331.
8 It is worth noting that, like Traill, Susanna Moodie wrote fiction while she was living in the backwoods, as for example, *Mark Hurdlestone, The Gold Worshipper* (1853). Unlike her sister, however, Moodie ignored Canada and Canadian life in her fiction, evidently preferring to employ English settings and to depict standard sentimental versions of the English lady of the nineteenth century. Moodie's reluctance to face the New World in her fiction enhances Traill's importance as a writer among her contemporaries for her inclusion of the New World and of the New-World woman in her fiction.
9 Rouslin, "Pioneering," 319.
10 Grove, *In Search of Myself*, 224, 223–4, 224.
11 Rouslin, "Pioneering," 319; see also Frye, *Bush Garden*, 251; Rouslin cites Dobbs, "Canadian Heroes?" 23.
12 Frye, *Bush Garden*, 232.

13 Frye, *Bush Garden*, 251.
14 Frye, *Bush Garden*, 250.

CHAPTER ONE

1 Susanna Moodie was a prolific writer of fiction. See for example, *Flora Lyndsay: or, Passages in an Eventful Life*; *Geoffrey Moncton: or, The Faithless Guardian*; *Mark Hurdlestone, The Gold Worshipper*; *Matrimonial Speculations*; "The First Debt: A Tale of Every Day."

One of Susanna Moodie's plot situations is quite similar to Traill's *The Young Emigrants*. In "Waiting for Dead Men's Shoes," one of the stories in *Matrimonial Speculations*, Moodie deals with the plight of a middle-class English family which is faced with the spectre of declining fortunes and reduced circumstances. As in Traill's *The Young Emigrants*, the family discusses the possibility of emigration. Some of the family members finally emigrate to Canada; some remain behind. But Moodie's development and treatment of this plot situation differs radically from Traill's. Moodie does not follow her characters to Canada, choosing instead to concentrate on the characters who remain behind in England and who preserve their status as middle-class gentlefolk. This may indicate that Moodie was unable or unwilling to reconcile a pioneer way of life with the concept of English gentility. The fact that Moodie wrote this story after her own emigration, and that she certainly could not claim ignorance of Canadian life, seems to indicate her choice to avoid Canada and the Canadian frontier in her fiction. This avoidance of the frontier illustrates the single most important difference in the Canadian-produced works of the Strickland sisters. On the one hand, Moodie, like Lot's wife, turns back to look at her English home and refuses to incorporate a Canadian setting into her fiction. In addition, if her non-fiction is to be trusted, she herself had a difficult time adjusting to Canada, since she could not reconcile her new role as a Canadian pioneer with her inherited status as an English lady. Traill, on the other hand, wrote *The Young Emigrants* before her settlement in Upper Canada. After her emigration, she commonly used a Canadian setting. Judging by the tone of her non-fiction (if her non-fiction is to be trusted), Traill had less difficulty than her sister adjusting to frontier conditions. Unlike Moodie, she could apparently continue to define herself as a lady no matter what her living conditions were like.

2 There are many studies dealing with the role of the British woman in fact and fiction; the points mentioned in this particular study reflect commonly accepted theories. For some typical analyses see: Patricia Branca, "Image and Reality: The Myth of the Idle Victorian Woman,"

in Hartman and Banner, eds., *Clio's Consciousness Raised*; Burman, ed., *Fit Work for Women*; Calder, *Women and Marriage in Victorian Fiction*; Colby, *Yesterday's Woman*; Crow, *The Victorian Woman*; Cunnington, *Feminine Attitudes in the Nineteenth Century*; Davidoff, *The Best Circles*; Dunbar, *The Early Victorian Woman*; Susan Gorsky, "The Gentle Doubters: Images of Women in Englishwomen's Novels, 1840–1920," in Cornillon, ed., *Images of Women in Fiction*; Hill, *Women in English Life from Medieval to Modern Times*; Mews, *Frail Vessels*; Siefert, *The Dilemma of the Talented Heroine*; Vicinus, ed., *Suffer and Be Still*.

3 For some representative definitions of the perfect lady from a late eighteenth-century or early nineteenth-century point of view, see the following books of advice: Ellis, *The Women of England, Their Social Duties, and Domestic Habits*; Gregory, *A Father's Legacy to His Daughters*; More, *Works*.

4 Dr Gregory, Hannah More, and Sarah Ellis offer invaluable advice to their gentle readers. Dr Gregory, for example, has the following words of wisdom about decorative accomplishments for women: "The intention of your being taught needle-work, knitting, and such like, is not on account of the intrinsic value of all you can do with your hands, which is trifling, but to enable you to judge more perfectly of that kind of work, and to direct the execution of it in others. Another principal end is to enable you to fill up, in a tolerably agreeable way, some of the many solitary hours you must necessarily pass at home. – It is a great article in the happiness of life, to have your pleasures as independent of others as possible." See Gregory, *Legacy*, 62–3.

5 Traill, *Little Downy; or, The History of a Field-Mouse. A Moral Tale*, 25. All further references to this work will have page numbers incorporated into the text.

6 For some example of working-class protagonists, see Eliot, *Adam Bede*; Gaskell, *Mary Barton*; Gaskell, *Ruth*.

7 For an important and influential literary source of the "virtue-rewarded" theme, see Richardson, *Pamela*.

8 Others of Traill's early works include a strong moral and didactic bias. See, for example, Traill, *Happy Because Good; The Tame Pheasant, and the Blind Brother and Kind Sister*; and *The Keepsake Guineas; or, The Best Use of Money*; and *Sketches From Nature; or, Hints to Juvenile Naturalists*.

9 Ruth Marks, Preface to Traill, *The Young Emigrants or Pictures of Canada*, xi–xii.

10 Thomas, "Traill's Canadian Settlers," 31. All future references to this work will have page numbers incorporated into the text.

11 Traill, *The Young Emigrants; or, Pictures of Canada*, 2–3. All future references to this work will have page numbers incorporated into the text.

12 Traill, *Lady Mary and Her Nurse; or, A Peep into the Canadian Forest,* 105. All further references to this work will have page numbers incorporated into the text.

13 Traill, *Canadian Crusoes, A Tale of the Rice Lake Plains,* 8. All further references to this work will have page numbers incorporated into the text.

14 For further analysis of the Crusoe theme in Traill's writing, see Mac-Lulich, "Crusoe in the Backwoods," 115–26; Thomas, "Crusoe and the Precious Kingdom," 58–64.

15 Moodie, *Geoffrey Moncton: or, The Faithless Guardian,* 232. All further references to this work will have page numbers incorporated into the text.

16 Moodie, "Waiting for Dead Men's Shoes," in *Matrimonial Speculations,* 70.

17 Moodie, *Flora Lyndsay: or, Passages in an Eventful Life,* 342.

18 *Flora Lyndsay* could be considered as a companion work to *Roughing It in the Bush.* There are many points of similarity between the protagonist of *Flora Lyndsay* and the narrator of *Roughing It in the Bush,* Susanna Moodie. Moreover, *Roughing It in the Bush* takes up the narrative where *Flora Lyndsay* ends – on board ship.

19 See Brown, *An Index to the "Literary Garland" (Montreal 1838–1851);* see also Klinck, "Literary Activity in Canada East and West (1841–1880)," in Klinck, ed., *Literary History of Canada,* I, 159–76.

20 Richardson, *The Canadian Brothers: or, The Prophecy Fulfilled: A Tale of the Late American War,* 47.

21 See Klinck, "Literary Activity in the Canadas (1812–1841)," in *Literary History of Canada,* I, 139–58; see also Klinck, "Literary Activity (1841–1880)," I, 159–76.

CHAPTER TWO

1 For an account of pioneer life in the Maritimes see Beavan, *Life in the Backwoods of New Brunswick;* For a listing of material available from prairie pioneer women, see chapter 3, note 1.

2 Traill, *The Backwoods of Canada: Being Letters from the Wife of an Emigrant Officer, Illustrative of the Domestic Economy of British America,* 16. All further references to this work will have page numbers incorporated into the text.

3 Mary O'Brien showed some of the same eager curiosity about her new surroundings. She comments in her journal: "Last night I undressed in the dark that I might more accurately observe the electrical phenomenon which occurs nightly and on all occasions. In taking off a linen garment quickly from over a flannel one, it appeared perfectly as if

smeared with phosphorus. Our cloth gowns are never clean. Every hair or particle of dust which we approach within a foot is attracted by them." See O'Brien, *The Journals of Mary O'Brien, 1828–1838*, 41. All other references to this work will have page numbers incorporated into the text.

4 Langton, *A Gentlewoman in Upper Canada: The Journals of Anne Langton*, 61. All future references to this work will have page numbers incorporated into the text.

5 See Moodie, *Roughing It in the Bush, or, Forest Life in Canada*, 111.

6 Jameson, *Winter Studies and Summer Rambles in Canada*, 11, 134. All other references to this work will have volume and page numbers incorporated into the text.

7 Moodie, *Life in the Clearings*, 554–5.

8 Traill, Preface, *The Canadian Settler's Guide*, xix. All further references to this work will have page numbers incorporated into the text.

9 Clara Thomas, Introduction to Traill, *The Canadian Settler's Guide*, xiii.

10 I have chosen "The Bereavement" rather than "The First Death in the Clearing" as a topic for critical discussion. The earlier work is more appealing. Later changes and revisions have altered the story only slightly and have not improved the narrative in any way.

11 Traill, "The Bereavement. A Fragment from Forest Gleanings," 69. All other references to this work will have page numbers incorporated into the text.

12 Catharine Traill wrote a number of "Floral Sketches" which were published in the *Literary Garland* in 1843. See Traill, "Floral Sketches: The Violet," 87–90; "The Rose," 129–31.

13 Traill, "The Bereavement," 71; see Milton, "Il Penseroso," 146:

But let my due feet never fail,
To walk the studious cloister's pale,
And love the high embowèd roof,
With antique pillars' massy proof,
And storied windows richly dight,
Casting a dim religious light.

14 For a listing of relevant source material concerning the literary history of the "lady" as character type, see chapter 1, notes 2 and 3.

CHAPTER THREE

1 There are many published accounts of pioneer life in western Canada written from a woman's point of view. For a representative listing see the following: Binnie-Clark, *A Summer on the Canadian Prairie* and

Wheat and woman; Caswell, *Pioneer Girl*; Cran, *A Woman in Canada*; Hall, *A Lady's Life on a Farm in Manitoba*; Hiemstra, *Gully Farm*; Jackel, ed., *A Flannel Shirt and Liberty*; McClung, *Clearing in the West* and *The Stream Runs Fast*; Morris, *An Englishwoman in the Canadian West*; Murphy, *Seeds of Pine*; Raber, *Pioneering in Alberta*; Sarah Ellen Roberts, *Of Us and the Oxen*; Saxby, *West-Nor'-West*; Strange, *With the West in Her Eyes*; Sykes, *A Home Help in Canada*; Weaver, *Canada and the British Immigrant*.

2 It becomes clear from her writing that Sara Jeannette Duncan defined herself both as a modern woman and as a traditionalist. Like many other Canadian feminists of the late nineteenth and early twentieth centuries, she was apparently unaware of any possible discrepancy in her views. Thomas E. Tausky has noted the dual emphasis in Duncan's writing, and comments on Duncan's awareness of herself as a modern pioneer: "Despite the variety of subjects, a consistent habit of mind manifests itself in Sara Jeannette Duncan's work, whatever the issue at hand. She was always conscious of being a modern woman, of being a pioneer in the struggle to evolve a new type of self-definition. Yet at the same time she had conservative instincts of loyalty to and faith in her country, and the social order. So, in discussing almost any issue, she seeks to discover what seems to her to be a sensible middle course, rejecting both the advanced position which she finds too radical, and the traditional position which she regards as outmoded." See Tausky, *Sara Jeannette Duncan, Novelist of Empire*, 20–1.

3 Early feminists were aware of the tension which existed between their role as reformers and their more traditional roles as wives and mothers. Consequently, efforts to effect change were explained as a natural evolution of a woman's role in a changing society; this theory is expressed by the Countess of Aberdeen, president of the National Council of Women of Canada, in her address to the delegates at the Council's first annual convention in 1894: "Our mothers, grandmothers and great-grandmothers have worked nobly along the lines open to them; and if we are to be worthy of them we must work on the lines which their experience has opened up for us." See National Council of Women of Canada, *Women Workers of Canada: Being a Report of the Proceedings of the First Annual Meeting and Conference of the National Council of Women of Canada*, 178.

4 Once again the National Council of Women provides a representative, if highly rhetorical, analysis of woman's role as it was perceived by the Canadian feminists of the late nineteenth century: "The old century is on the wane. Through the shadow of the globe we shall usher into the new century a splendid army of organized womanhood, and in that glorious dawn we catch a vision of a brighter day. When the interests

here represented shall be wrought out into living truths, it will bring humanity into more harmonious relations by infusing justice into citizenship, purity into social relations, and the spirit of the Golden Rule into all life." See National Council, *Women Workers*, 17.

5 The optimism of the Canadian feminists did not last past the Depression and the Second World War, but for many years, women actually had hoped to change the world and to usher in a golden age. Nellie McClung remembers the spirit of the times in her autobiography: "I knew life had reached a pinnacle and we were standing on a high place, a place easier to achieve than to maintain. We were in sight of the promised land, a land of richer sunshine and brighter fruitage, and our heads and hearts were light. Whatever else can be said about us, one fact remains: We were in deadly earnest and our one desire was to bring about a better world for everyone ... Ours was not a rage, it was a passion." See McClung, *Stream*, 134.

6 Virtually every leading feminist claimed to be conservative in her views. Letitia Youmans, an advocate of temperance laws and of the vote for women, was being more honest than many when she admitted, "I saw, in this respect, the necessity of being as wise as a serpent and as harmless as a dove." See Youmans, *Campaign Echoes*, 206.

As an interesting parallel study, for an analysis of the connection between feminist theory, social history, and the gradual evolution of female characters in British fiction, see Thomson, *The Victorian Heroine*. Thomson posits that writers of British fiction began to incorporate, almost imperceptibly, feminist theories and the "new woman" into their fiction, and that the work of even the most conservative writers reflects changing interpretations of woman's role at home and in society.

For a more radical interpretation of the "new woman" and her impact on English fiction, see Cunningham, *The New Woman and the Victorian Novel*.

7 One of the most frequently cited passages from Traill's *Canadian Settler's Guide* concerns the necessity for taking immediate action during an emergency: "In cases of emergency, it is folly to fold one's hands and sit down to bewail in abject terror: it is better to be up and doing." See Traill, *The Canadian Settler's Guide*, 204.

8 Traill has much to say about the need for a cheerful acceptance of one's duty on the frontier. The following is only one example among many: "The greatest heroine in life is she who knowing her duty, resolves not only to do it, but to do it to the best of her abilities, with heart and mind bent upon the work." See Traill, *Settler's Guide*, 4.

9 It is difficult to isolate the various aspects of Traill's definition of the personality of the ideal pioneer woman. The anecdote found in *The Canadian Settler's Guide* of the woman who manages to plant and to

harvest the first crop of Indian corn serves to reinforce her recommen-
dation of immediate activity in the face of an emergency and to point
out the important qualities of fortitude, courage, and pragmatism: "At
first she was inclined to fret, and give up in despair, but when she
looked upon her sick husband and her helpless babe, she remembered
that duty required better things from her than to lie down and weep,
and lament: she knew that other women had their trials, and she
braced up her mind to do what was before her, praying to God to give
her strength to do her duty, and she went on cheerfully and with a
brave spirit." See Traill, *Settler's Guide,* 114.

10 See Traill, *The Backwoods of Canada*; *The Canadian Settler's Guide.*

11 In her creation of the character of Mrs Murchison, Duncan generally
adheres to the definition of the ideal pioneer established by Traill in
The Backwoods of Canada and *The Canadian Settler's Guide.* For example,
Mrs Murchison is clearly aware that usefulness and beauty should ideally coexist in household objects. Yet Duncan's interpretation of the
relationship between a woman and her house indicates a major difference in the focus of the two writers. Traill objectifies her house in her
backwoods writing. Her home is a thing which contains both useful
and decorative items. Furthermore, when Traill includes herself as narrator and as character in her writing, as for example in "The Bereavement. A Fragment from Forest Gleanings," she seems perpetually to be
looking out of the house, to be venturing outside, and to be describing
external events. Duncan's approach is quite different. She personifies
the homes of her characters, or, rather, makes the houses and their
inhabitants mirror images of each other. The interiors assume greater
significance, and the appearance of the home becomes a vital element
in the delineation of character. As will be noted in a later chapter, in
The Man From Glengarry (1901) and *Glengarry School Days* (1902), Ralph
Connor also uses the interior of a house to indicate the personality of
the homemaker.

12 Clara Thomas has also commented on the symbol of the house. Her
analysis includes the importance of the home to Mr Murchison and the
Murchison children: "The house is unique among houses in Elgin and it
is a very real symbol of John Murchison's place in his own concept of
Canada, and even more so, of his idea of the future progress of his
family in Canada. The house is a fitting shelter for his family, a setting
for their growth and a launching-point for their future. By so far had
John Murchison come from his origin in Scotland to become a leading
citizen of Elgin, by so much the farther did he have every reason to
believe that his children would progress in prosperity and in influence
from Elgin, their centre, to all Canada beyond." See Thomas, "Canadian
Social Mythologies in Sara Jeannette Duncan's *The Imperialist,*" 41–2.

13 Like the Murchison home, the store has also changed with the times. Its transition from carrying a "light stock" to a "heavy stock," from selling a "kitchen stove that burned wood," to selling a "new gas cooking-stove" indicates the improvement in the Murchison family fortunes. In addition, the expansion of the store and its increased emphasis on "luxury" items parallel the change in Elgin as it evolves from a frontier town into a prosperous manufacturing town. Finally, the advancement in technology indicated by the modern cooking stoves sold by Mr Murchison points to the greater freedom from domestic drudgery, and the corresponding increase in leisure time, enjoyed by Canadian women at the turn of the century as pioneer days came to an end. See Duncan, *Imperialist*, 23–4.

14 Duncan, *The Imperialist*, 31–2. Future references to this work will have page numbers incorporated into the text.

15 When the Murchisons set up housekeeping, Elgin is still a relatively new town. What the narrator of *The Imperialist* says of Mr Murchison and Dr Drummond applies equally well to Mrs Murchison: "So the two came, contemporaries, to add their labour and their lives to the building of this little outpost of Empire. It was the frankest transfer, without thought of return; they were there to spend and be spent within the circumference of the spot they had chosen, with no ambition beyond. In the course of nature, even their bones and their memories would enter into the fabric. The new country filled their eyes; the new town was their opportunity, its destiny their fate." See Duncan, *The Imperialist*, 21–2.

16 In *The Canadian Settler's Guide*, Traill mentions rag carpets. Like Duncan's Mrs Murchison, Traill is aware that these carpets have both a useful and decorative function: "To the more wealthy class this humble manufacture may seem a very contemptible affair; but it is not for the gay and luxurious that such things are suitable; though I have seen them in the houses of some of our best settlers, who were wise enough, like the wife of the rector, to value whatever was comfortable, and save buying. When well assorted, I assure you these rag-carpets make by no means a despicable appearance, on the rough floors of a Canadian farmer's house." See Traill, *Settler's Guide*, 182.

17 For an analysis of the combination of romance and realism in Duncan's work, see Tausky, *Duncan, Novelist of Empire*.

18 The advantages of the modern woman was a recurring theme in Duncan's writing. For a representative sampling of Duncan's non-fiction, see Duncan, *Sara Jeannette Duncan: Selected Journalism*, ed. Tausky.

19 Mrs Crow of *The Imperialist*, like Mrs Murchison, is evidently more at home in the kitchen than in the parlour; Mrs Crow is a capable woman who plays an active role in the daily work of the farm. Yet, she greets

her company in the formal room of the house – the parlour: "She sat on the sofa in her best black dress with the bead trimming on the neck and sleeves, a good deal pushed up and wrinkled across the bosom, which had done all all that would ever be required of it when it gave Elmore and Abe their start in life. Her wiry hands were crossed in her lap in the moment of waiting: you could tell by the look of them that they were not often crossed there. They were strenuous hands; the whole worn figure was strenuous, and the narrow set mouth, and the eyes which had looked after so many matters for so long, and even the way the hair was drawn back into a knot in a fashion that would have given a phrenologist his opportunity. It was a different Mrs Crow from the one that sat in the midst of her poultry and garden-stuff in the Elgin market square; but it was even more the same Mrs Crow, the sum of a certain measure of opportunity and service, an imperial figure in her bead trimming, if the truth were known." See Duncan, *Imperialist*, 188.

20 Traill, *Backwoods*, 177–8; *Settler's Guide*, 3.

21 The social historian S.D. Clark has noted the tendency of frontier groups to break away from traditional values and to develop new behaviours and new ideas more relevent to their frontier surroundings: "In a sense, such people moved out to the margins of society, and, while they carried with them some of the habits of thought and behaviour which had been implanted by previous forms of control, they had to leave behind, or cast off on the way, the great body of habits not fitted to the new conditions of life. Habits, like tools, were abandoned through non-usage because they failed to work. Whether this represented a failure to maintain conditions of life which had been considered desirable, or a release from social obligations which had been felt as irksome, the effect was to emancipate the individual from controls to which he had been accustomed. He was left to work out by himself a code of conduct and philosophy of life which more nearly satisfied his present needs. The immediate reaction was one of uneasiness, relieved partly by a feeling of exhilaration. The ultimate result, if new group attachments failed to be forged, was complete personal disorganization. Problems of mental health and suicide, and to some extent of intemperance, in periods of rapid social development, were an indication of the failure of individuals to resolve the personal crisis in face of radically new conditions of living." See Clark, *The Developing Canadian Community*, 11.

22 In her article "Canadian Social Mythologies in Sara Jeannette Duncan's *The Imperialist*," Clara Thomas has noted the polarization of two racial strains – Scottish and English – in Duncan's social mythology: "In Canada she shows the Scotch and their offspring to be builders, men to

usher in the future; the English are reactionary, cautious, conservative and ridiculously class-ridden in a society which sees itself as classless. In effect, Duncan polarizes the two racial strains to the point of substituting her own elite establishment, Scotch and Presbyterian, for the old colonial elitism of British and Anglican." See Thomas, "Social Mythologies," 42.

23 For a similar view of a Canadian meritocracy see Traill, *Backwoods*, 81. In both *The Backwoods of Canada* and *The Canadian Settler's Guide*, Traill describes the dislocation of the pioneer which is combined with the inevitable social levelling that takes place in a frontier society. Traill provides advice on the best method of dealing with the situation. She is somewhat ambivalent about the levelling process and the subsequent removal of class barriers. Her defence of the social equality found in Canada contrasts with her own sense of superiority, and her resentment of the assumption of independence by the lower-class emigrants contrasts with her personal appreciation of freedom from social restraint and "Grundyism." Despite some evidence of her distaste for the loss of Old-World standards of class distinction, however, in her published work Traill appears to be an optimistic social observer. She anticipates the rebuilding and restructuring of society to form a meritocracy; she advocates social advancement which is based on personal worth rather than on birth or wealth.

   Unlike Traill, Duncan writes of the pioneer process and the restructuring of society with the authority of hindsight. On the one hand, she criticizes the Milburn women, who attempt to maintain what they believe to be Old-World customs and values. On the other hand, she praises the Murchison family, who cheerfully help to create a new social edifice, a structure, incidentally, which closely resembles Traill's vision of a Canadian meritocracy.

24 For an example of one of the few Canadian coquettes in fiction, see Holmes, *Belinda, or, The Rivals*; see also the character of Maimie St Clair in Connor, *The Man from Glengarry*; and see Brooke, *The History of Emily Montague*. The protagonists of this last work are worth mentioning in spite of the fact that they are merely visitors to Canada. Like Lady Mary of Traill's *Lady Mary and Her Nurse* (1856), Emily and Arabella are affected in only a peripheral way by their period of residence in Canada, and they return to England with their gentility intact. Thus, while Brooke's Arabella is undoubtedly a coquette (although more sympathetically portrayed than any of the others listed here), she remains an English rather than a Canadian figure.

25 Canadian reformers tried to reassure their opponents that they were not unfeminine. Letitia Youmans, for example, actively campaigned for temperance regulations and often spoke in public. But she defined her

role as a feminine one: "It seemed imperative that I should define my position; accordingly I assured the audience that I had not come there to advocate women's rights, but that I had come to remonstrate against women's and children's wrongs. But there is one form of women's rights in which I firmly believe, and that is, the right of every woman to have a comfortable home, of every wife to have a sober husband, of every mother to have sober sons." See Youmans, *Campaign Echoes*, 128.

26 Tausky, *Duncan, Novelist of Empire*, 20–1.

27 See Goethe, *Faust, Part Two*, 203: "The eternal in woman is the gleam we follow."

28 Tausky, *Duncan, Novelist of Empire*, 34.

29 See McClung, *Stream*; National Council of Women, *Women Workers*; Strong-Boag, "The Roots of Modern Canadian Feminism," 22–33; Roberts, "'Rocking the Cradle for the World': The New Woman and Maternal Feminism, Toronto, 1877–1914," in Kealey, ed., *A Not Unreasonable Claim*, 15–45.

Female reformers genuinely perceived their role as a maternal one. Nellie McClung's sentiments were typical of the turn-of-the-century feminist in Canada: "Women must be made to feel their responsibility. All this protective love, this instinctive mother love, must be organized some way, and made effective. There was enough of it in the world to do away with all the evils which war upon childhood, undernourishment, slum conditions, child labor, drunkenness. Women could abolish these if they wanted to." See McClung, *Stream*, 27.

30 Traill, *Backwoods*, 182; *Settler's Guide*, 4.

31 Traill, *Settler's Guide*, 204.

32 Traill, *Backwoods*, 270–1.

33 Traill, *Backwoods*, 269–70; *Settler's Guide*, 46.

34 Claude Bissell, Introduction to Duncan, *The Imperialist*, viii.

35 Bissell, Introduction to *Imperialist*, viii.

36 For further reading on the early women's movement in Canada, see the following: Acton et al., eds., *Women at Work*; Cleverdon, *The Woman Suffrage Movement in Canada*; Wayne Roberts, *Honest Womanhood*; Trofimemkoff and Prentice, eds., *The Neglected Majority*.

37 Montgomery, *Anne of Green Gables*, 30. Future references to this work will have page numbers incorporated into the text.

38 Montgomery, *Emily of New Moon*, 63. Future references to this work will have page numbers incorporated into the text.

39 McClung, *The Second Chance*, 64.

40 McClung, *The Stream Runs Fast*, 210–11.

41 McCourt, *The Canadian West in Fiction*, 86.

42 Stead, *The Homesteaders*, 7. Future references to the work will have page numbers incorporated into the text.

CHAPTER FOUR

1 Thompson and Thompson, "Ralph Connor and the Canadian Identity," 159.

2 Gordon, *Postcript to Adventure: The Autobiography of Ralph Connor*, 150. All future references to this work will have page numbers incorporated into the text. See also Gordon Roper, "New Forces: New Fiction, 1880–1920," in Klinck, ed., *Literary History of Canada*, 1, 286.

3 Gordon, *Postscript*, 150; Gordon Roper, Beharriell, and Schieder, "Writers of Fiction, 1880–1920," in Klinck, ed., *Literary History of Canada*, 1, 336.

4 Gordon, *Postscript*, 150.

5 See Gordon Roper, Schieder, and Beharriell, "The Kinds of Fiction, 1880–1920," in Klinck, ed., *Literary History of Canada*, 1, 298–326.

6 McCourt, *The Canadian West in Fiction*, 41.

7 In Duncan's *The Imperialist* (1904), the frontier becomes redefined to include contemporary social issues. Both Connor and Duncan accept and extend the use in fiction of the frontier and the frontier woman. Yet each writer pursues a different direction.

8 McCourt, *Canadian West*, 28–9.

9 McCourt, *Canadian West*, 41.

10 Connor's novels generally have two complementary religious spokesmen, one male, one female. They work differently to achieve the same end – salvation of souls. The exception to the general rule is *The Sky Pilot: A Tale of the Foothills* (1899), where the minister (the "sky pilot" of the title) is an oddly androgynous figure in the midst of Connor's generally clearly defined male and female characters. The sky pilot is a gentle, feminine, yet crusading and passionate missionary; he is a character who combines both masculine and feminine traits.

11 Traill, in *The Backwoods of Canada* (1836) and *The Canadian Settler's Guide* (1855), stresses the importance of adding beauty to the backwoods dwelling, saying, for example: "It is a great mistake to neglect those little household adornments which will give a look of cheerfulness to the very humblest home." See Traill, *Canadian Settler's Guide*, 13.

12 Watt, "Western Myth," 29.

13 Connor, *The Man from Glengarry*, 24. All future references to this work will have page numbers incorporated into the text.

14 Lizars and Lizars, *Committed to His Charge*, 50. Future references to this work will have page numbers incorporated into the text.

15 Connor, *Glengarry School Days: A Story of Early Days in Glengarry*, 170–1. Future references to this work will have page numbers incorporated into the text.

Connor's use of the house as mirror to the woman's soul extends to this non-fiction as well. In *Postscript to Adventure*, for example, he describes his visits to two homes in the foothills. The garden of the "good" woman is characterized by its beauty and its neatness. It has been carefully tended. The house and its mistress are welcoming, and the woman is evidently a good Christian. Set in contrast to this is Gordon's visit to a neighbouring house. At the second home, the character of the homemaker is established by the state of the neglected, weed-filled garden. The house is wretched and crude; the homemaker is not as friendly as the first woman; she is evidently not a good Christian. See Gordon, *Postscript*, 118–22.

16 Knowles, *The Singer of the Kootenay: A Tale of Today*, 27. Future references to the work will have page numbers incorporated into the text.

17 Cody, *The Frontiersman: A Tale of the Yukon*, 96. Future references to the work will have page numbers incorporated into the text.

18 Withrow, *The King's Messenger; or, Lawrence Temple's Probation. A Story of Canadian Life*, 6. Future references to the work will have page numbers incorporated into the text.

19 Gordon, *Postscript*, 412.

20 Keith, *Duncan Polite*, 229. Future references to the work will have page numbers incorporated into the text.

21 Charles Gordon's sympathies and personal religious beliefs appear to have been more closely allied to those of his female characters. For example, he was an advocate of church union and was a leading figure in the discussions which led to the formation of the United Church of Canada.

22 Keith, *The Silver Maple*, 21.

23 Withrow, *Barbara Heck: A Tale of Early Methodism*, 27. Future references to the work will have page numbers incorporated into the text.

24 Watt, "Western Myth," 34.

25 Gordon supported the women's rights movement. At a women's suffrage rally in London, England, he spoke of the heroic work of Canadian women: "I took as my theme 'Canadian Women in Public Affairs in Canada.' I told of their work in social service, of their remarkable work in the church, and so on and so on. I told them yarns of my mother in the old Glengarry days, of the heroic women of the foothill country. I had plenty of stuff and I served it up hot, and right from my heart." See Gordon, *Postscript*, 190.

26 See Strong-Boag, "The Roots of Modern Canadian Feminism," 22–33.

27 National Council of Women of Canada, *Women Workers of Canada: Being a Report of the Proceedings of the First Annual Meeting and Conference of the National Council of Women of Canada*, 11.

28 National Council of Women, *Women Workers*, 11.

29 National Council of Women, *Women Workers*, 219.
30 See McClung, *The Stream Runs Fast*. McClung discusses her sense of disillusionment with the women's movement when it failed to achieve its high goals.

CHAPTER FIVE

1 Laurence, "My Final Hour," 188.
2 Laurence, "Ivory Tower or Grassroots?" 24–5.
3 See Traill, "Introductory Remarks", in *The Canadian Settler's Guide*, 1–47.
4 Traill refers to "Grundyism" in *The Backwoods of Canada*, 270.
5 See McClung, *The Stream Runs Fast*; National Council of Women of Canada, *Women Workers of Canada: Being a Report of the Proceedings of the First Annual Meeting and Conference of the National Council of Women of Canada*; Youmans, *Campaign Echoes*.
6 For an overview of the typical traits of a nineteenth-century lady, see chapter 1, notes 2 and 3.
7 Laurence, *The Stone Angel*, 292. Future references to this work will have page numbers incorporated into the text.
8 For an analysis of the difficulties encountered by the English lady on the Canadian frontier, see Traill's *The Canadian Settler's Guide*.
9 This movement places Hagar within the tradition of the Crusoe element in Canadian fiction; see MacLulich, "Crusoe in the Backwoods," 115–26; Thomas, "Crusoe and the Precious Kingdom," 58–64; Traill, *Canadian Crusoes: A Tale of the Rice Lake Plains*.
10 Wilson, *Swamp Angel*, 40. Future references to this work will have page numbers incorporated into the text.
11 Montgomery, *The Blue Castle*, 5–6. Future references to this work will have page numbers incorporated into the text.
12 Beresford-Howe, *The Book of Eve*, 1–2. Future references to this work will have page numbers incorporated into the text.
13 van Herk, *Judith*, 116. Future references to this work will have page numbers incorporated into the text.
14 Barfoot, *Abra*, 109. Future references to this work will have page numbers incorporated into the text.
15 Laurence, "Gadgetry or Growing," 58.
16 Laurence, *A Jest of God*, 181. Future references to this work will have page numbers incorporated into the text.
17 For some discussions of the mother-daughter relationship in Laurence's fiction, see Nancy Bailey, "Margaret Laurence, Carl Jung and the Manawaka Women," 306–21; Buss, *Mother and Daughter Relationships in the Manawaka Works of Margaret Laurence*; Maeser, "Finding the Mother," 151–66.

18 Govier, *Between Men*, 191. Future references to this work will have page numbers incorporated into the text.

19 Laurence, "Ten Years' Sentences," 14.

20 Laurence, "A Place to Stand On," in *Heart of a Stranger*, 6.

21 Thomas, *The Manawaka World of Margaret Laurence*, 135.

22 Laurence, *The Diviners*, 135. Future references to the work will have page numbers incorporated into the text.

23 Frederick Sweet discusses these three major focuses in "Margaret Laurence," 53.

24 Laurence, *Diviners*, 97; Traill, *Settler's Guide*, 204.

25 Laurence, "Final Hour," 188.

26 Traill, *The Backwoods of Canada*, 268.

Bibliography

Acton, Janice, et al., eds. *Women at Work: Ontario, 1850–1930*. Introd. Linda Kealey. Toronto: Canadian Women's Educational Press 1974.

Adam, Ruth. *A Woman's Place, 1910–1975*. London: Chatto and Windus 1975.

Allen, Richard, ed. *Man and Nature on the Prairies*. Regina: Canadian Plains Studies Centre 1976.

– *A Region of the Mind: Interpreting the Western Canadian Plains*. Regina: Canadian Plains Studies Centre, University of Saskatchewan 1973.

Armstrong, F.H., et al., eds. *Aspects of Nineteenth-Century Ontario: Essays Presented to James J. Talman*. Toronto: University of Toronto Press in association with the University of Western Ontario 1974.

Atwood, Margaret. *The Journals of Susanna Moodie*. Toronto: Oxford University Press 1970.

– *Survival: A Thematic Guide to Canadian Literature*. Toronto: Anansi 1972.

Austen, Jane. *Emma*. Ed. Stephen M. Parrish. New York: W.W. Norton 1972.

– *Pride and Prejudice*. New York: W.W. Norton 1966.

Bailey, Alfred G. "The Historical Setting of *The Imperialist*." In *Beginnings, A Critical Anthology*, ed. John Moss, 129–42. The Canadian Novel, vol. 2. Toronto: New Canada Publications 1980.

Bailey, Mary C. "Reminiscences of a Pioneer." *Alberta Historical Review* 15, no. 4 (1967): 17–25.

Bailey, Nancy. "Fiction and the New Androgyne: Problems and Possibilities in *The Diviners*." *Atlantis* 4, no. 1 (Fall 1978): 10–17.

– "Margaret Laurence, Carl Jung and the Manawaka Women." *Studies in Canadian Literature* 2, no. 2 (Summer 1977): 306–21.

Ball, Rosemary R. "A Perfect Farmer's Wife: Women in Nineteenth-Century Rural Ontario." *Canada: An Historical Magazine* 3, no. 2 (Dec. 1975): 3–21.

Ballstadt, Carl. "Susanna Moodie and the English Sketch." *Canadian Literature* no. 51 (Winter 1972): 32–8.

Bannerman, Jean. *Leading Ladies: Canada 1639–1967.* Belleville: Mika Publishing 1977.

Barfoot, Joan. *Abra.* Toronto: McGraw-Hill Ryerson 1978.

Bassett, Isabel. *The Parlour Rebellion: Profiles in the Struggle for Women's Rights.* Toronto: McClelland and Stewart 1975.

Beavan, Mrs Frances. *Life in the Backwoods of New Brunswick.* London 1845; rpt. St Stephen, New Brunswick. Print'N Press 1980.

Beer, Patricia. *Reader, I Married Him: A Study of the Women Characters of Jane Austen, Charlotte Brontë, Elizabeth Gaskell and George Eliot.* London: Macmillan 1974.

Bennett, Donna A. "The Failure of Sisterhood in Margaret Laurence's Manawaka Novels." *Atlantis* 4, no. 1 (Fall 1978): 103–9.

Benson, Mary Sumner. *Women in Eighteenth-Century America: A Study of Opinion and Social Usage.* 1935; rpt. New York: AMS Press 1976.

Bentley, D.M.R. Afterword. *The Backwoods of Canada,* by Catharine Parr Traill, 291–301. Toronto: McClelland and Stewart 1989.

Bercuson, D.J., and P.A. Buckner, eds. *Eastern and Western Perspectives.* Toronto: University of Toronto Press 1981.

Beresford-Howe, Constance. *The Book of Eve.* Toronto: Macmillan 1973.

Bergmann, Helena. *Between Obedience and Freedom: Woman's Role in the Mid-Nineteenth Century Industrial Novel.* Goteborg University: Gothenburg Studies in English 1979.

Berton, Laura Beatrice. *I Married the Klondike.* Pref. Robert Service. 1967; rpt. Toronto: McClelland and Stewart 1972.

Binnie-Clark, Georgina. *A Summer on the Canadian Prairie.* London: Edward Arnold 1910.

– *Wheat and Woman.* Introd. Susan Jackel. Toronto: University of Toronto Press 1979.

Bird, Isabella Lucy. *The Englishwoman in America.* Foreword Andrew Hill Clark. Toronto: University of Toronto Press 1966.

Blair, Karen J. *The Clubwoman as Feminist: True Womanhood Redefined, 1868–1914.* New York: Holmes and Meier 1980.

Blewett, David. "The Unity of the Manawaka Cycle." *Journal of Canadian Studies* 13, no 3 (Fall 1978): 31–9.

Blom, Margaret Howard, and Thomas E. Blom, eds. *Canada Home: Juliana Horatia Ewing's Fredericton Letters, 1867–1869.* Vancouver: University of British Columbia Press 1983.

Booth, General Bramwell. *Census Surplus and Empire.* London: Salvation Army International Emigration Office 1911.

Bradley, Mary. "Mary Bradley's Reminiscences: A Domestic Life in Colonial New Brunswick." *Atlantis* 7, no. 1 (1981): 92–101.

Branca, Patricia. *Silent Sisterhood: Middle Class Women in the Victorian Home.* London: Croom Helm 1975.

Bredwold, Louis I. *The Natural History of Sensibility.* Detroit: Wayne State University Press 1962.

Brissenden, R.R. *Virtue in Distress: Studies in the Novel of Sentiment from Richardson to Sade.* London: Macmillan 1974.

British Columbia Women's Institute. *Modern Pioneers, 1909–1959.* Vancouver: British Columbia Women's Institute 1960.

Brooke, Frances. *The History of Emily Montague.* Introd. Carl F. Klinck. New Canadian Library, no. 27. Ed. Malcolm Ross. Toronto: McClelland and Stewart 1961.

Brookes, Alan A., and Catharine A. Wilson. "'Working Away' from the Farm: The Young Women of North Huron 1910–30." *Ontario History* 77, no. 4 (Dec. 1985): 281–300.

Brown, Robert Craig, and Ramsay Cook. *Canada 1896–1921: A Nation Transformed.* Toronto: McClelland and Stewart 1974.

Brown, Herbert Ross. *The Sentimental Novel in America, 1789–1860.* Durham, North Carolina: Duke University Press 1940.

Brown, Mary Markham. *An Index to the "Literary Garland" (Montreal 1838–1851).* Toronto: Bibliographical Society of Canada 1962.

Brydon, Diana. "The Colonial Heroine: The Novels of Sara Jeannette Duncan and Mrs. Campbell Praed." *Canadian Literature* no. 86 (Autumn 1980): 41–8.

Bumsted, J.M., ed. *Canadian History before Confederation: Essays and Interpretations.* 2nd ed. 1972; rpt. Georgetown: Irving-Dorsey 1979.

Burman, Sandra, ed. *Fit Work for Women.* Canberra: Australian National University Press 1979.

Burnet, Jean, ed. *Looking into My Sister's Eyes: An Exploration in Women's History.* Toronto: Multicultural History Society of Ontario 1986.

Burnett, John, ed. *Useful Toil: Autobiographies of Working People from the 1820s to the 1920s.* London: Allen Lane 1974.

Buss, Helen M. "Margaret Laurence – A Bibliographical Essay." *American Review of Canadian Studies* 11, no. 2 (Autumn 1981): 1–14.

– *Mother and Daughter Relationships in the Manawaka Works of Margaret Laurence.* English Literary Studies. Victoria: University of Victoria 1985.

Butler, Major W.F. *The Great Lone Land: A Narrative of Travel and Adventure in the North-West of America.* 6th ed. 1872; rpt. London: Sampson Low, Marston, Searle, & Rivington 1874.

Calder, Jenni. *Women and Marriage in Victorian Fiction.* London: Thames and Hudson 1976.

Campbell, Bonnie, et al. *Women Unite! An Anthology of the Canadian Women's Movement.* Discussion Collective no. 6. Toronto: Canadian Women's Educational Press 1972.

Caroll, John. *My Boy Life, Presented in a Succession of True Stories.* Toronto: W. Briggs 1882.

Caswell, Maryanne. *Pioneer Girl.* Pref. Grace Lane. Toronto: McGraw-Hill 1964.

Chambers, Robert D. "The Women of Margaret Laurence." *Journal of Canadian Studies* 18, no. 2 (Summer 1983): 18–26.

Clark, S.D. *The Developing Canadian Community.* 2nd ed. 1968; rpt. Toronto: University of Toronto Press 1970.

Cleverdon, Catherine L. *The Woman Suffrage Movement in Canada.* Introd. Ramsay Cook. 2nd ed. Social History of Canada, no. 18. Ed. Michael Bliss. 1974; rpt. Toronto: University of Toronto Press, 1978.

Cody, H.A. *The Frontiersman: A Tale of the Yukon.* Toronto: William Briggs 1910.

Cloie, Mack. *The Old Orchard.* Toronto: William Briggs 1903.

Colby, Vineta. *Yesterday's Woman: Domestic Realism in the English Novel.* Princeton: Princeton University Press 1974.

Coldwell, Joan. "Hagar as Meg Merrillies, The Homeless Gipsy." *Journal of Canadian Fiction,* no. 27 (Fall 1980): 92–100.

Connor, Ralph. *Beyond the Marshes.* Toronto: Westminster 1900.

– *Black Rock: A Tale of the Selkirks.* Toronto: Westminster 1898.

– *Corporal Cameron of the North West Mounted Police: A Tale of the Macleod Trail.* Toronto: Westminster 1912.

– *The Doctor: A Tale of the Rockies.* Toronto: Westminster 1906.

– *The Friendly Four and Other Stories.* New York: George H. Doran 1926.

– *Glengarry School Days: A Story of Early Days in Glengarry.* Introd. S. Ross Beharriell. NCL, no. 118. Ed. Malcolm Ross. 1902; rpt. Toronto: McClelland and Stewart 1975.

– *The Man from Glengarry.* Introd. S. Ross Beharriell. NCL, no. 14. Ed. Malcolm Ross. 1901; rpt. Toronto: McClelland and Stewart 1969.

– *The Prospector: A Tale of the Crow's Nest Pass.* Toronto: McClelland and Stewart 1904.

– *The Sky Pilot: A Tale of the Foothills.* Introd. Robin W. Winks. Lexington: University Press of Kentucky 1970.

– *The Sky Pilot in No Man's Land.* Toronto: McClelland and Stewart 1919.

– *Torches Through the Bush.* Toronto: McClelland and Stewart 1934.

Conrad, Margaret. *Recording Angels: The Private Chronicles of Women From the Maritime Provinces of Canada, 1750–1950.* CRIAW Papers, no. 4. Ottawa: Canadian Research Institute for the Advancement of Women 1982.

Cook, Ramsay, and Wendy Mitchinson, eds. *The Proper Sphere: Woman's Place in Canadian Society.* Toronto: Oxford University Press 1976.

Cooley, Dennis. "Antimacassared in the Wilderness: Art and Nature in *The Stone Angel.*" *Mosaic* 11, no. 3 (Spring 1978): 29–46.

Cornillon, Susan Koppelman, ed. *Images of Women in Fiction: Feminist Perspectives.* Bowling Green: Bowling Green Popular Press 1972.

Cowan, Helen I. *British Emigration to British North America: The First Hundred Years.* 2nd ed. Toronto: University of Toronto Press 1928.

Cran, Mrs Georges. *A Woman in Canada.* London: W.J. Ham-Smith 1911.

Creighton, Donald. *Dominion of the North: A History of Canada.* 1944; rpt. Toronto: Macmillan 1977.

Cross, Michael J., ed. *The Frontier Thesis and the Canadas: The Debate on the Impact of the Canadian Environment.* Toronto: Copp Clark 1970.

Crow, Duncan. *The Victorian Woman.* New York: Stein and Day 1972.

Cunningham, Gail. *The New Woman and the Victorian Novel.* London: Macmillan 1978.

Cunnington, Dr C. Willett. *Feminine Attitudes in the Nineteenth Century.* New York: Haskell House 1973.

Davidoff, Lenore. *The Best Circles: Society Etiquette and the Season.* London: Croom Helm 1973.

Davidson, Cathy N. "Past and Perspective in Margaret Laurence's *The Stone Angel.*" *American Review of Canadian Studies* 8, no. 2 (Autumn 1978): 61–9.

Davis, Marilyn I. "Anglo-Boston Bamboozled on the Canadian Thames, Holmes; *Belinda; or, The Rivals.*" *Journal of Canadian Fiction* 2, no. 3 (Special Issue, Summer 1973): 56–61.

– "*Belinda, or The Rivals* – A Burlesque of Sentimental Fiction." Diss. University of Western Ontario 1963.

Daymond, Douglas, and Leslie Monkman, eds. *Canadian Novelists and the Novel.* Ottawa: Borealis 1981.

Defoe, Daniel. *Robinson Crusoe.* Ed. Michael Shinagel. New York: W.W. Norton 1975.

de la Roche, Mazo. *Delight.* Introd. Desmond Pacey. NCL, no. 21. Ed. Malcolm Ross. Toronto: McClelland and Stewart 1970.

Dembski, Peter E. Paul. "Jenny Kidd Trout and the Founding of the Women's Medical Colleges at Kingston and Toronto." *Ontario History* 77, no. 3 (Sept. 1985): 183–206.

Demetrakopoulos, Stephanie A. "Laurence's Fiction, A Revisioning of Feminine Archetypes." *Canadian Literature* no. 93 (Summer 1982): 42–57.

Djwa, Sandra. "False Gods and the True Covenant: Thematic Continuity between Margaret Laurence and Sinclair Ross." *Journal of Canadian Fiction* 1, no. 4 (Fall 1972): 43–50.

Dobbs, Kildare. "Canadian Heroes?" In *Canada: A Guide to the Peaceable Kingdom,* ed. William Kilbourn, 22–5. Toronto: Macmillan 1970.

Dooley, D.J. *Moral Vision in the Canadian Novel.* Toronto: Clarke, Irwin 1979.

Dufferin, Lady. *My Canadian Journal, 1872–1878, Extracts from My Letters Home.* London 1891; rpt. Toronto: Coles Canadiana Collection 1971.

Dunbar, Janet. *The Early Victorian Woman: Some Aspects of Her Life (1837–57)*. London: George G. Harrap 1953.

Duncan, Sara Jeannette. *Cousin Cinderella: A Canadian Girl in London*. Toronto: Macmillan 1908.

– *A Daughter of Today: A Novel*. New York: D. Appleton 1894.

– *The Imperialist*. Introd. Claude Bissell. NCL, no. 20. Ed. Malcolm Ross. 1904; rpt. Toronto: McClelland and Stewart 1971.

– *Sara Jeannette Duncan: Selected Journalism*. Ed. Thomas E. Tausky. Ottawa: Tecumseh 1978.

– *A Social Departure*. London: Chatto and Windus 1890.

Dunlop, William. *Tiger Dunlop's Upper Canada*. Introd. Carl F. Klinck. NCL, no. 55. Ed. Malcolm Ross. Toronto: McClelland and Stewart 1967.

Eakin, Paul John. *The New England Girl: Cultural Ideals in Hawthorne, Stowe, Howells and James*. Athens: University of Georgia Press 1976.

Earnest, Ernest. *The American Eve in Fact and Fiction, 1775–1914*. Urbana: University of Illinois Press 1974.

Edgar, Matilda, ed. *Ten Years of Upper Canada in Peace and War, 1805–1815, Being The Ridout Letters*. Toronto: William Briggs 1890.

Eggleston, Wilfrid. *The Frontier and Canadian Letters*. Introd. D.O. Spettigue. Carleton Library, no. 102. Ed. Michael G. Gnarowski. Toronto: McClelland and Stewart 1977.

Eliot, George. *Adam Bede*. Introd. Robert Speaight. 1966; rpt. London: Dent, Everyman 1973.

– *Middlemarch: A Study of Provincial Life*. Afterword Frank Kermode. New York: New American Library 1964.

Ellice, Jane. *The Diary of Jane Ellice*. Ed. Patricia Godsell. Ottawa: Oberon 1975.

Ellis, Sarah Stickney. *The Women of England, Their Social Duties, and Domestic Habits*. 12th ed. London: Fisher, Son 1839.

Engel, Marian. "Steps to the Mythic: *The Diviners* and *A Bird in the House*." *Journal of Canadian Studies* 13, no. 3 (Fall 1978): 72–4.

Fabre, Michel. "Words and the World: *The Diviners* as an Exploration of the Book of Life." *Canadian Literature* no. 93 (Summer 1982): 60–78.

Fairbanks, Carol, and Sara Brooks Sundberg. *Farm Women on the Prairie Frontier: A Sourcebook for Canada and the United States*. Metuchen, N.J.: Scarecrow Press 1983.

Faithfull, Emily. *Three Visits to America*. Edinburgh: David Douglas 1884.

Falk, Robert. *The Victorian Mode in American Fiction, 1865–1885*. Michigan State University Press 1965.

Fernando, Lloyd. *"New Women" in the Late Victorian Novel*. Pennsylvania State University Press 1977.

Forman, Denyse, and Uma Parameswaran. "Echoes and Refrains in the Canadian Novels of Margaret Laurence." *Centennial Review* 16, no. 3 (Summer 1972): 233–53.

Fowler, Marian. *The Embroidered Tent: Five Gentlewomen in Early Canada.* Toronto: Anansi 1982.
– *Redney: A Life of Sara Jeannette Duncan.* Toronto: Anansi 1983.
Francis, R. Douglas. "Changing Images of the West." *Journal of Canadian Studies* 17, no. 3 (Fall 1982): 5–19.
Fraser, Joshua. *Shanty, Forest and River Life in the Backwoods of Canada.* Montreal: John Lovell and Son 1883.
Fraser, W.A. *The Lone Furrow.* New York: D. Appleton 1907.
Frye, Northrop. *The Bush Garden: Essays on the Canadian Imagination.* Toronto: Anansi 1971.
– *Divisions on a Ground: Essays on Canadian Culture.* Ed. James Polk. Toronto: Anansi 1982.
Gagnon, D., ed. *Prairie Perspectives.* Toronto: Holt, Rinehart and Winston 1970.
Gairdner, William D. "Traill and Moodie: The Two Realities." *Journal of Canadian Fiction* no. 2 (Spring 1972): 35–42.
Galt, John. *Bogle Corbet.* Ed. and with an introd. by Elizabeth Waterston. NCL, no. 135. Ed. Malcolm Ross. Toronto: McClelland and Stewart 1977.
Gaskell, Elizabeth. *Mary Barton: A Tale of Manchester Life.* Harmondsworth: Penguin 1978.
– *Ruth.* London: Dent, Everyman 1967.
– *Wives and Daughters: An Every Day Story.* London: Smith, Elder 1867.
Geike, John C., ed. *Life in the Woods: A Boy's Narrative of the Adventures of a Settler's Family in Canada.* Boston: Crosby and Ainsworth 1865.
Godsell, Jean W. *I Was No Lady.* Toronto: Ryerson 1959.
Goethe, Johann Wolfgang von. *Faust, Part Two.* Trans. Barker Fairley. Toronto: University of Toronto Press 1970.
Goldie, Terry. "Folklore, Popular Culture and Individuation in *Surfacing* and *The Diviners*." *Canadian Literature* no 104 (Spring 1985): 95–108.
Gom, Leona M. "Laurence and the Use of Memory." *Canadian Literature* no. 71 (Winter 1976): 48–58.
Gordon, Charles W. *Postscript to Adventure: The Autobiography of Ralph Connor.* New York: Farrar and Rinehart 1938.
Gordon, Charles, Jr. "Ralph Connor and the New Generation." *Mosaic* 3, no. 3 (Spring 1970): 11–18.
Gorham, Deborah. *The Victorian Girl and the Feminine Ideal.* London: Croom Helm 1982.
Gottlieb, Lois C., and Wendy Keitner. "Demeter's Daughters: The Mother-Daughter Motif in Fiction by Canadian Women." *Atlantis* 3, no. 1 (Fall 1977): 130–44.
Govier, Katherine. *Between Men.* Markham, Ontario: Penguin 1987.
Grace, Sherrill. "A Portrait of the Artist as Laurence Hero." *Journal of Canadian Studies* 13, no. 3 (Fall 1978): 64–71.

Greg, William Rathbone. "Why Are Women Redundant?" In *Literary and Social Judgments*, 274–308. New York: Henry Holt 1876.

Gregory, Dr. *A Father's Legacy to His Daughters*. 1774; rpt. London: Minerva Press n.d.

Griffiths, N.E.S. *Penelope's Web: Some Perceptions of Women in European and Canadian Society*. Toronto: Oxford University Press 1976.

Grove, Frederick Philip. *In Search of Myself*. Introd. D.O. Spettigue. NCL, no. 94. Ed. Malcolm Ross. Toronto: McClelland and Stewart 1974.

Guillet, Edwin A. *Early Life in Upper Canada*. 1933; rpt. Toronto: University of Toronto Press 1963.

– *The Pioneer Farmer and Backwoodsman*. 2 vols. Toronto: Ontario Publishing Co. 1963.

Hall, Mrs Cecil. *A Lady's Life on a Farm in Manitoba*. London: W.H. Allen 1884.

Hamil, Fred C. "A Pioneer Novelist of Kent County." *Ontario History* 39 (1947): 101–14.

Hammerton, A. James. *Emigrant Gentlewomen, Genteel Poverty and Female Emigration, 1830–1914*. Totowa, New Jersey: Rowman and Littlefield; London: Croom Helm 1979.

Harrison, Dick. *Unnamed Country: The Struggle for a Canadian Prairie Fiction*. Edmonton: University of Alberta Press 1977.

Harshaw, Josephine Perfect. *When Women Work Together: A History of the Young Women's Christian Association in Canada*. Toronto: Young Women's Christian Association of Canada 1966.

Hartman, Mary S., and Lois Banner. *Clio's Consciousness Raised: New Perspectives on the History of Women*. New York: Harper and Row 1974.

Hedenstrom, Joanne. "Puzzled Patriarchs and Free Women: Patterns in the Canadian Novel." *Atlantis* 4, no. 1 (Fall 1978): 2–9.

Henly, W.J. *Women of Red River, Being A Book Written From the Recollections of Women Surviving From the Red River Era*. 1923; rpt. Winnipeg: Women's Canadian Club of Winnipeg 1977.

Herrington, W.S. *Pioneer Life among the Loyalists in Upper Canada*. Toronto: Macmillan 1915.

Hill, Georgiana. *Women in English Life from Medieval to Modern Times*. 2 vols. London: Richard Bentley 1896.

Hiemstra, Mary. *Gully Farm*. Toronto: McClelland and Stewart 1955.

Hilts, Rev. Joseph H. *Among the Forest Trees or, How the Bushman Family Got Their Homes. Being a Book of Facts and Incidents of Pioneer Life in Upper Canada, Arranged in the Form of Story*. Toronto: William Briggs 1888.

Hodgins, Jack, ed. *The Frontier Experience*. Themes in Canadian Literature. Ed. David Arnason. Toronto: Macmillan 1975.

Holcombe, Lee. *Victorian Ladies at Work: Middle-Class Working Women in England and Wales, 1850–1914*. Hamden, Connecticut: Archon Books 1973.

Holmes, Abraham S. *Belinda, or, The Rivals.* Introd. Carl F. Klinck. Vancouver: Alcuin Society 1971.

Horn, Pamela. *The Rise and Fall of the Victorian Servant.* Dublin: Gill and Macmillan 1975.

Howells, William Dean. *Heroines of Fiction.* 2 vols. New York: Harper and Brothers 1901.

Howes, E.A. *With a Glance Backward.* Toronto: Oxford University Press 1939.

Huggett, Frank E. *Life below Stairs: Domestic Servants in England from Victorian Times.* London: John Murray 1977.

Hughes, Kenneth James. "Politics and *A Jest of God*." *Journal of Canadian Studies* 13, no. 3 (Fall 1978): 40–54.

Hughes, Patricia. "Towards the Development of Feminist Theory." *Atlantis* 5, no. 1 (Fall 1979): 15–28.

Inderwick, Mary E. "A Lady and Her Ranch." *Alberta Historical Review* 15, no. 4 (1967): 1–9.

Innis, Mary Quayle. *Unfold the Years: A History of the Young Women's Christian Association in Canada.* Toronto: McClelland and Stewart 1949.

Innis, Mary Quayle, ed. *The Clear Spirit: Twenty Canadian Women and Their Times.* 1966; rpt. Toronto: University of Toronto Press 1973.

Irvine, Lorna. "Hostility and Reconciliation: The Mother in English Canadian Fiction." *American Review of Canadian Studies* 8, no. 1 (Spring 1978): 56–64.

Jackel, Susan, ed. *A Flannel Shirt and Liberty: British Emigrant Gentlewomen in the Canadian West, 1880–1914.* Vancouver: University of British Columbia Press 1982.

Jameson, Anna. *Shakespeare's Heroines: Characteristics of Women, Moral, Poetical, and Historical.* Philadelphia: Henry Altemus n.d.

– *Studies, Stories, and Memoirs.* Boston: Houghton, Mifflin and Company 1888.

– *Winter Studies and Summer Rambles in Canada.* 3 vols. London 1838; rpt. Toronto: Coles Canadiana Collection 1972.

Jeffrey, David L. "Biblical Hermeneutic and Family History in Contemporary Canadian Fiction: Wiebe and Laurence." *Mosaic* 11, no. 3 (Spring 1978): 87–106.

Johnson, E. Pauline. *The Mocassin Maker.* Toronto: W. Briggs 1913.

Johnson, Stanley C. *A History of Emigration from the United Kingdom to North America, 1763–1912.* London 1913; rpt. New York: A.M. Kelley 1966.

Johnston, Eleanor. "The Quest of the Diviners." *Mosaic* 11, no. 3 (Spring 1978): 107–18.

Johnston, Jean. *Wilderness Women: Canada's Forgotten History.* Toronto: Peter Martin Associates 1973.

Jones, D.G. *Butterfly on Rock: A Study of Themes and Images in Canadian Literature.* 1970; rpt. Toronto: University of Toronto Press 1979.

Katz, Michael B., and Paul H. Mattingly, eds. *Education and Social Change: Themes from Ontario's Past.* New York: New York University Press 1975.

Katz, Michael B. *The People of Hamilton, Canada West, Family and Class in a Mid-Nineteenth-Century City.* Cambridge: Harvard University Press, 1975.

Kealey, Linda, ed. *A Not Unreasonable Claim: Women and Reform in Canada, 1880s–1920s.* Toronto, Women's Educational Press 1979.

Kearns, Judy. "Rachel and Social Determinism: A Feminist Reading of *A Jest of God." Journal of Canadian Studies* no. 27 (Fall 1980): 101–23.

Kechnie, Margaret. "The United Farm Women of Ontario: Developing a Political Consciousness." *Ontario History* 77, no. 4 (Dec. 1985): 267–80.

Keith, Marian. *Duncan Polite, The Watchman of Glenoro.* Toronto: McClelland, Goodchild and Stewart 1905.

– *'Lizbeth of the Dale.* Toronto: Westminster 1910.

– *The Silver Maple: A Study of Upper Canada.* Toronto: Westminster 1908.

Kertzer, J.M. "*The Stone Angel*: Time and Responsibility." *Dalhousie Review* 54, no. 3 (Autumn 1974): 499–509.

King, Basil. *The Street Called Straight.* 5th ed. London: Methuen 1912.

Klassen, Henry C., ed. *The Canadian West: Social Change and Economic Development.* Calgary: Comprint Publishing 1977.

Klinck, Carl F. "A Gentlewoman of Upper Canada." *Canadian Literature,* no. 1 (1959): 75–7.

Klinck, Carl F., ed. *Literary History of Canada: Canadian Literature in English.* 3 vols. 2nd ed. 1976; rpt. Toronto: University of Toronto Press 1977.

Klinck, Carl F. Introduction. *Roughing It in the Bush,* by Susanna Moodie. NCL, no. 31. Ed. Malcolm Ross. Toronto: McClelland and Stewart 1970.

Knowles, R.E. *St. Cuthbert's. A Novel.* Toronto: Fleming H. Revell Company 1905.

– *The Singer of the Kootenay: A Tale of Today.* Toronto: Fleming H. Revell Company 1911.

Kolodny, Annette. *The Lay of the Land: Metaphor as Experience and History in American Life and Letters.* Chapel Hill: University of North Carolina Press 1975.

– "Some Notes on Defining a 'Feminist Literary Criticism.'". *Critical Inquiry* 2, no. 1 (Autumn 1975): 75–92.

Kostash, Myrna, et al. *Her Own Woman: Profiles of Ten Canadian Women.* Toronto: Macmillan 1975.

Kreisel, Henry. "A Familiar Landscape." *Tamarack Review,* no. 55 (Spring 1970); 91–2, 94.

Labonte, Ronald. "Laurence and Characterization: The Humanist Flaw." *Journal of Canadian Fiction* no. 33 (1981–82): 107–11.

Langdon, Eustella. *Pioneer Gardens at Black Creek Pioneer Village.* Toronto: Holt, Rinehart and Winston 1972.

Langton, Anne. *A Gentlewoman in Upper Canada: The Journals of Anne Langton.* Ed. H.H. Langton. Toronto: Clarke, Irwin 1950.

Latham, Barbara, and Cathy Kess, eds. *In Her Own Right: Selected Essays on Women's History in B.C.* Victoria: Camosun College 1980.

Laurence, Margaret. *The Diviners.* Toronto: Bantam 1975.

– "Gadgetry or Growing: Form and Voice in the Novel." *Journal of Canadian Fiction* no. 27 (Fall 1980): 54–62.

– *Heart of a Stranger.* Toronto: McClelland and Stewart-Bantam 1980.

– *A Jest of God.* Introd. G.D. Killam. 1974; rpt. Toronto: McClelland and Stewart 1986.

– "Ivory Towers or Grassroots? The Novelist as Socio-Political Being." In *A Political Art: Essays and Images in Honour of George Woodcock,* ed. William H. New, 15–25. Vancouver: University of British Columbia Press 1978.

– "Letter to Bob Sorfleet, from Margaret Laurence." *Journal of Canadian Fiction* no 27 (Fall 1980): 52–3.

– "My Final Hour." *Canadian Literature* no. 100 (Spring 1984): 187–97.

– *The Stone Angel.* Introd. William H. New. NCL, no. 59. Ed. Malcolm Ross. Toronto: McClelland and Stewart 1968.

– "Ten Years' Sentences." *Canadian Literature* no. 41 (Summer 1969): 10–16.

Lawson, Mrs J.K. *The Harvest of Moloch: A Story of To-Day.* Toronto: John M. Poole 1908.

Lennox, John Watt. "Manawaka and Deptford: Place and Voice." *Journal of Canadian Studies* 13, no. 3 (Fall 1978): 23–30.

Lever, Bernice. "Margaret Laurence Interview, November 20, 1974." *Waves* 3, no. 2 (Winter 1975): 4–12.

Light, Beth, and Alison Prentice, eds. *Pioneer and Gentlewomen of British North America, 1713–1867.* Documents in Canadian Women's History, vol. 1. Toronto: New Hogtown Press 1980.

Light, Beth, and Veronica Strong-Boag. *True Daughters of the North, Canadian Women's History: An Annotated Bibliography.* Toronto: Ontario Institute for Studies in Education 1980.

The Literary Garland. Montreal: John Lovell 1838–51.

Lizars, Robina, and Kathleen MacFarlane Lizars. *Committed to His Charge.* Toronto: George N. Morang 1900.

– *In The Days of the Canada Company: The Story of the Settlement of the Huron Tract and a View of the Social Life of the Period.* Introd. G.M. Grant. 1896; rpt. Toronto: Coles Canadiana Collection 1972.

M.E.R. "Sara Jeannette Duncan." *Canadian Literature* no. 27 (Winter 1966): 15–19.

MacDonagh, Oliver, ed. *Emigration in the Victorian Age: Debates on the Issue from Nineteenth-Century Critical Journals.* Germany: Gregg International Publishers 1973.

MacDonald, R.D. "Design and Purpose." *Canadian Literature* no. 51 (1972): 20–31.

Machar, Agnes Maule. *Roland Graeme: Knight*. Montreal: Wm Drysdale 1892.

MacLulich, T.D. "*Anne of Green Gables* and the Regional Idyll." *Dalhousie Review* 63, no. 3 (Autumn 1983): 488–501.

– "Crusoe in the Backwoods: A Canadian Fable?" *Mosaic* 9, no. 2 (Winter 1976): 115–26.

MacMurchy, Helen. *The Mother, The Children and the New World Order. An address given at the Eighth Biennial Meeting of the Federated Women's Institutes of Canada and the Twenty-Second Meeting of the Women's Institutes of Manitoba.* Winnipeg: Women's Institute 1933.

MacMurchy, Marjory. *The Canadian Girl at Work: A Book of Vocational Guidance.* Toronto: A.T. Wilgress 1919.

MacNab, Sophia. *The Diary of Sophia MacNab*. Ed. Charles Ambrose Carter and Thomas Melville Barley. Hamilton: W.L. Griffin 1968.

Macnaughton, S. *My Canadian Memories*. London: Chapman and Hall 1920.

Macpherson, Lydia E. *Historical Sketch of the Woman's Christian Temperance Union of British Columbia, Commemorating Seventy Years of Service, 1883–1953.* British Columbia: Women's Christian Temperance Union 1953.

Maeser, Angelika. "Finding the Mother: The Individuation of Laurence's Heroines." *Journal of Canadian Fiction* no. 27 (Fall 1980): 151–66.

Mandel, Eli, ed. *Contexts of Canadian Criticism*. Chicago 1971; rpt. Toronto: University of Toronto Press 1977.

Mathews, Robin. "Susanna Moodie, Pink Toryism, and Nineteenth Century Ideas of Canadian Identity." *Journal of Canadian Studies* 10, no. 3 (1975): 3–15.

Manitoba Women's Institute. *The Great Human Heart: A History of the Manitoba Women's Institute, 1910–1980.* Manitoba: Manitoba Women's Institute 1980.

Matheson, Gwen, ed. *Women in the Canadian Mosaic*. Toronto: Peter Martin Associates 1976.

Matthews, John Pengwerne. *Tradition in Exile: A Comparative Study of Social Influences on the Development of Australian and Canadian Poetry in the Nineteenth Century.* Toronto: University of Toronto Press 1962.

McAlister, Lottie. *Clipped Wings*. Toronto: William Briggs 1899.

McBride, Theresa M. *The Domestic Revolution: The Modernisation of Household Service in England and France, 1820–1920.* London: Croom Helm 1976.

McClung, Nellie L. *All We Like Sheep, and Other Stories*. Toronto: Thomas Allen 1926.

– *Clearing in the West: My Own Story*. Toronto: Thomas Allen 1976.

– *Painted Fires*. Toronto: Thomas Allen 1925.

– *Purple Springs*. Toronto: Thomas Allen 1921.

– *The Second Chance*. Toronto: William Briggs 1910.

– *Sowing Seeds in Danny*. New York: Doubleday, Page 1908.
– *The Stream Runs Fast: My Own Story*. Toronto: Thomas Allen 1945.
McConnachie, Kathleen. "Methodology in the Study of Women in History: A Case Study of Helen MacMurchy, M.D." *Ontario History* 75, no. 1 (March 1983): 61–70.
McCourt, Edward. *The Canadian West in Fiction*. Toronto: Ryerson 1970.
McGillivray, Royce. "Novelists and the Glengarry Pioneer." *Ontario History* 65, no. 2 (June 1973): 61–8.
McKee, Mrs S.G.E. *Jubilee History of the Ontario Woman's Christian Temperance Union 1877–1927*. Whitby: C.A. Goodfellow 1927.
McKenna, Isobel. "Women in Canadian Literature." *Canadian Literature* no. 62 (August 1974): 69–78.
McKenzie, Ruth. "Life in a New Land: Notes on the Immigrant Theme in Canadian Fiction." *Canadian Literature* no. 7 (1961): 24–33.
McKibbin, Rev. Archibald. *The Old Orchard*. Toronto: William Briggs 1903.
McKishnie, Archie P. *Willow, The Wisp*. Toronto: Thomas Allen 1918.
McLeod, Carol. *Legendary Canadian Women*. Huntsport, N.S.: Lancelot Press 1983.
McMullen, Lorraine. "Images of Women in Canadian Literature: Woman as Hero." *Atlantis* 2, no. 2 (Conference Issue, Spring 1977): 134–42.
Metcalf, John, ed. *The Narrative Voice: Short Stories and Reflections by Canadian Authors*. Toronto: McGraw-Hill Ryerson 1972.
Mews, Hazel. *Frail Vessels: Woman's Role in Women's Novels from Fanny Burney to George Eliot*. London: Athlone Press 1969.
Miles, Angela R., and Geraldine Finn, eds. *Feminism in Canada: From Pressure to Politics*. Montreal: Black Rose Books 1982.
Mill, John Stuart, and Harriet Taylor Mill. *Essays on Sex Equality*. Ed. Alice S. Rossi. Chicago: University of Chicago Press 1970.
Millett, Kate. "The Debate over Women: Ruskin versus Mill." *Victorian Studies* 14, no. 1 (Sept. 1970): 63–82.
Milton, John. "Il Penseroso." In *The Poems of John Milton*, ed. John Carey and Alastair Fowler, 146. Longmans Annotated Poets. Ed. F.W. Bateson. London: Longmans, Green 1968.
Mitchell, Juliet, and Ann Oakley, eds. *The Rights and Wrongs of Women*. Harmondsworth: Penguin 1976.
Monck, Frances. *My Canadian Leaves*. Toronto: Canadian Library Service, University of Toronto Press 1963.
Monk, Samuel H. *The Sublime: A Study of Critical Theories in Eighteenth-Century England*. New York: MLA 1935.
Montgomery, L.M. *Anne of Green Gables*. Toronto: McGraw-Hill Ryerson 1968.
– *The Blue Castle*. 1972; rpt. Toronto: McClelland and Stewart 1977.
– *Emily of New Moon*. Afterword Alice Munro. NCL. Ed. David Staines. 1923; rpt. Toronto: McClelland and Stewart 1989.

Moodie, Susanna. *Flora Lyndsay: or, Passages in an Eventful Life.* New York: DeWitt and Davenport n.d.

— *Geoffrey Moncton: or, The Faithless Guardian.* New York: DeWitt and Davenport 1855.

— *Life in the Clearings.* Ed. Robert L. McDougall. Toronto: Macmillan 1959.

— *Mark Hurdlestone, The Gold Worshipper.* 2 vols. London: Richard Bentley 1853.

— *Matrimonial Speculations.* London: Richard Bentley 1854.

— *Roughing It in the Bush, or, Forest Life in Canada.* 1913; rpt. Toronto: Coles Canadiana Collection 1980.

Moodie, Susanna, and J.W.D. Moodie, eds. *The Victoria Magazine, 1847–1848.* 1848; rpt. Vancouver: University of British Columbia Library 1968.

More, Hannah. *The Works of Hannah More.* 2 vols. New York: Harper 1854.

Morgan, Henry J. *Bibliotheca Canadensis: or A Manual of Canadian Literature.* Ottawa: G.E. Desbarats 1867.

Morley, Patricia. "Canada, Africa, Canada: Laurence's Unbroken Journey." *Journal of Canadian Fiction* no. 27 (Fall 1980): 81–91.

— "The Long Trek Home: Margaret Laurence's Stories." *Journal of Canadian Studies* 11, no. 4 (November 1976): 19–26.

— "Margaret Laurence's Early Writing: 'a world in which others have to be respected.'" *Journal of Canadian Studies* 13, no. 3 (Fall 1978): 13–16.

Morris, Audrey Y. *The Gentle Pioneers: Five Nineteenth-Century Canadians.* Don Mills: General Publishing, PaperJacks 1973.

Morris, Elizabeth Keith. *An Englishwoman in The Canadian West.* London: Simpkin Marshall 1913.

Morrison, T.R. "'Their Proper Sphere': Feminism, The Family and Child-Centered Social Reform in Ontario, 1875–1900, Part 1." *Ontario History* 68, no. 1 (March 1976): 45–64.

— "'Their Proper Sphere': Feminism, The Family and Child-Centered Social Reform in Ontario, 1875–1900, Part 2." *Ontario History* 68, no. 2 (June 1976): 65–74.

Mortlock, Melanie. "The Religion of Heritage: *The Diviners* as a Thematic Conclusion to the Manawaka Series." *Journal of Canadian Fiction* no. 27 (Fall 1980): 132–42.

Morton, W.L., ed. *God's Galloping Girl: The Peace River Diaries of Monica Storrs, 1929–1931.* Vancouver: University of British Columbia Press 1979.

Moss, John. *Patterns of Isolation in English Canadian Fiction.* Toronto: McClelland and Stewart 1974.

Moss, John, ed. *Beginnings: A Critical Anthology* . Canadian Novel, vol. 2. Toronto: New Canada Publications 1980.

Murphy, Emily. *Janey Canuck in the West.* Introd. Isabel Bassett. Heritage Books, no. 2. Ed. Clara Thomas. Toronto: McClelland and Stewart 1975.

— *Seeds of Pine.* Toronto: Musson 1922.

National Council of Woman of Canada. *Women of Canada, Their Life and Work.* 1900; rpt. Ottawa: National Council of of Women of Canada 1975.

– *Women Workers of Canada: Being a Report of the Proceedings of the First Annual Meeting and Conference of the National Council of Women of Canada.* Ottawa: National Council of Women of Canada 1894.

– *Women Workers of Canada, 1900: Report of the Seventh Annual Meeting of the National Council of Women of Canada.* Ottawa: National Council of Women of Canada 1900.

Neff, Wanda Fraiken. *Victorian Working Women: An Historical and Literary Study of Women in British Industries and Professions.* New York: AMS Press 1966.

New, W.H. *Articulating West: Essays on Purpose and Form in Modern Canadian Literature.* Toronto: New Press 1972.

– "Every Now and Then: Voice and Language in Lawrence's [sic] *The Stone Angel.*" *Canadian Literature* no. 93 (Summer 1982): 79–96.

– "Frances Brooke's Chequered Gardens." *Canadian Literature* no. 52 (1972): 24–38.

– "Text and Subtext: Laurence's "The Merchant of Heaven."" *Journal of Canadian Studies* 13, no. 3 (Fall 1978): 17–22.

Noonan, G. "Susanna and Her Critics: A Strategy of Fiction for *Roughing It in the Bush.*" *Studies in Canadian Literature* 5, no. 2 (Fall 1980): 280–9.

Northey, Margot. *The Haunted Wilderness: The Gothic and Grotesque in Canadian Fiction.* Toronto: University of Toronto Press 1976.

O'Brien, Mary. *The Journals of Mary O'Brien, 1828–1838.* Ed. Audrey Saunders Miller. Toronto: Macmillan 1968.

Ormsby, Margaret A., ed. *A Pioneer Gentlewoman in British Columbia: The Recollections of Susan Allison.* Vancouver: University of British Columbia Press 1976.

Osachoff, Margaret Gail. "Moral Vision in *The Stone Angel.*" *Studies in Canadian Literature* 4, no. 1 (Winter 1979): 139–53.

Ostenso, Martha. *Wild Geese.* Introd. Carlyle King. NCL, no. 18. Ed. Malcolm Ross. Toronto: McClelland and Stewart 1961.

Otty, Marianne Grey. *Fifty Years of Women's Institutes in New Brunswick, Canada, 1911–1961.* New Brunswick: New Brunswick Women's Institute 1961.

Owram, Douglas. *Promise of Eden: The Canadian Expansionist Movement and the Idea of the West, 1856–1900.* Toronto: University of Toronto Press 1980.

Oxley, J. MacDonald. *The Young Woodsman or Life in the Forests of Canada.* London: T. Nelson 1895.

Paradis, Suzanne. *Femme Fictive, Femme Réelle, Le Personnage Féminin dans Le Roman Féminin Canadien-Français, 1884–1966.* Québec: Garneau 1968.

Packer, Miriam. "The Dance of Life: *The Fire-Dwellers.*" *Journal of Canadian Fiction* no. 27 (Fall 1980): 124–31.

Parr, Joy. "The Significance of Gender among Emigrant Gentlefolk." *Dalhousie Review* 62, no. 4 (Winter 1982–83): 693–9.

Pesando, Frank. "In a Nameless Land: The Use of Apocalyptic Mythology in the Writing of Margaret Laurence." *Journal of Canadian Fiction* 2, no. 1 (Winter 1973): 53–7.

Peterman, Michael. "Catharine Parr Traill." in *Profiles in Canadian Literature*, vol. 3, ed. Jeffrey M. Heath, 25–32. Toronto: Dundurn Press 1982.

– "Humour and Balance in *The Imperialist:* Sara Jeannette Duncan's 'Instinct of Presentation.'" *Journal of Canadian Studies* 11, no. 2 (May 1976): 56–64.

Peterson, M. Jeanne. "The Victorian Governess: Status Incongruence in Family and Society." *Victorian Studies* 14, no. 1 (Sept. 1970): 7–26.

Pinchbeck, Ivy. *Women Workers and the Industrial Revolution.* 1930; rpt. London: Frank Cass 1969.

Portlock, Rosa. *Twenty-Five Years of Canadian Life With a Study on Bible Prophecy.* Toronto: William Briggs 1901.

Prentice, Alison. *The School Promoters: Education and Social Class in Mid-Nineteenth Century Upper Canada.* Toronto: McClelland and Stewart 1977.

Prentice, Alison L., and Susan E. Houston, eds. *Family, School and Society in Nineteenth-Century Canada.* Toronto: Oxford University Press 1975.

Prince Edward Island Women's Institute. *Through the Years: The Women's Institutes of Prince Edward Island, 1913–1963.* Prince Edward Island: Prince Edward Island Women's Institute 1963.

Raber, Jessie Browne. *Pioneering in Alberta.* New York: Exposition Press 1951.

Rasmussen, Linda, et at., eds. *A Harvest Yet to Reap: A History of Prairie Women.* Toronto: Woman's Press 1976.

Rasporich, Anthony W., and Henry C. Klassen, eds. *Frontier Calgary, Town, City, and Region, 1875–1914.* Calgary: McClelland and Stewart West 1975.

Rasporich, Anthony W., ed. *Western Canada, Past and Present.* Calgary: McClelland and Stewart West 1975.

Rasporich, A.W., and H.C. Klassen, eds. *Prairie Perspectives 2: Selected Papers of the Western Canadian Studies Conferences, 1970, 1971.* Toronto: Holt, Rinehart and Winston 1973.

Read, S.E. "The Maze of Life." *Canadian Literature* no. 27 (Winter 1966): 5–14.

Rees, Barbara. *The Victorian Lady.* London: Gordon and Cremonesi 1977.

Reid, Diane, et al. *A Bridge to the Future: A History of the Council of Women of Ottawa and Area.* Ottawa: Council of Women of Ottawa 1976.

Richardson, John. *The Canadian Brothers; or, The Prophecy Fulfilled: A Tale of the Late American War.* 1840; rpt. Toronto: University of Toronto Press 1976.

– *Wacousta, A Tale of the Pontiac Conspiracy.* Toronto: McClelland and Stewart 1923.

– *Wacousta or The Prophecy.* Ed. Carl F. Klinck. NCL, no. 58. Ed. Malcolm Ross. Toronto: McClelland and Stewart 1967.

Richardson, R.L. *Colin of the Ninth Concession: A Tale of Scottish Pioneer Life in Eastern Ontario.* Toronto: George N. Morang 1903.

Richardson, Samuel. *Clarissa, or The History of a Young Lady in Four Volumes.* Introd. John Butt. London: J.M. Dent, Everyman 1962.
- *Familiar Letters on Important Occasions.* English Library. Ed. J. Isaacs. London: George Routledge and Sons 1928.
- *Pamela, or Virtue Rewarded.* Introd. William M. Sale. New York: W.W. Norton 1958.
Ricou, Laurence. *Vertical Man/Horizontal World: Man and Landscape in Canadian Prairie Fiction.* Vancouver: University of British Columbia Press 1973.
Roberts, Charles G.D. *The Heart of the Ancient Wood.* New York: A. Wessels 1906.
- *The Last Barrier and Other Stories.* Introd. Alec Lucas. NCL, no. 7. Ed. Malcolm Ross. Toronto: McClelland and Stewart 1970.
Roberts, Sarah Ellen. *Of Us and the Oxen.* Saskatoon: Modern Press 1968.
Roberts, Wayne. *Honest Womanhood: Feminism, Femininity and Class Consciousness among Toronto Working Women, 1893–1914.* Toronto: New Hogtown Press 1976.
Rooke, Constance. "A Feminist Reading of *The Stone Angel.*" *Canadian Literature* no. 93 (Summer 1982): 26–41.
Ross, Catherine Sheldrick. "Calling Back the Ghost of the old-Time Heroine: Duncan, Montgomery, Atwood, Laurence, Munro." *Studies in Canadian Literature* 4, no. 1 (Winter 1979): 43–58.
Rouslin, Virgina Watson. "The Intelligent Woman's Guide to Pioneering in Canada." *Dalhousie Review* 56, no. 2 (Summer 1976): 319–35.
Ruskin, John. "Of Queens' Gardens." In *Sesame and Lilies,* 83–133. Toronto: W.J. Gage, 1981.
Russell, Lois S. "The First Canadian Cooking Stove." *Canada, An Historical Magazine* 3, no. 2 (1975): 34–5.
Ryerson, Egerton. *My Dearest Sophie: Letters from Egerton Ryerson to his Daughter.* Ed. C.B. Sissons. Toronto: Ryerson 1955.
Sainte-Marie-Eleuthère, Soeur. *La Mère dans le Roman Canadien Français.* Québec: Les Presses de l'Université Laval 1964.
Samuel, Raphael, ed. *Village Life and Labour.* History Workshop Series. London: Routledge and Kegan Paul 1975.
Saxby, Jessie M.E. *West-Nor'-West.* London: James Nisbet 1890.
Scott, Lloyd M. "The English Gentlefolk in the Backwoods of Canada." *Dalhousie Review* 39, no. 1 (Spring 1959): 56–69.
Seton, Ernest Thompson. *Two Little Savages, Being the Adventures of Two Boys Who Lived as Indians and What They Learned.* New York: Dover 1962.
Shaw, Rosa L. *Proud Heritage: A History of the National Council of Women of Canada.* Toronto: Ryerson 1957.
Shields, Carol. *Susanna Moodie: Voice and Vision.* Ottawa: Borealis Press 1977.
- "Three Canadian Women: Fiction of Autobiography." *Atlantis* 4, no. 1 (Fall 1978): 49–54.

Shortt, Adam. *The Life of the Settler in Western Canada before the War of 1812*. Bulletin of the Departments of History and Political and Economic Science in Queen's University, no. 12. Kingston: Queen's University 1914.

Siefert, Susan. *The Dilemma of the Talented Heroine: A Study in Nineteenth Century Fiction*. Monographs in Women's Studies. Ed. Sherri Clarkson. Montreal: Eden Press 1978.

Silverman, Eliane Leslau. *The Last Best West: Women on the Alberta Frontier 1880–1930*. Montreal: Eden Press 1984.

Simcoe, Mrs John Graves. *The Diary of Mrs. John Graves Simcoe, Wife of the First Lieutenant-Governor of the Province of Upper Canada, 1792–6*. With Notes and a Biography by J. Ross Robertson. 1911; rpt. Toronto: Coles Canadiana Collection 1973.

Skelton, Isabel. *The Backwoodswoman: A Chronicle of Pioneer Home Life in Upper and Lower Canada*. Toronto: Ryerson 1924.

Smith, A.J.M., ed. *The Colonial Century: English-Canadian Writing Before Confederation*. Toronto: Gage 1973.

– ed. *Masks of Fiction: Canadian Critics on Canadian Prose*. NCL, no. 2. Ed. Malcolm Ross. Toronto: McClelland and Stewart 1961.

Smith, Allan. "Metaphor and Nationality in North America." *Canadian Historical Review* 51, no. 3 (September 1970): 247–75.

Springett, Evelyn Cartier. *For My Children's Children*. Montreal: Unity Press 1937.

Stang, Richard. *The Theory of the Novel in England, 1850–1870*. New York: Columbia University Press 1959.

Stead, Robert. *The Cow Puncher*. Toronto: Musson 1918.

– *Grain*. Introd. Thomas Saunders. NCL, no. 36. Ed. Malcolm Ross. Toronto: McClelland and Stewart 1963.

– *The Homesteaders*. Introd. Susan Wood Glicksohn. Toronto: University of Toronto Press 1973.

– *Neighbours*. Toronto: Hodder and Stoughton 1922.

– *The Smoking Flax*. Toronto: McClelland and Stewart 1924.

Stephen, Donald G., ed. *Writers of the Prairies*. Vancouver: University of British Columbia Press 1973.

Stephenson, Marylee, ed. *Women in Canada*. Toronto: New Press 1973.

Stevenson, Warren. "The Myth of Demeter and Persephone in *A Jest of God*." *Studies in Canadian Literature* 1, no. 1 (Winter 1976): 120–3.

Stewart, Frances. *Our Forest Home, being Extracts from the Correspondence of the Late Frances Stewart*. Ed. E.S. Dunlop. 2nd ed. Montreal: Gazette Printing and Publishing 1902.

Stouck, David. "'Secrets of the Prison House': Mrs. Moodie and the Canadian Imagination." *Dalhousie Review* 34, no. 3 (Autumn 1974): 463–72.

Strange, Kathleen. *With the West in Her Eyes*. Toronto: George J. McLeod; New York: Dodge Publishing 1937.

Stringer, Arthur. *The Prairie Child*. Toronto, McClelland and Stewart 1922.
– *The Prairie Mother*. Toronto: McClelland and Stewart 1920.
– *The Prairie Wife*. New York: A.L. Burt n.d.
Strong-Boag, Veronica. "Canadian Feminism in the 1920s: The Case of Nellie L. McClung." *Journal of Canadian Studies* 12, no. 4 (Summer 1977): 35–57.
– *The Parliament of Women: The National Council of Women of Canada, 1893– 1929*. Ottawa: National Museums of Canada 1976.
– "The Roots of Modern Canadian Feminism: The National Council of Women, 1893–1929." *Canada, An Historical Magazine* 3, no. 2 (1975): 22–33.
Swainson, Donald, ed. *Oliver Mowat's Ontario*. Toronto: Macmillan 1972.
Sweet, Frederick. "Margaret Laurence." In *Profiles in Canadian Literature*, vol. 2, ed. Jeffrey M. Heath, 49–56. Toronto: Dundurn Press 1980.
Sykes, Ella. *A Home Help in Canada*. London: G. Bell 1912.
Tausky, Thomas E. "The American Girls of William Dean Howells and Sara Jeannette Duncan." *Journal of Canadian Fiction* 4, no. 1 (1975): 146–58.
– *Sara Jeannette Duncan, Novelist of Empire*. Port Credit: P.D. Meany 1980.
Teskey, Adeline M. *Where the Sugar Maple Grows: Idylls of a Canadian Village*. Toronto: Musson 1901.
Thomas Clara. Introduction. *The Backwoods of Canada*, by Catharine Parr Traill. NCL, no. 51. Ed. Malcolm Ross. Toronto: McClelland and Stewart 1971.
– "Canadian Social Mythologies in Sara Jeannette Duncan's *The Imperialist*." *Journal of Canadian Studies* 12, no. 2 (Spring 1977): 38–49.
– "The Chariot of Ossian: Myth and Manitoba in *The Diviners*." *Journal of Canadian Studies* 13, no. 3 (Fall 1978): 55–63.
– "A Conversation about Literature: An Interview with Margaret Laurence and Irving Layton." *Journal of Canadian Fiction* 1, no. 1 (Winter 1972): 65–8.
– "Crusoe and the Precious Kingdom: Fables of Our Literature." *Journal of Canadian Fiction* 1, no. 2 (Spring 1972): 58–64.
– "Happily Ever After: Canadian Women in Fiction and Fact." *Canadian Literature* no. 34 (Autumn 1967): 43–53.
– "Heroinism, Feminism and Humanism: Anna Jameson to Margaret Laurence." *Atlantis* 4, no. 1 (Fall 1978): 19–29.
– "Journeys to Freedom." *Canadian Literature* no. 51 (Winter 1972): 11–19.
– *The Manawaka World of Margaret Laurence*. NCL, no. 131. Ed. Malcolm Ross. Toronto: McClelland and Stewart 1976.
– "The Novels of Margaret Laurence." *Studies in the Novel* 4, no. 2 (Summer 1972): 154–64.
– "Pilgrims' Progress: Margaret Laurence and Hagar Shipley. *Journal of Canadian Studies* 17, no. 3 (Fall 1982): 110–16.
– "Proud Lineage: Willa Cather and Margaret Laurence." *Canadian Review of American Studies* 2, no. 1 (Spring 1971): 3–12.

– "Traill's Canadian Settlers." *Canadian Children's Literature* nos. 5 and 6 (1976): 31–9.
– "Women Writers and the New Land." In *The New Land, Studies in a Literary Theme*, ed. Richard Chadbourne and Hallvard Dahlie, 45–60. Waterloo: Wilfrid Laurier University Press 1978.
Thompson, Anne. "The Wilderness of Pride: Form and Image in *The Stone Angel*." *Journal of Canadian Fiction* 4, no. 3 (1975): 95–110.
Thompson, Eric. "Prairie Mosaic: The Immigrant Novel in the Canadian West." *Studies in Canadian Literature* 5, no. 2 (Fall 1980): 236–59.
Thompson, J. Lee, and John H. Thompson. "Ralph Connor and the Canadian Identity." *Queen's Quarterly* 79, no. 2 (Summer 1972): 159–70.
Thompson, Samuel. *Reminiscences of a Canadian Pioneer for the Last Fifty Years, 1833–1883*. Toronto: McClelland and Stewart 1968.
Thomson, Patricia. *The Victorian Heroine: A Changing Ideal, 1837–1873*. London: Oxford University Press 1956.
Tinkler, John F. "Canadian Cultural Norms and Australian Social Rules: Susanna Moodie's *Roughing It in the Bush* and Marcus Clarke's *His Natural Life*." *Canadian Literature* no. 94 (Autumn 1982): 10–22.
Tivy, Louis, ed. *Your Loving Anna: Letters from the Ontario Frontier*. 1972; rpt. Toronto: University of Toronto Press 1974.
Toronto Council of Women. *Nothing New Under the Sun: A History of the Toronto Council of Women in Federation with Provincial Council of Women of Ontario, National Council of Women of Canada, International Council of Women*. Toronto: Local Council of Women of Toronto 1978.
Traill, Catharine Parr. *The Backwoods of Canada: Being Letters from the Wife of an Emigrant Officer, Illustrative of the Domestic Economy of British America*. London 1836; rpt. Toronto: Coles Canadiana Collection 1971.
– "The Bereavement. A Fragment from Forest Gleamings." *Literary Garland* ns 4 (Feb. 1846): 69–72.
– *Canadian Crusoes: A Tale of the Rice Lake Plains*. Ed. Rupert Schieder. Ottawa: Carleton University Press 1986.
– *The Canadian Settler's Guide*. Introd. Clara Thomas. NCL, no. 64. Ed. Malcolm Ross. Toronto: McClelland and Stewart 1969.
– *Canadian Wild Flowers*. 1868; rpt. Toronto: Coles Canadiana Collection 1972.
– *Cot and Cradle Stories*. Ed. Mary Agnes Fitzgibbon. Toronto: William Briggs 1895.
– "Floral Sketches: The Violet." *Literary Garland* ns 1 (March 1843): 87–90.
– "Flowers, and Their Moral Teaching." *Journal of Canadian Fiction* 2, no. 3 (Special Issue, Summer 1973): 82–5.
– *Happy Because Good; The Tame Pheasant, and the Blind Brother and Kind Sister*. London: Thomas Dean n.d.
– *The Keepsake Guineas; or, The Best Use of Money*. London: A.K. Newman 1828.

– *Lady Mary and Her Nurse; or, A Peep into the Canadian Forest.* London: Arthur Hall, Virtue 1856.
– *Little Downy; or, The History of a Field-Mouse. A Moral Tale.* London: Dean and Munday 1822.
– *Pearls and Pebbles; or, Notes of an Old Naturalist.* Toronto: William Briggs 1894.
– "The Rose." *Literary Garland* ns 1 (March 1843): 129–31.
– *Sketches from Nature; or, Hints to Juvenile Naturalists.* London: Harvey and Darton 1830.
– *The Tell-Tale: An Original Collection of Moral and Amusing Stories.* London: Harris and Son 1823.
– *The Young Emigrants; or, Pictures of Canada.* London 1826; rpt. Wakefield, England: S.R. Publishers; New York: Johnson Reprint Corporation 1969.
Trofimenkoff, Susan Mann, and Alison Prentice, eds. *The Neglected Majority: Essays in Canadian Women's History.* Toronto: McClelland and Stewart 1977.
van Herk, Aritha. *Judith.* Toronto: McClelland and Stewart-Bantam, Seal Books 1979.
Vicinus, Martha, ed. *Suffer and Be Still: Women in the Victorian Age.* Bloomington: Indiana University Press 1972.
Vipond, M. "Blessed Are the Peacemakers: The Labour Question in Canadian Social Gospel Fiction." *Journal of Canadian Studies* 10, no. 3 (August 1975): 32–43.
Warwick, Susan J. "A Laurence Log." *Journal of Canadian Studies* 13, no. 3 (Fall 1978): 75–83.
– "Margaret Laurence, An Annotated Bibliography." In *The Annotated Bibliography of Canada's Major Authors,* vol. 1, ed. Robert Lecker and Jack David, 47–102. Downsview: ECW Press 1979.
Wasserton, William. *Heiress of All the Ages; Sex and Sentiment in the Genteel Tradition.* Minneapolis: University of Minnesota Press 1959.
Waterston, Elizabeth. *Survey: A Short History of Canadian Literature.* Toronto: Methuen 1973.
Watt, F.W. "Western Myth: The World of Ralph Connor." *Canadian Literature* no. 1 (Summer 1959): 29–36.
Watters, Reginald Eyre. *A Checklist of Canadian Literature and Background Materials, 1628–1960.* 2nd ed. Toronto: University of Toronto Press 1972.
– "Original Relations: A Genographic Approach to the Literature of Canada and Australia." *Canadian Literature* no. 7 (Winter 1961): 6–17.
Weaver, Emily. *Canada and the British Immigrant.* London: Religious Tract Society 1914.
Westfall, William. "Order and Experience: Patterns of Religious Metaphor in Early Nineteenth Century Upper Canada." *Journal of Canadian Studies* 20, no. 1 (Spring 1985): 5–24.
Williams, Helen E. *Spinning Wheels and Homespun.* Toronto: McClelland and Stewart 1923.

Willeson, Marjory MacMurchy. *The Woman – Bless her. Not as Amiable a Book as it Sounds*. Toronto: S.B. Gundy 1916.

Wilson, Ethel. *Swamp Angel*. Introd. Desmond Pacey. NCL, no. 29. Ed. Malcolm Ross. Toronto: McClelland and Stewart, 1954.

Wilson, Keith. *Charles William Gordon*. Manitobans in Profile. Winnipeg: Pegasus Publishers 1981.

Winthrow, W.H. *Barbara Heck: A Tale of Early Methodism*. Toronto: William Briggs n.d.

Withrow, W.H. *The King's Messanger; or, Lawrence Temple's Probation. A Story of Canadian Life*. Toronto: William Briggs 1897.

– *Neville Trueman, the Pioneer Preacher*. Toronto: William Briggs 1900.

Wollstonecroft, Mary. *A Vindication of the Rights of Women*. Ed. Carol H. Poston. New York: W.W. Norton 1975.

Wood, Joanna E. *Judith Moore; or, Fashioning a Pipe*. Toronto: Ontario Publishing Co. 1898.

– *The Untempered Wind*. 3rd ed. New York: J. Selwin Tait 1894.

Woodcock, George. "Many Solitudes: The Travel Writings of Margaret Laurence." *Journal of Canadian Studies* 13, no. 3 (Fall 1978): 3–12.

Woodcock, George, ed. *The Canadian Novel in the Twentieth Century: Essays from Canadian Literature*. NCL, no. 115. Ed. Malcolm Ross. Toronto: McClelland and Stewart 1975.

Yonge, Charlotte M. *The Clever Woman of the Family*. 2 vols. London, 1865; rpt. New York: Garland 1975.

Youmans, Letitia. *Campaign Echoes: The Autobiography of Mrs. Letitia Youmans, The Pioneer of the White Ribbon Movement in Canada*. Introd. Frances E. Willard. 2nd ed. Toronto: William Briggs 1893.

Young, E. Ryerson. *Duck Lake: Stories of the Canadian Backwoods*. London: the Religious Tract Society 1920.

Zaremba, Eve, ed. *Privilege of Sex: A Century of Canadian Women*. Toronto: Anansi 1974.

Zezulka, Joseph M. "*The Imperialist:* Imperialism, Provincialism, and Point of View." In *Beginnings: A Critical Anthology*, ed. John Moss, 143–57. Canadian Novel, vol. 2. Toronto: New Canadian Publications 1980.

Zichy, Francis. "Sara Jeannette Duncan." In *Profiles in Canadian Literature*, vol. 1, ed. Jeffrey M. Heath, 33–40. Toronto: Dundurn Press 1980.

Index

DATE DUE